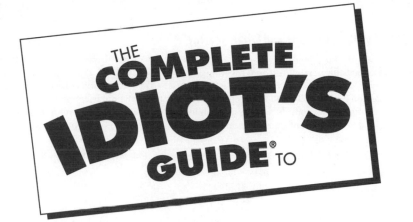

THE COMPLETE IDIOT'S GUIDE® TO

Gambling Like a Pro

Third Edition

Stanford Wong and Susan Spector

ALPHA

A Pearson Education Company

International Standard Book Number: 0-02-864485-9
Library of Congress Catalog Card Number: 2002115299

04   03   02   8   7   6   5   4   3   2   1

Interpretation of the printing code: The rightmost number of the first series of numbers is the year of the book's printing; the rightmost number of the second series of numbers is the number of the book's printing. For example, a printing code of 02-1 shows that the first printing occurred in 2002.

Printed in the United States of America

Note: This publication contains the opinions and ideas of its authors. It is intended to provide helpful and informative material on the subject matter covered. It is sold with the understanding that the authors and publisher are not engaged in rendering professional services in the book. If the reader requires personal assistance or advice, a competent professional should be consulted.

The authors and publisher specifically disclaim any responsibility for any liability, loss, or risk, personal or otherwise, which is incurred as a consequence, directly or indirectly, of the use and application of any of the contents of this book.

For marketing and publicity, please call: 317-581-3722

The publisher offers discounts on this book when ordered in quantity for bulk purchases and special sales.

For sales within the United States, please contact: Corporate and Government Sales, 1-800-382-3419 or corpsales@pearsontechgroup.com

Outside the United States, please contact: International Sales, 317-581-3793 or international@pearsontechgroup.com

Publisher: *Marie Butler-Knight*
Product Manager: *Phil Kitchel*
Managing Editor: *Jennifer Chisholm*
Acquisitions Editor: *Gary Goldstein*
Development Editor: *Ginny Bess Munroe*
Copy Editor: *Cari Luna*
Illustrator: *Chris Eliopoulos*
Cover/Book Designer: *Trina Wurst*
Indexer: *Tonya Heard*
Layout/Proofreading: *Megan Douglass, Becky Harmon*

Contents at a Glance

Contents

Foreword

With the proliferation of gaming throughout the United States in recent years, the activity of gaming itself has become a common and very accepted pastime and means of recreation. Make no mistake; any recreational "gamers" should look upon this activity strictly as recreation. In doing so I will share with you that which you may already be aware of: Knowledge is strength.

As you enter the world of the casino your first time, you may find yourself somewhat overwhelmed by the lights, distractions, and fast pace associated with gaming activities. In fact, I have known some very sophisticated individuals who avoided casinos because they were intimidated by the glitz factor. I say, "fear no more!" Prepare yourself and prepare yourself well. In terms of preparation, I highly recommend this *Complete Idiot's Guide*, as it will give you a sense of security in what might be considered a somewhat insecure setting. Armed with information contained in this easy-to-read—and most important, understandable—publication, you will walk into the world of the casino with a sense of knowledge and confidence that will help ensure you have the most enjoyable casino experience possible.

The Complete Idiot's Guide to Gambling Like a Pro, Third Edition, contains something for everyone. As an experienced gaming executive, I found the guide an enjoyable refresher. Somewhat recently, I had occasion to utilize the first printing on a project as required reading for the training of casino surveillance officers. These gentlemen had absolutely no casino background and with the help of the *Complete Idiot's Guide* they were speaking and understanding "casino-ese" in an accelerated time frame. The book proved to be the tool to provide a "bridge" for our uninitiated to reach the "promised land."

Dive into this book and you'll understand how the games work, what your expectations are, and protocol and etiquette in casinos. This book helps sweep away the "cloak" and mystery surrounding this exciting world and translates for all into lay terms. I truly wish this publication had been available years ago for me to recommend to the many clients, customers, and friends I have met during my career.

There are many books on the shelves these days, many are written for the already savvy gambler and are advanced. There are also "intro" books out there but all too often they are incomplete in some fashion. I give *The Complete Idiot's Guide to Gambling Like a Pro, Third Edition*, my highest rating due to the comprehensive, easy to digest, applicable approach of the author.

If you are going to invest dollars on a gaming table or in a slot machine, invest in this book first and do your homework—it might save you a fortune.

Lastly, after reading, comprehending, and learning, gamble responsibly and have a great time.

GOOD LUCK!

—James William Tuthill Jr.

James William Tuthill Jr. is a second generation casino executive who has held VP of Operations, VP of Gaming, and VP/Casino Manager positions for properties such as the Sands in Atlantic City and The Casino at the Ritz Carlton in San Juan. Mr. Tuthill has traveled and worked on behalf of companies in Australia, Aruba, Florida, Nevada, Puerto Rico, and New Jersey.

Mr. Tuthill entered the gaming industry in the mid-1970s and has held virtually every position relating to table games in the casino. He has been placed in charge of marketing, slots, and credit departments in recent years.

Mr. Tuthill is currently licensed as a Vice President and key qualifier in New Jersey and as a Vice President in Puerto Rico. He has conducted and participated in seminars related to gaming instruction, and has guest lectured for Hospitality Division and Gaming Administration classes for Drexel University in Philadelphia, Pennsylvania, and Atlantic Cape Community College in Atlantic County, New Jersey. Mr. Tuthill has also participated on one of the first Advisory Boards for the Hospitality Division at Atlantic Community College.

Mr. Tuthill attended the University of Nevada at Las Vegas' College of Hotel Administration from 1968 through 1972.

Preface

Susan and I complement each other. She enjoys gambling, and I look at casino games the way an investor looks at stocks. She believes in luck, and I believe in probabilities. She believes in streaks, and I believe in randomness. She is a professional writer and training consultant, and I know as much as anybody about how the games are played and how to beat them. Over the years, I've written many gambling books that are geared to the expert player—professionals and semi-professionals who are committed to finding an edge and winning. The strategies I have developed have proven successful many times over.

Susan came to me with the idea for this book after recognizing that gambling was sweeping the country, and more and more people were interested in what proven professionals like me had to say on the subject. She believed that by working together, we could create a simple, easy-to-use, and entertaining guide that the average player could enjoy and use to enhance his or her gambling knowledge and skills.

Although it's mostly Susan's voice that you'll be reading in this book, all of the playing strategy and tips are mine, as relayed to her. Of course, Susan likes to have fun when she gambles, so there's plenty about how to do that sprinkled throughout. But, to make sure that all of the technical details are correct and that she didn't go too far in extolling the virtues of luck, I carefully reviewed and edited every chapter.

What you have in your hands is a book aimed at gambling newcomers. Its purpose is to inform you about how these games are played, how the odds work against you (that is, where and why the house makes money in each game), and where you can possibly get an edge if there's an edge to get. If you want to find a game for yourself, we'll show you what makes each game attractive so you can figure out which one's for you.

We also tell you the rules of the game, and give you the rudiments of strategy. We'll tell you which games can be beaten, and how to find more detailed information on beating them if that's your goal. You won't be able to support yourself as a professional gambler after just reading this book, but you will be able to get the maximum enjoyment out of your next visit to a casino.

Gambling is fun, for most people. But you have to watch yourself. Most activities you pursue for fun come with prices you can figure out in advance. If you want to treat someone to a football game, you can figure out in advance how much it will cost you for parking, tickets, program, and food. Your day at the game won't cost you much more than you planned unless something drastic happens, like coming across a souvenir you can't resist.

Casino gambling is different from attending a football game or most other leisure activities in a major way: Gambling has a variable cost. The good news is *you* are in charge of the cost. The bad news is if you're unable to control it, the cost can get out of hand. My advice is if you want to gamble, determine the cost in advance. Then, when you're inside the casino, surrounded by new and exciting sights, sounds, and smells, stick to the cost you set in advance. Do not, under any circumstance, pay more than what you decided ahead of time was a reasonable price for the fun you're having.

If, once inside a casino, you realize you budgeted too little for gambling—tough. Live with the amount you already set. Then, when you're away from the excitement and being logical, if you think a higher expenditure is justified you can set a higher gambling budget for the next trip.

I would also like to caution you against borrowing or lending money in a casino. I once even refused to lend $500 to my own father in a casino. I told him if he were home and asked for $500—or even $5,000—I would lend or give it to him, but not in a casino. I told him he decided before he came to Reno how much he could afford to risk, and I wasn't going to enable him to exceed that amount.

My father is well-off enough that I wasn't worried about his ability to pay me back. But in general, when you lend money to someone in a casino, you must accept the fact that there's a good chance you won't be paid back. I never make loans in casinos, but I have friends who are softer touches than me. They know from sad experience that loans made in casinos frequently turn out to be gifts.

So, have fun in casinos using the information you glean from this book, and keep the cost of the entertainment under your control. In fact, I hope you have so much fun taking on the casinos that you buy the rest of my books to learn how to get an edge at the "beatable" games.

—Stanford Wong

Pi Yee Press
7910 Ivanhoe #34
La Jolla, CA 92037-4502
619-456-4080 voice
619-456-8076 fax

Introduction

Although *The Complete Idiot's Guide to Gambling Like a Pro, Third Edition*, can't promise to make everybody a winner, we can help you get more enjoyment and satisfaction from the games you play. You're almost certain to become an "informed" player. To us, an informed player is a smart player. He or she is someone who:

♦ Takes the time to learn the basics *before* jumping into a game.

♦ Understands that without risk, it wouldn't be gambling.

♦ Knows what he or she is up against (the house edge and odds) in every game he or she plays.

♦ Knows how and where to get an "edge," when there's an edge to get.

♦ Is smart enough to set a gambling limit for him or herself.

♦ Is responsible enough to call it quits when that limit is reached.

How to Use This Book

There's a lot to cover, and you probably want to hurry up and start playing. So, let's go:

In **Part 1, "On Becoming a Gambler,"** we take you on a very quick tour through the history of gambling to show you that, as a gambler, you're in very good company! Then, we segue into the present to explain many of the options available to you in today's world of legalized gambling. We illustrate why the odds are stacked against you in most games of chance, and if you're still with us after that, we'll help you find the games that best fit your personality and playing style. There's even a paragraph or two about luck and divine intervention thrown in to entertain me and, hopefully, you as well.

By the time you finish Part 1, you will probably know which games you want to play, and the chapters in Parts 2 through 5 will show you how. The chapters are grouped into Parts, or sections of the book, according to types of games. For example, **Part 2, "Taking a Chance,"** contains all of the games that don't require any thinking or skill at all. They're purely games of "chance." Chapters in **Part 3, "The Competitive Edge (Games of Skill),"** cover all of the games that DO require some skill. These are the games that professional gamblers like Stanford are known to play because they're "beatable"! **In Part 4, "The ROYALS (A Lot of Ways to Play Poker),"** we cover nothing but poker (and the search for the Royal Flush). There are hundreds of poker games out there and this section covers the ones you'll find played in most American casinos. For those of you who have a lot of lucky numbers (or perhaps just one that's *really* lucky), **Part 5, "Nothing But Numbers,"** covers all of the games of chance that require you to pick numbers. In case you'd like to learn about gambling within the comforts of your own home on the Internet, we discuss online gambling in **Part 6, "Virtual Gambling (The Last Frontier?)."** We even have a chapter that teaches you how to surf the web and find interesting gambling websites and news-groups.

We wouldn't want to let you loose in the casino without discussing money, so we've included **Part 7, "Money Management,"** to wrap things up. Part 7 is all about the responsible management of your gambling money. It contains information on every-thing from creating an annual gambling budget to cashing in on casino freebies as a way to stretch your gambling dollars and maybe even double your pleasure. There are also chapters on casino etiquette and protecting yourself in a gambling environ-ment because you can never be too careful when there's money involved.

For those who need more, we've thrown in some safety nets. At the very end of the book, you'll find a glossary containing all of the gambling terms that we've explained in each chapter—and then some—as well as a brief bibliography to guide you if you'd like to read more.

Basically, the order in which you read this book doesn't matter. If you've never set foot inside a casino, you'll probably benefit most by starting at the beginning. If you've been playing for years and just want to brush up on some old skills or learn a new game, you can zip right to the appropriate chapter. If you happen to gamble a lot and lose often, you might find Chapter 3 a particularly interesting place to start. By the same token, if you're ready to change what you've been doing and want to learn a new game, read Chapter 4 to get an idea of other games that might suit you.

Extra Help

As you read you'll find boxes scattered throughout the chapters. Each type of box contains different information that you'll find interesting and useful in different situations.

Risky Business

As the name implies, these boxes point out riskier bets that you might want to avoid, and warn you against making costly mistakes. Also, if there's something you *shouldn't* do because of etiquette, it'll be mentioned here as well.

Gamb-lingo

You'll look less like a novice if you sprinkle some of your casino conversation with the words contained in these boxes. You'll also be able to understand what everyone else is talking about if you check here every once in a while.

Best Bet

If there's a right and a wrong way to do something in a casino, we'll tell you the right way right here. You'll also find special gambling tips and the more favorable bets to make.

Bet You Didn't Know ...

These boxes contain stuff we thought was interesting that we "bet you didn't know." Though this information probably won't help you with your game, it might help you strike up a conversation in a hotel elevator.

Acknowledgments

We'd like to thank everyone who has contributed to *The Complete Idiot's Guide to Gambling Like a Pro, Third Edition,* and the thousands of informed players who have made *The Complete Idiot's Guide to Gambling Like a Pro* such a success!

Special thanks to Anthony Curtis, publisher of *Las Vegas Advisor* at Huntington Press in Las Vegas, for answering all our questions related to his town and to Brian Spector for his great graphic support and quick turnaround.

Sue would also like to thank her favorite gambling partners; Mom, Dad, and Scott for always being there when the money runs out!

Trademarks

All terms mentioned in this book that are known to be or are suspected of being trademarks or service marks have been appropriately capitalized. Alpha Books and Pearson Education, Inc., cannot attest to the accuracy of this information. Use of a term in this book should not be regarded as affecting the validity of any trademark or service mark.

Part 1

On Becoming a Gambler

So you want to be a gambler. How about becoming an informed player, first? Most of us informed, recreational players know what we're up against when we gamble, and we tend to give it our best shot. Before you jump into the world of legalized gambling, read Chapter 1 to learn about the long line of gamblers who came before you. In Chapter 2, learn about the games you're most likely to encounter in today's casinos. Find out which games require some skill, and which don't, which games you can eventually beat, and which games will eventually beat you. And, most importantly, find out why you are more likely to win some games and not others.

By the time you finish reading about odds and the mathematics of gambling in Chapter 3, you may be a little overwhelmed. That's why we'll lift your spirits in Chapter 4 and show you how to find the games that will give you the most pleasure. Now isn't that rewarding enough for you? (Well, an informed player knows that sometimes you just have to base your winnings on how much fun you had!)

A Brief History of Gambling

In This Chapter

- How far back can we trace the roots of gambling?
- The earliest forms of gambling
- What *really* makes this period in history unique in gambling?

I became interested in writing this book shortly after I began to notice that my favorite Las Vegas casinos were filling up in the summertime—a time of year that used to guarantee me an almost private swimming pool and a lot of one-on-one time with the blackjack dealer. When riverboat gambling was legalized in many states along the Mississippi, I knew that gambling had really taken off. It was no coincidence that we were legalizing gambling all over the place just when more people were entering their retirement years with more time and money on their hands than ever before.

After doing some research, I found out that I was right about the skyrocketing popularity of gambling *and* the aging of America. But I was also relieved to learn that it didn't mark the decline of civilization (or personal financial ruin), as some might think. People all over the world have actually been gambling since the beginning of recorded time with no real ill effects on society. The history of gambling is actually kind of fascinating, and I'd like to share it with you in this chapter. (Then we'll get right down to business and start teaching you how to gamble! I promise.)

Once Upon a Time

The earliest gamblers were primitive witch doctors who were often called upon to divine the future by reading the way sacred sticks, stones, or the knucklebones of sheep or cows landed when tossed to the ground. This practice grew out of a reverence for whatever higher power controlled our fate and a desire to predict the future. To determine the will of the gods, they posed questions about the future or current affairs and found their answers in the way things landed. Perhaps face up meant *yes*, and face down meant *no*, or the direction in which a stick landed told them which path to take.

Gamb-lingo

Coins have two sides, so you can **flip a coin** and bet on which side will land face-up. The Bible speaks often of **casting lots,** which is tossing or rolling objects that can be counted, measured, or numbered to decide a winner. A **lottery** is a drawing in which prizes are distributed to the winners among all those who purchased chances. The word *lottery* is derived from the word *lots*.

Gamb-lingo

The game of **craps** played in casinos today probably evolved from ancient **dice** games in which an object or objects were tossed in the air and people wagered on which side(s) would land face-up.

Later civilizations also believed fate and destiny controlled the outcome of each toss, but they learned it was more fun to *wager* on the result than to make predictions. The appearance of similar tossing games and paraphernalia in different cultures during different periods of civilization indicate that similar games of chance may have been passed from one civilization to another, perhaps as treasured gifts.

As Alice Fleming tells us in *Something for Nothing: A History of Gambling*, early Egyptians enjoyed wagering on a game much like the one kids play today when they try to guess whether the number of fingers extended by two people will be odd or even. The ancient Romans *flipped coins* and held *lotteries*, which they may have learned from the Chinese. Greek men and women played the equivalent of a coin-flip game, using sea shells, and rolled primitive dice to take their minds off their hunger during times of famine. It's likely, too, that the Greeks passed their knowledge of dice on to the Romans, for the New Testament tells us that as they guarded Jesus on the cross, the Romans *cast lots*, or rolled dice, to decide who would win his clothes.

Dice was a popular game in ancient Rome. Emperors, like Nero and Claudius, played religiously. Their subjects enjoyed the game so much that little else got done, so gambling was eventually restricted to special holidays. Historians believe that knowledge of dice disappeared with everything else during the fall of the Roman Empire, but was reintroduced to Europe centuries later by crusaders who learned the game at the Arab fortress of Hazart.

After dice were reintroduced to Europe by returning crusaders in the late 1100s, dice games flourished again. In fact, many kings of England and France lost fortunes playing a dice game called *hazard*, which was probably named for the place of its origin during the Crusades. By the eighteenth century, hazard was still going strong as a popular European diversion for kings and countrymen alike.

> **Bet You Didn't Know ...**
>
> No one is certain about the origin of dice, but it's widely believed that primitive witch doctors were the first to toss four-sided knucklebones of sheep or cows with an interest in which side landed face-up. The Greeks probably picked up the knucklebone idea, added markings on each side, and used them for entertainment in a game similar to dice. By the time the Greeks passed their dice on to the Romans, dice had evolved into six-sided cubes that were usually made of wood, stone, animal teeth, or ivory. Today's dice are made of colored plastic, marked with dots that indicate numbers, and tossed two at a time.

Marco Polo's Greatest Discovery

Sometime during the fourteenth century, card games also found their way into European culture, and it is assumed that the first cards were brought back by explorers and merchants who visited China. The earliest European cards were made in Italy and contained 78 beautifully hand-painted pictures, similar to today's tarot cards. As cards became more and more popular for entertainment and wagering, the deck changed. When mass printing was invented, more people could afford playing cards and their popularity spread quickly. By the fifteenth century, the French reduced the number of cards in a deck to 56 and began manufacturing cards for all of Europe.

By this time in world history, the Crusades had long ago ended, the Dark Ages had given way to the Renaissance, and the Age of Enlightenment had begun. For the first time in the history of civilization, even commoners had idle time to play and possessions to wager. Games of chance—including lotteries, raffles, card games, and dice—flourished. Sporting events and horse racing also took their place among popular forms of recreation, especially among the elite. Gambling became such a popular pastime that by the sixteenth century it was restricted by law (but rarely enforced) to weekends and/or certain holidays for the working classes in both England and France. Noblemen, on the other hand, were permitted to gamble at will. By the seventeenth and eighteenth centuries, a man's nobility and aristocracy were often measured by his propensity to wager small fortunes.

Bet You Didn't Know ...

Today's 52-card deck of playing cards is a direct descendant of the cards first manufactured in France in the 1400s. The French cards contained four suits of 13 cards each, plus four wild cards. Each suit depicted one of the four classes of French society: Hearts represented the church, spades symbolized the army, diamonds depicted the merchants, and clubs symbolized the peasants and farmers.

The English later improved playing cards by printing the suit and rank at both the top and bottom of a card, so that players would no longer have to tip their hand by turning kings, queens, and jacks upside down to read them.

Gambling Discovers America

Early American settlers in the mid-1600s were no doubt surprised to find the Iroquois Indians and other North American tribes already playing their own dice game with stones. Perhaps the Native Americans learned of dice from Columbus's men, who were also credited with bringing the first playing cards to America in 1492. Reports from early settlers indicate that whole tribes of Indians often held high-stakes dice games in which players heroically wagered all their earthly possessions. They bet on horse races with the same fervor.

Although the Pilgrims fled England in search of religious freedom and a puritanical way of life, colonists and fur traders who followed were not free of idleness and vice. In fact, the Puritans tried unsuccessfully to ban gambling and card playing in the colonies. But by the late 1600s, gambling became legal and as acceptable as it was in Europe.

Many of our country's founding fathers were avid card players and gamblers. George Washington often played for money. Thomas Jefferson enjoyed a game similar to poker and recorded his winnings and losses in a journal. Benjamin Franklin enjoyed cribbage and a game called Boston, which was probably a predecessor of today's game of bridge. President Andrew Jackson was very fond of card playing, cockfighting, and horse racing.

Rolling on the River

Although more conservative Americans along the eastern seaboard accepted horse racing as a form of recreation and private lotteries as a means of raising much-needed capital, they were generally ambivalent about the vices of alcohol and gambling. The more adventurous freedom-loving citizens began to move west, and brought to the new frontier a desire and willingness to gamble.

Besides the small saloons that sprang up in settlements along frontier trails, Mississippi riverboats offered the greatest opportunity for gamblers. Wealthy businessmen from the Northeast and plantation owners from the South regularly traveled the riverboats with large sums of money, on their way to or from the markets. Professional gamblers and cheats preyed on these unsuspecting "marks," wagering large sums in floating poker games and other games of chance. Towns catering to merchants and riverboat gamblers sprang up along the river. Sometimes the biggest money wagered on riverboats was not at the poker tables, but by gamblers and spectators watching along the shore and betting on which of two boats traveling the same course would make it to the designated port first.

One of the most successful river towns was New Orleans, which became the unofficial gambling capital of the new frontier in the early 1800s. Lousiana's first settlers were French and Spanish colonists who brought from their homeland games of chance like poker, faro, vingt-et-un (blackjack), roulette, and craps, which were unfamiliar to the more conservative Yankees. American soldiers passing through town on their way back from the Mexican War introduced three-card monte, which later became another staple of gamblers up and down the river. By the mid-1800s, New Orleans had more than 400 gaming halls and five horse-racing tracks.

Go West, Young Man

As commerce developed, railroads and steamboats replaced more leisurely riverboat travel, and many professional gamblers decided to seek their fortunes farther west. As they established roots, the citizens of the Southwest ran the gamblers out of town to preserve the "good life."

However, although the people of the Southwest were able to rid their cities of gamblers, crooks, and cheats, they had no real interest in getting rid of gambling entirely. In fact, the games that originated in New Orleans and the riverboats spread to gaming halls in the East and Midwest. The professional gamblers scattered to those locations and lined the trade routes throughout the western frontier. The more daring set out for California's Gold Rush country to part the forty-niners from their newfound wealth.

The Rest Is History

San Francisco and Reno originated as frontier gambling towns. Since many of the miners were already onto the tricks of the professional cheats who had plied their trade on the riverboats, the professionals had to rely less on trickery and more on percentages and odds to win.

In the late nineteenth and early twentieth centuries, gambling moved south to Los Angeles, and then about 300 miles east to a tiny town in the middle of the Mojave Desert: Las Vegas, Nevada. Las Vegas prospered as a waystation for passing travelers. But in the late 1940s, a mobster named Benny ("Bugsy") Siegel had the vision, desire, and money to take a chance building the largest and most lavish casino in America in that lonely desert town.

More than 50 years later, Las Vegas is still growing by leaps and bounds. Gambling has been legalized in one form or another in most of our 50 states, and regulation has made one of the world's oldest forms of recreation relatively safe from mobsters and cheats.

Epilogue

People have always had a fascination with whatever higher power controls our destiny and fate. If we weren't reading tea leaves or pick-up sticks to predict the future, we were betting on the outcome of events as though we *could*. History has proved time and again that whenever laws are written to regulate or limit the human appetite for games of chance, they have been largely unenforceable.

What makes this current period of American history unique is not that so many of us gamble. It's that for the first time in our nation's history, there are ample laws and regulations in place to provide a safe and honest environment in which to test the hands of fate. And more knowledge and information is available on the subject than ever before.

In the chapters that follow, we will give you some of that information, and we hope you'll gain a more thorough understanding of the odds you're up against, as well as a more realistic expectation of your results. We also hope you'll learn enough to win more often. In the end, however, no one can predict the future, and what you make of your own propensity to gamble is entirely up to you. Good luck!

The Least You Need to Know

- People in all walks of life and throughout recorded history have enjoyed gambling.

- Whenever attempts to outlaw gambling have been made, they've failed.

- The legitimate regulation of gambling in America today makes this an opportune time to find and enjoy an honest game of chance.

Chapter 2

LIFE Is a Gamble

In This Chapter

- What is gambling?
- Games of chance versus games of skill
- Why games of chance are not always a 50-50 proposition
- Where is it safest to play?

Webster defines gambling as an activity that involves an element of *risk*—the possibility of incurring a loss. With this definition in mind, you can see why you don't always have to be in a casino to gamble. But in this chapter, we'll show you why you might have a lot more fun if you are!

We'll also explain the difference between games of chance and games of skill and why—if you really like casinos and like to gamble—you might want to invest your time and energy in learning a game or two that require some skill.

Risk and Reward

There are infinite ways to gamble. The stock market is one; driving on a rainy day in Southern California is another. Gambling always involves the risk of losing something—whether it be your money, your life, or anything you hold dear. People take risks because they think it's "worth it." They believe the chances of being rewarded for taking the risk are greater than the chances of incurring the loss.

The amount of risk we are willing to take is usually proportional to the amount of reward we expect. The greater the reward, the more risk we're likely to take. Would you buy a junk bond that pays only 5 percent annual interest when you could get a government-backed treasury bond that pays the same? If you'd never parachuted out of an airplane, would you consider doing it because someone dared you to? What if they offered you a million dollars or more?

Gamb-lingo _____

Your **bet** is the money you put up, wager, or risk in a gambling game in hopes of winning a reward. **Odds** describe the mathematical probability that an event will occur. The amount you collect if your bet wins is your **payoff** (called **payout** when referring to slot and video machines).

The point is, almost everything we do is a gamble, a constant comparison of potential loss versus potential reward. Gambling in a casino is no different. Even though you risk only the money you've set aside for entertainment, it still involves levels of risk and potential rewards that you can assess logically. Your potential *reward* can be as little as a day's entertainment or as great as a multimillion-dollar jackpot. Your level of *risk* is the amount of money you're willing to wager, or *bet*, to pursue the reward. The amount of uncertainty involved equates to the *odds* that are stacked against you in different games.

Because the risk and potential rewards of gambling vary with each game you play, it's important to know what you're getting into, how much you're willing to spend, and what your chances of winning are *before* you lay down your hard-earned cash! In the remainder of this book, we'll help you understand the risks involved in each game and the potential *payoffs*, or rewards. We'll also explain the odds against you and where you're most likely to find an edge in each game. But first, let's take a quick look at the gambling options we'll be covering.

Heads It's Chance, Tails It's Skill

There are two types of gambling games: games of chance, and games of chance that also involve skill. *All* honest gambling games are games of chance, or "equal-opportunity" games, because theoretically, if you played forever, you would have as much chance or likelihood of winning as any other player.

Some games of chance also provide the opportunity for skilled players to increase their likelihood of winning by making smart playing decisions. These are the casino *skill* games, and they're the ones you should really take the time to learn well if you want to be a serious player.

In this section, we'll describe the games that involve chance alone and those in which you can improve your chances of winning by investing some time and practice.

All I Need Is a Miracle (Games of Chance)

People are more familiar with and can usually be found playing the obvious games of chance, such as slot machines, roulette, and keno. That's not because these are "no-brainers," but because they often offer the highest payouts and give you the greatest excitement for the least amount of money. As the name implies, there's little you can do to influence a game of chance, except guess right and pray.

A slight edge in a game of chance isn't entirely out of the question when you know how the game works and what you're getting into. You'll learn what that means when we cover individual games of chance in later chapters:

Lottery   A numbers game used by states to generate money. You can choose from many kinds of lotteries: Pick 3, Pick 4, scratch-offs, and so on. Lottery games are not played in a casino; they are sponsored by state governments. You can buy lottery tickets in supermarkets, convenience stores, vending machines, and other locations. We'll explain the different kinds of lottery games in detail in Chapter 23.

Bingo   Another numbers game, played with a field of 75 numbers. Players purchase their own game boards; each game board contains a different, random selection of 25 of the 75 possible numbers. The person running the game calls out the numbers, which are pulled one by one from a rotating bin. The player's objective is to be the first to fill a designated pattern on his or her board by covering each called number. Bingo is explained in Chapter 24.

Keno   A lottery-type numbers game you play as you wait to be served in casino restaurants or in special keno lounges. Players select anywhere from 1 to 20 of the 80 possible numbers on a keno board. If, say, 6 of the 10 numbers you picked matches any of the 20 that were randomly selected for that game—you win. Sounds pretty easy, doesn't it? Check out Chapter 22 to find out why it's *not* always as easy as it sounds.

Baccarat   A card game *de France*, in which two hands are dealt and players bet whether the player's hand or the house's hand (the banker) will be closer to a total of 9. An elegant no-brainer that requires only one decision. Find out how the dealer does all the work while you kick back and watch the game in Chapter 9.

Roulette   A game played with a spinning wheel of either 37 (European version) or 38 (American version) numbers. Players bet on the outcome of the next spin of the wheel. Fortunately, you don't have to guess the *number* all the time. You can just bet the color (red or black), too! Learn all your roulette betting options in Chapter 8.

Slot machines   Commonly referred to as "one-armed bandits," these machines literally built Las Vegas and every other gambling mecca of today—and tomorrow. Players bet that each spin of the mechanical reels will result in a jackpot, or at least a payout. Just getting your coins back counts as a win! Find out why they're so hard to beat—yet still enticing—in Chapters 5 and 6.

When Practice Can *Almost* Make Perfect (Games of Skill)

In games of skill, which include all sports and most card games, a player has meaningful decisions to make. If there are no meaningful decisions, it is not a game of skill. Your knowledge of the game, ability to make the right playing decisions, and consistent use of proven playing and betting strategies can significantly increase your odds of winning a skill game. That's why most professional gamblers stick to these games, and most casinos strive to limit how they play by imposing very calculated rules, betting limits, and *payout schedules*, a.k.a. the *house edge*. (We'll talk more about the house edge in the next chapter.)

Gamb-lingo

Regulars fondly call a casino the **house**—their gaming "home away from home." You bet against the house in most casino games. The **house edge** is the small percentage of each bet (win or lose) that the house takes. It's regarded as income—your payment for playing, like an entertainment tax. The **payout schedule** is how much a winning hand, roll of the dice, or combination on a slot machine will pay.

Here's a list of the "chancy" games of skill you'll learn more about in this book:

Poker   A five- or seven-card game in which players bet against each other rather than the house. The objective is to win the pot of money that players bet as they try to achieve a winning hand by buying new cards, or as they raise the stakes to make other players think they already have one. A winning hand consists of the highest ranking combination of cards. The skill is in knowing how to play your cards—when to bet and when to fold. There are many variations of poker, and the two most popular ones are covered in Chapter 15.

Pai gow poker   A seven-card game played with a deck of 52 cards plus the joker. The game is actually based on the combination of a Chinese domino game called *pai gow* and good old American poker. The skill comes in knowing how to arrange the seven cards into a five-card poker hand and a two-card hand. Unravel the mysteries of pai gow poker in Chapter 19.

Blackjack   A card game in which players play against a dealer (the house). The objective is to hold a hand that adds up to more than the dealer's hand, without going over 21. The skill comes in knowing when to *hit* (take more cards), *stand* (stop taking cards), *double down* (double your bet and take only one more card), or *split* (make two separate hands out of the original cards dealt)—and when to bet more. Blackjack is clearly Stanford's game, and we'll share his proven strategy and tips with you in Chapters 10 and 11.

Craps   A game played with a pair of dice on a special table. Players bet on the outcome of the next roll of the dice. While this is truly a game of chance, knowing how and when to place your bets is a workable skill that can greatly influence how much money you get to take home. For details, see Chapter 12.

Sports betting   Betting on the outcome of sporting events, including college and professional football, baseball, basketball, and more. The skill comes in analyzing information about each team and finding betting situations that can give you an advantage. Remember, however, that you bet against professionals whose job is analyzing sports-related information. For details, see Chapter 14.

Horse racing   You guessed it—wagering on the outcome of horses racing against each other. The objective, of course, is to pick the winning horse, or at least the top three. The skill is in "reading the sheets," evaluating the odds, placing your bets, and finding the one horse (and jockey) that are skillful enough to beat all the others! We'll share Stanford's special strategies in Chapter 13.

Video poker   Video card games share a lot of similarities with basic slot machines, which makes them risky. However, if you know how the machine works, you can increase your chances of winning. The skill in video poker is knowing which machines to play and which cards to hold. Stanford has a whole book on the subject, and the advice you'll find in Chapter 16 has already saved me a fortune!

Betting Strategy

Now that you know the difference between a game of chance and the games of skill that require more thought and decision making, you might find it useful to know how a betting strategy can affect your gambling outcome. A *betting strategy* is the rhyme or reason (you could say method) by which a player places his or her bets. Most casino games have a minimum and maximum allowed bet. Even slot machines let you play with one, two, three, or more coins per spin (depending on the type of machine). It's your choice!

The perfect betting strategy is one in which you always lower your bet when you're *cold* (losing all the time) and raise it when you get *hot* (predominantly winning).

Gamb-lingo

Calculate your **rate of return** by dividing the amount of money you win (minus commissions, fees, and so on) by the amount you bet. A positive rate of return means you have an edge over the casino, and a negative rate of return means the casino has an edge over you.

Unfortunately, few of us are intuitive or aware enough of our actions to recognize when we're hot and when we're not—or consistent enough to apply that simple logic faithfully.

Different betting strategies have been developed to help players get through the ups and downs of some games less traumatically and, hopefully, increase their *rate of return*. Unfortunately, most betting strategies don't work. For games like blackjack, in which a betting strategy can give you an edge, we'll show you how and why in that game's chapter.

Put Me in Coach, I'm Ready to Play!

These days there are so many places to gamble that it wouldn't be practical—or even possible—to list them all. And Stanford (our roving professional) says we really shouldn't cite particular places and states where gambling is legal (other than Las Vegas and Atlantic City) because the gambling scene changes so quickly.

Risky Business

When gambling at your favorite Native American Indian casino, keep in mind that you are no longer protected by local, state, and federal laws and regulations. Most Indian casinos are located on tribal land, which means they are self-governing sovereign nations and you must abide by their laws.

What we *can* tell you is that anything goes in Nevada. Reno, Lake Tahoe, Las Vegas, and many towns elsewhere in the state offer all the games covered here. The same is true of Atlantic City. These well-known meccas, by the way, are generally your safest bets because they are so well organized and heavily regulated to protect you against cheating.

For the most part, this book explains how the pros play in Nevada and points out minor variations you'll find in Atlantic City. If you plan to play in other cities and states, it's worth the extra time to check the casino rules and how they differ before you start.

Ask the dealer or casino personnel what the house rules are for the game you want to play. Sometimes you'll find the rules printed on the top of the gaming table or on a placard on the side of a table or video machine. Whenever you're in doubt about any rules or betting requirements, don't hesitate to ask a casino employee.

Bet You Didn't Know ...

You shouldn't have to go too far to find a live bingo game. Many local churches play religiously on Tuesday or Thursday nights. And if you're feeling lucky today but still have to work, why not pick up a lottery ticket (with your donut and coffee) on the way in?

The Least You Need to Know

- Every day new and bigger opportunities to gamble open up. Before you rush in, know what you're getting into.

- When you gamble, you're evaluating a potential reward and what you're willing to risk to get it.

- All casino games and state lotteries are games of chance.

- Some casino games, such as poker and blackjack, require an element of skill, which (if you have it) can improve your odds of winning. Likewise, your lack of skill can reduce your odds of winning.

- Gambling is heavily regulated to protect you in Nevada and Atlantic City. Everywhere else—enjoy yourself, but know the local gaming rules!

An Odds Way of Looking at Things

In This Chapter

- ◆ How to tell if a bet is a good one to make
- ◆ What "true odds" are, and why you don't get paid accordingly when you gamble
- ◆ Why you *can't* beat a negative-expectation game in the long run, but can sometimes succeed in the short run

Pay careful attention to this chapter. If you read nothing else in this book, you'll be missing out on a lot of sound playing strategy and advice, but at least you'll understand why it's so hard to get your picture posted on the Winner's Wall. We'll show you what you're really up against when you gamble and why it's never quite as easy as it looks!

You'll find out how the house makes its money in most games. We'll even explain *why* you can sometimes beat the house in the short run, but they'll always win in the long run—unless you know which games to play and learn to play them well. This isn't the most encouraging chapter in the book, but it may be the most important!

Playing the Percentages

Say we flipped a coin for money, and every time it landed on heads you paid us a dollar, and every time it landed on tails, we paid you a dollar. Who do you think would be ahead after 20 tosses?

If you said you really can't predict the outcome of only 20 tosses, you're way ahead of the game! But you can apply what you already know about *probability* to determine whether the bet is a good one to make. For example, because a coin has only two sides, you know for certain that you have 1 chance out of 2 possible outcomes (heads or tails) of winning each coin toss. This fact can be expressed in terms of probability as 1/2. A probability of 1/2 means you have a 50 percent chance of winning the game, which makes it an even, 50–50 proposition.

Gamb-lingo

Probability is a branch of mathematics that measures the likelihood that an event will occur. Probabilities are expressed as numbers between 0 and 1. The probability of an impossible event is 0, and for an event that is certain to occur is 1. The fractions in between represent the probability of an event's occurrence.

If we offer to pay you $10 if you pick a queen from a well-shuffled deck of 52 playing cards, and all it costs you is $1 for each try, should you play? Figure out the odds!

You know there are 52 cards in the deck, which includes four queens. Your probability of picking the exact card (four queens out of 52 cards) is 4/52, or 1/13. In gambling, your chances are expressed as the odds against an event occurring. Your odds of picking a queen are 48 to 4, or 12:1 against.

Gamb-lingo

The **true odds**, commonly referred to as **odds**, are the ratio of the number of times an unfavorable event will occur compared to the number of times a favorable event will occur.

We are offering to pay you odds of 9 to 1 (you win $9—our $10 minus the $1 you wagered) to pick a queen. If we played fair, we'd pay you the *true odds* of 12 to 1. We would then expect to collect $1 from you 12 times (on the average) before we'd finally have to let you keep your original $1 wager and pay you $12 for winning. In the long run, we would all wind up even, or close to it.

But if we pay you only $10, we'll make $3 ($13 minus $10) every time you play 13 times, which is a hefty 23 percent profit. From where you sit, that means every dollar you wager at 9:1 costs you an average of about 23 cents. That's our *edge*, or advantage, over you if we play this game our way. (By the way, if we keep taking 23 cents from every dollar you bet, win or lose, how long do you think you'll be able to keep playing our game before you run out of money?)

When a casino offers you a reduced *payoff* like this, the difference between the true odds and the odds paid is called the *house edge*. The house edge varies from game to game—even from one bet to another in a game like craps. Sometimes, instead of reducing the correct payoff, the house charges a commission on certain bets, as in baccarat, or a fee for playing, as in most poker rooms. We'll show you how the house makes its money on each game, and which games and bets are the most favorable for *you*.

In this book, the house edge is sometimes shown as a *player expectation*, which is the amount of money a player can expect to win or lose from every dollar he or she wagers against the house. (The player expectation in our "pick a card" example would be stated as minus 23 percent—you'd expect to lose 23 cents for every dollar you bet.) In the long run, it's impossible for you to win a game with a negative expectation for the player. We'll show you why this is true in the next section.

However, we also know it's not altogether *hopeless* in the short run, or people would cease to gamble and the casinos would shut down—and that's clearly not happening! In gambling centers all over the world, there are winners every minute. We cannot show you how to win all the time—no one can possibly do that. But we can and will show you how to maximize your opportunities while minimizing your risks, so that you can continue to enjoy the game and perhaps wind up a winner in the short run!

Great Expectations (for the House)

The following table gives you a sample of some of your gambling options and what the house *expects* to keep from each dollar wagered (win *or* lose), by virtue of the rules of the game and what it pays off on winning bets.

The *player's expectation* refers to the percentage of each dollar wagered that you can expect to win or lose, in the long run. A *positive* expectation (+) is the percentage you can expect to win, and a *negative* expectation (–) is what you can almost count on losing, over time. (When a range is indicated, it means that the player's expectation varies depending on the bets made, level of skill, and the rules of the game and/or playing conditions. There is a large variance for most games, which is why we didn't include them all on the chart.)

Blackjack (under favorable conditions), bingo (in Las Vegas), sports wagering (when you

Gamb-lingo

Your **payoff**, or **payback**, is the return you receive on a wager, which equals 100 percent minus the house edge. The **house edge** is a percentage of each bet you make that the house takes in. It's regarded as payment for letting you play, like an entertainment tax. For the house to get this edge, winning bets are paid off at less than the true odds.

know how to find opportunities), and video poker (when playing the "right" machine) are the only games on the chart that actually allow a skilled player to enjoy a positive expectation at times. Poker can be another positive expectation game, but only when played with a great deal of experience and skill.

What You Can Expect to Win or Lose from Particular Games

	Approximate Expected Win (+) or Loss (–)	Expected Earnings Game from a $100 Bet
Baccarat	–1.2%	$98.80
Bingo	–15% to +0%	$85 to $100 or more
Blackjack (single deck)	–6% to +1.5%	$94 to $101.50
Caribbean Stud	–5.2% to –2.6%	$95 to $97.40
Craps	–13% to –.6%	$87 to $99.40
Keno	–27% (average)	$73
Let It Ride	–3.5%	$97
Lottery	–50%	$50
Roulette	–5.3%	$94.70
Slot machines	–20% to –2.7%	$80 to $97.30
Sports wagering	–10% to +0%	$90 to $100 or more
Video poker (progressives)	–6.3% to +1%	$93.70 to $101.00

You'll find out where your best opportunities lie in each game as we explain the rules and strategies in individual chapters. For now, what you need to know is that when you have a positive expectation, you're playing with an *advantage* and can expect to win the longer you play under the right conditions. When you're playing with a negative expectation, you are at a *disadvantage*, and the longer you play, the more likely you are to lose.

For Whom the Bell Tolls

A *bell curve* is a symmetrical distribution of numbers around its *mean*, or average. Statisticians make predictions about the outcome of events by using the standard bell curve as a reference.

All this talk about long runs and short runs and player expectations can best be explained by looking at a simple bell curve of a typical negative expectation game.

The bell curve in the next illustration shows a player's chances of winning or losing after playing 100 trials (or plays) of a hypothetical game that has a –5 percent player expectation. Each point on the curve shows the probability that you will win or lose a specific percentage of your money.

The horizontal axis represents the percentage of every dollar that a player can either win (+) or lose (–). The vertical axis shows the probability that a specific win or loss on the horizontal axis will occur. A line drawn down the center of the curve touches the horizontal axis at –5 percent because this is the *average* result (or player expectation) that any of us can expect to get playing this game in the long run.

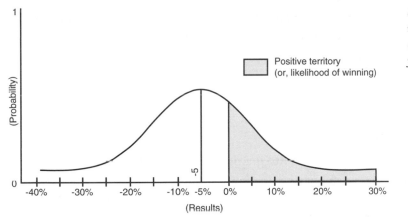

Self-fulfilling prophecy: The more you play a negative-expectation game, the greater your chances of losing.

If we were to continue playing this game forever, as we played more and more hands the curve would narrow, getting closer and closer to the average expectation of –5 percent, which means that if we were to add all our winning and losing hands, we'd wind up losing about 5 percent of each bet. In general, as the number of plays increases, a player is more likely to reach the expected outcome, which in this case is negative. If the player were playing a positive-expectation game, the center line (which represents the average, or player expectation) of the curve would be plotted in positive territory and he or she would have less expectation of losing and more expectation of winning.

What's it all mean? Basically, the old adage about coming out ahead in the long run just isn't true in negative-expectation games (although it is true when playing a positive-expectation game).

Risky Business

A game that is a negative expectation for the player is a positive expectation for the house. That means the longer you play, the more certain the house is of getting its share of your money.

Sure, on different occasions your bankroll may fall into positive territory, but if you play a negative-expectation game long enough, you can't help but wind up back in negative territory. The only one guaranteed to win a negative-expectation game the longer you play is the house. (That's because what's negative for a player is positive for the house.)

You can do only two things to reduce your risk when playing a negative-expectation game:

> **Don't play too long.** Make fewer bets, hope for the best, and quit while you're ahead.

> **Play games that offer smart bettors a higher expectation.** You can expect to lose less money in the long run playing a game with only a –1.2 percent expectation than one in which your expectation is –10 percent or worse.

You can also start out armed with the knowledge of probabilities so that you are not emotionally or financially devastated if and when the inevitable losses mount up.

Deviating from the Norm

Most recreational gamblers won't begin to get the *leveling* effect of increased trials on their bankroll because they won't be able to play enough on a single outing. You'll probably experience a combination of wins and losses that leave you within one or two standard deviations of the player expectation.

The *standard deviation* (SD) is another tool statisticians use. It can help gamblers figure out how much they are likely to win or lose based on the bell curve. The curve shown next is the same one we created for the –5 percent expectation game. The standard deviations have been calculated and drawn in to show you how much you are most likely to win or lose in 100 hands of play. Each vertical line is the border of a single standard deviation (SD). As you can see, you will experience the player expectation (–5 percent) plus or minus 1 SD about 68 percent of the time. Your actual outcome will be worse than 1 SD below the expectation about 16 percent of the time and better than 1 SD above the expectation about 16 percent of the time.

If you make 100 plays of $1 each, the odds are you will lose $5. There is a 68.26 percent (2 times 34.13 percent) chance you will end up somewhere between losing $15 and winning $5. You have only a 15.87 percent chance (13.59 percent + 2.14 percent + 0.14 percent) of winning more than $5 or losing more than $15.

Now that you've seen how the odds are stacked against you mathematically, you should be better prepared to assess the risk and find games that are right for your bankroll and tolerance of risk, based on the house edge and player expectation. In the next chapter, we'll discuss the psychology of gambling and what it takes to win from that perspective. It makes sense that if you play games suited to your personality, you'll enjoy yourself more and improve your fun factor! Who knows—maybe we'll start seeing more smiling faces in those hotel elevators.

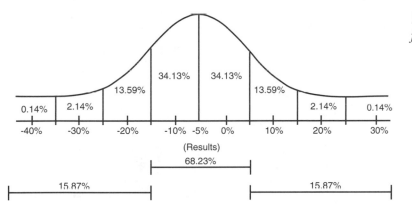

Your standard deviation from the norm.

The Least You Need to Know

♦ Casinos generally pay you less than the true odds when you win a bet. That's how they make their money. If they don't reduce the payout, then they charge a commission or fee.

♦ Most casino games are negative-expectation games, which means that the rules and payout schedules have been calculated in the house's favor. In negative-expectation games, the house always wins in the long run.

♦ You can win occasionally, but the longer you play a negative-expectation game, the more likely you are to wind up losing.

♦ The best advice for casino gambling is first, don't play too long, and second, play games that offer a higher expectation, such as blackjack, baccarat, and some bets in craps. (We'll point out games in which you can get an edge throughout the remainder of this book.)

Chapter 4

What It Takes to Win

In This Chapter

- Finding games that suit your style
- What do winners look like?
- Establishing gambling goals and parameters
- Where Lady Luck and divine intervention fit in

When I was a kid, the best part of a vacation was playing pinball at the end of a long day of sightseeing—and charging milkshakes to the room when I could get away with it. Today, give me room service, good food, and the opportunity to play, and I'm a happy camper! I play the games I enjoy, when I want to play them. If I win—great! If I lose, I skip the shrimp cocktail. Life goes on.

In this chapter, Stanford and I will help you figure out what it takes for *you* to be a winner, or at least a happy camper. Although we explained in Chapter 3 why you *shouldn't* expect to win too often, now we're going to look at what can help you improve your chances, from an emotional and psychological perspective. And, of course, there's always *luck*—which in some people's view (forgive me, Stanford!) is no small part of the equation.

You Can't Win If You Don't Play

First, to be a winner you need to find the game that interests you. Winners invest their time and money doing what they enjoy. It makes no sense to spend your hard-earned cash gambling if you don't have fun. Neither does it make a whole lot of sense to play games you don't enjoy simply because you read about someone else's good fortune or have a friend who paid for a great vacation with the winnings.

We assume, however, that if you're reading this book, you're already committed to playing—and learning how to win. The best place to start, then, is to find the games you're most suited for emotionally and psychologically. Players who enjoy what they're doing are more inclined to learn as much about their game as they can. They're more likely to give it their best shot and count the hours of pleasure the game provides among the rewards.

A Taxonomy of Games

Gambling is almost a science. Not only can you analyze games mathematically, as we showed you in the last chapter, you can also categorize them according to the type of player they attract. For instance, crap shooters like company. They're social beings who probably enjoy team sports and group activities. Slot players, on the other hand, are usually the Greta Garbos of the world who "vant to be alone!"

Best Bet _____

Diversify your gaming portfolio by learning to play different games. That way, if you're having a bad run in one game, you can always try your luck at something else.

Stanford and I have classified each game according to a broad psychological characterization of the majority of its players. Basically, there are five categories:

- ◆ Sociable games
- ◆ Analytical games
- ◆ Games you can beat
- ◆ Escapes from reality
- ◆ Patience games

In the next sections, take a look at which games fit into which categories. It's up to you to find the category of games that best suits your own personality, playing style, and preferences, and then learn to play those games well by reading the chapter that's listed beside the game.

Bet You Didn't Know ...

From the casino's perspective, there's a lot of psychology to gambling. When you sit down at a gaming table, for example, the first thing you do is lay down the money you want to play with, and the dealer gives you the equivalent amount in casino chips. It's easier for dealers to collect bets and make payoffs with chips instead of cash. But, more importantly, you're less likely to regard those bright, stackable chips as real money, so you spend more of them as a result (especially after you take advantage of all those "free" cocktails!).

For Party Animals and Social Beings

In *sociable games*, everyone wins or loses together. Players go up against the luck of the draw or the luck of the house, but not against each other. You'll generally find players laughing, talking—and sometimes even sweating it out—together. Like the Knights of the Round Table, it's one for all and all for one in these games. Although sociable players want to win, they know that if they don't, at least they had a good time trying. Sociable games include:

- Craps (Chapter 12)
- Roulette (Chapter 8)
- Baccarat (Chapter 9)
- Blackjack (Chapters 10 and 11)
- Pai gow poker (Chapter 19)
- Let It Ride (Chapter 17)
- Caribbean Stud (Chapter 20)

For Number Crunchers

Analytical games attract the more "cerebral" types who generally like to analyze data, read the fine print, draw their own conclusions, and might even be accused of "thinking too much"! If you love scouring the paper, aren't satisfied with just one account of an event, and like to find contradictions and formulate your own opinions, you'll probably love playing the horses or betting on sports. For you, the joy comes in doing your homework and then watching your prediction come true at the finish line or in the closing seconds of a game. These are the analytical games:

- Horse races (Chapter 13)
- Sports betting (Chapter 14)

For Those Who Play Only to Win

Some of the *games you can beat* are also sociable games, like blackjack and pai gow poker, but for the most part, these games attract serious players who want to get an edge. The typical "games you can beat" player is generally competitive and likes to win. S/he is also willing to put forth the extra time and effort it takes to master the game and tip the scales in his or her favor.

In most games you can beat, winning requires learning to play skillfully by using a basic or expert strategy and reading everything you can about beating your opponent. Most importantly, games you can beat involve making the right playing decisions, so you have to like making decisions in the first place. You also need to be discriminating about the conditions under which you play.

In games you can beat, you're the captain of your own ship and you're out there strictly on your own. It makes no difference how other people play or how many opponents you have to beat in order to win. Your goal is to come out ahead, period. The games you can beat with a little bit of luck and a whole lot of skill include:

◆ Blackjack (Chapters 10 and 11)

◆ Poker (Chapter 15)

◆ Pai gow poker (Chapter 19)

◆ Video poker (Chapter 16)

◆ Sports betting (Chapter 14)

◆ Horse races (Chapter 13)

When You Want to Get Away from It *All*

Everyone likes an occasional *escape from reality*, especially in a casino. That's probably why slots and video game machines are as popular as they are today. Play one of these games long enough and you won't even remember where you are. Plant me in front of one, and I'm mesmerized—totally unable to think of anything but the outcome of each spin, and winning. For other people, each spin takes them farther and farther away from their immediate surroundings … perhaps to a world where they've already won ….

Whatever the reason, players enjoy not only the mental and emotional escape that slot and video games provide, but the extraordinary potential for tremendous returns. To get a return that's equivalent to the thousands of dollars you can win on one successful pull of the handle or push of a button, you would have to wager very large sums of money on each hand or roll of the dice in another game.

The only problem with escape-from-reality games is that eventually they end—and more often than not, you lose. It takes a good deal of willpower and self-control to walk away from an escape mechanism. If you can understand and respect the discipline and psychological control these games require, you're more likely to leave a winner and enjoy the experience. The escape-from-reality games include:

- All slot machines (Chapters 5 and 6)

- All video games, such as keno, poker, blackjack, and so on (Chapters 16 and 26)

For Those with Time on Their Hands

If you like to relax when you play, you'll probably enjoy playing *patience games*. These are games in which players wait patiently for their numbers to come up. People who like to take things slowly—but still enjoy a little action now and then—prefer the calmer surroundings in which these games are played. If you like to take a chance without getting your adrenaline all worked up and have a handful of numbers that seem to work for you, consider playing one of these games:

 Best Bet

If you have a set of lucky numbers you like to play, you'll enjoy keno and lottery, or even roulette, which is a little faster-paced. When you play bingo, you don't get to choose your own numbers. The numbers you play are preprinted on the bingo game boards you purchase for each bingo session.

- Bingo (Chapter 24)

- Keno (Chapter 22)

- Lottery (Chapter 23)

Know Thyself

If you want to approach gambling as a professional, you have to choose your games carefully and devote weeks of study, practice, and *discipline* to becoming successful. Even then, you still have occasional losing sessions. Perhaps a better measure of success for a recreational player is not what it takes to win, but what it takes to make you *happy* when you play. Are you content to walk away from a game or a machine knowing you've given it your best shot and entertained yourself in the attempt? Or do you have to go for broke and win tons of money before you're satisfied?

Part of being a winner is setting realistic goals for yourself and then learning what you need to know to achieve them. In the average gambling session, you often have the opportunity to stop while you're ahead—or at least even—and walk away a winner. If that doesn't happen, you still have the opportunity to quit when you reach your limit, but many players don't take advantage of these stopping points and keep playing beyond their limit and their means. If this sounds like you, ask yourself if you have any intention of being a smart player and possibly a winner, or if you really just want to play. There *is* a difference.

A smart player knows his or her monetary and emotional limits and understands that there will be other days and other opportunities to win. A foolish player is more likely to gamble beyond his or her limits like there's no tomorrow—and go to sleep regretting the experience. If you're going to gamble, play smart: Set appropriate limits and stick to them.

I've noticed that when many people gamble, they forgo other simple pleasures—and even some necessities, like eating and sleeping! When I gamble, I like to stay in the best hotel I can afford because it's part of the whole gaming experience. But I never used to take advantage of the amenities available because they cut into my playing time and money.

> **⚠ CAUTION**
>
> **Risky Business**
>
> You learned in Chapter 3 why you're not likely to win back money you've lost by continuing to play with money you didn't plan on spending. Playing beyond your limit is a dangerous precedent that can transform gambling from recreation to a problem. Win or lose, be disciplined and stay within the time and monetary limits you set for yourself.

Now, as I've gotten older, I've learned there's more to having fun than gambling all the time. I've also learned that if I deny myself those simple pleasures, like good food, a sauna and massage (to relieve that video-poker shoulder!), or hanging out at the pool, I don't relax and—oddly enough—I don't win, either. Consequently, I've learned to strike a happy balance between relaxing and gambling. Not only do I feel better and play better when I take care of myself, I seem to win more often, too.

Respect the Lure of the Game

As we mentioned in Chapter 1, the proliferation of gambling in America is nothing new. We were a land of gamblers and risk-takers long before we were a nation. What's new is the legalization and regulation of gambling, which has lifted it out of the back rooms and alleys and into the mainstream. More people gamble today than ever before, and with those numbers come inevitable casualties.

Results of studies conducted in states that have recently legalized gambling show a rise in the number of gamblers with a gambling problem. According to Rachel Vobolerg of Gemini Research, Inc., in 1989, when the only form of legal gambling in Iowa was the state lottery, approximately 1.7 percent of the population had a moderate to severe gambling problem. Today, with the legalization of all forms of gambling on Indian reservations and riverboats, and the inclusion of slot machines at many horse-racing tracks in Iowa, that figure has more than tripled to 5.4 percent, largely as the result of video and slot machine play.

Ironically, losing doesn't cause gambling problems. Many compulsive gamblers start down the wrong path by *winning*, initially. The thrill of victory can be so enticing to some that after they have a substantial taste, they are unable to stop and are willing to risk everything in the pursuit of more.

Gambling has a serious downside that all recreational players need to be aware of. Gambling can be fun, thrilling, exciting, glamorous, even provocative at times, but it is also a serious game played for money, with real-life consequences. Most of us, fortunately, will never know the problems gambling can cause those who unwittingly take it beyond the sphere of entertainment and recreation and into the realm of addiction. But it's important to know yourself, know your limits, and resist any temptation to play beyond your means. If you suspect you or a loved one has a gambling problem, seek the help of organizations such as Gamblers Anonymous.

Gamblers Anonymous (GA) is a twelve-step recovery program patterned after Alcoholics Anonymous. The only requirement for membership in GA is a desire to stop gambling. If you want to get in touch with your local GA chapter, consult your local telephone directory or write to Gamblers Anonymous, P.O. Box 17173, Los Angeles, CA 90017, for the chapter nearest you.

What About *Luck?*

A chapter on winning wouldn't be complete without giving Lady Luck her due. As a group, recreational gamblers tend to be a superstitious bunch. They like to thank their lucky stars now and then, and more often than not, pin their losses on someone else. Poor Ms. Luck fits the bill on both counts. Whether you believe in luck or not,

CAUTION

Risky Business _____

Luck is big business. You can buy your "lucky numbers" and good luck charms from magazine ads, call psychic hotlines to divine your future, and even check your biorhythms on the information superhighway. The value of any of these resources is questionable. Proceed with caution and a sense of humor. You may be looking for luck in all the wrong places.

sometimes things happen that seem to defy explanation. How else can you explain hitting a jackpot with your last dollar? Winning the lottery with your first ticket? Being dealt a royal flush? These things happen, and to believers, no explanation other than luck will suffice.

Sure, a mathematician might watch an even number come up 20 times in a row on a roulette wheel and explain its occurrence by the randomness theory, which says that even unlikely events will occur occasionally. In fact, anything within the realm of possibility is likely to happen at least once over a long enough period. But a mathematician isn't likely to play roulette, and the guy who just collected a small fortune letting his bet ride on even knows that it was luck, and he'd be a fool to press it any further.

If the same roulette player took his or her winnings over to a slot machine and proceeded to win a few thousand dollars more in only a few pulls, he or she and everyone else would know for sure he or she was *hot!* Mathematicians, on the other hand, would claim these were just clusters of unlikely events that happened in a short span of time.

There's no way to predict whether the fortunate run will continue, just as there's no way to know when an odd number will finally come up. Certainly no one can debate that logic. But many gamblers believe that when you're hot, you're hot—and when you're not, you're not! And 'tis better to tempt the hand of fate when you happen to be running hot!

It does no good to debate who's right and who's wrong, but it's interesting to note the many ways gamblers try to court the lady. Some won't enter a casino without a lucky charm or an article of clothing they wore the last time they won, or without checking their horoscope and biorhythms first. Others believe in lucky numbers, and the games they play, such as keno, lotto, and roulette, allow them to indulge their beliefs.

Some players take foolish delight in tempting fate and testing their luck. One of my favorite blackjack buddies used to make my heart stand still by doubling down on 12 (which isn't a very smart thing to do), but 9 times out of 10—at least when I was sitting next to him—he'd win. I've seen blackjack players who did everything wrong but couldn't stop winning. I've even experienced some mindless runs myself, when the cards seemed to play themselves. Was it probability? Maybe. Was I due? Always. Was it luck? No doubt!

If you believe in luck, look for the signs and gauge your play accordingly. I like to find a video poker machine whenever I happen to notice the mileage on my car turning to four of a kind, full house, or a straight. I tend to hit a royal flush around my birthday. If I find a coin heads up, I keep it. If it's heads down, I turn it over and leave it for the next lucky person to find.

The bottom line on luck is this: It's fun to ponder and it's fun to have—but you can't take it to the bank. Unfortunately, even if Ms. Luck does exist, we never know when she's about to arrive because she doesn't make appointments. If you want to gamble, and you want to win, be prepared to do it on your own.

> **Best Bet**
>
> A casino is a great place to test your intuition. If you get occasional hunches, try paying attention to the ones involving slot machines, roulette wheels, or other games of chance and see what happens. I once dropped two bucks into a slot machine that caught my eye on the way to the snack bar and walked away with $1,000 *on one pull*. Remember, winning also involves knowing when to quit!

The Least You Need to Know

- When you play games you enjoy, you reap the psychological rewards that come from giving yourself time to play, compete, meet people, be alone, or just relax.

- To be a smart player, play the games you're attracted to and will enjoy playing. If you enjoy some of the beatable games, take the time to learn them well. Always set your limits and stick to them.

- It doesn't hurt to believe in luck (or divine intervention?) as long as you recognize it's just part of the game, not something to depend on.

Part 2

Taking a Chance

All gambling games are games of chance—some to a greater extent than others. In this part, we're going to show you how to play some of the most "chancy" games of all—those that require absolutely no skill. Chapters 5 and 6 cover slot machines, the most common and certainly the most popular games of chance today. They also happen to be among the riskiest. That's why we think they're worthy of two chapters.

Chapter 7 introduces you to the newest slot machines—mega-jackpots. And, Chapter 8 shows you how to play the very American and "sophisticated" roulette. Then Chapter 9 teaches you about the game that has no strategy—mini-baccarat.

Chapter 5

Slots–The Reel Story

In This Chapter

- ◆ Where slot machines came from and how they evolved
- ◆ Calculating your odds of winning
- ◆ Two kinds of slot machines—which is the best?
- ◆ Deciding how many coins to play

Charles Fey invented the first slot machine in the late 1800s, but don't blame him! Bugsy Siegel started the craze when he furnished his Flamingo Hilton hotel with slots back in the late 1940s as entertainment for the wives and girlfriends of his high-rolling friends. The rest is history. America can't seem to build slot palaces fast enough!

Slot machines have a universal appeal because, unlike other casino games, you can play them at your own pace and they don't require any skill. In this chapter, we'll examine enough interesting facts about slot machine odds and percentages to make your head spin. Then we'll try to help you find a machine that's right for you and get into a playing strategy in the next chapter.

The Machine Age

Slot machines, commonly referred to as "one-armed bandits," are unmistakably games of chance. They evolved from simple mechanical devices with three spinning *reels* into today's computer-controlled devices with three to five spinning reels. The reels, which have symbols printed on them, are the spinning wheels you see inside a slot-machine window.

Gamb-lingo

The **payline** is the line on a slot-machine window where the symbols from each reel must line up. Slot machines can have as many as eight (or more!) paylines, although most have only one. The more paylines, the more coins you need to play.

The old-style reel had 20 symbols on it, but with today's technology, a reel can have hundreds—it's actually very hard to tell! Your goal, whether playing an old machine or a new one, is to spin the reels so that the symbols on all of them line up on the *payline* in a winning combination, like the one shown in the following figure. If they do, you win according to the payout table posted on the front of the machine. The payout table tells you what each winning symbol combination pays for the number of coins played. If the symbols don't line up in a winning combination, you try again!

It doesn't get much better than this!

This payout table tells you what symbols need to line up and how much you win when they do.

This is a winning combination of symbols, lined up on the payline.

The reels spin simultaneously, but each one stops individually.

Odds Are, There's a Catch

It doesn't matter at all what type of symbols a machine has, such as wild cherries, bars, double bars, double diamonds, 7s, and so on. What *does* matter is how many reels a machine has and how many symbols are on each reel. The more reels and symbols, the harder it is to hit the *jackpot* or even a winning combination.

Gamb-lingo

The **jackpot** is the moment you've been waiting for. It's the biggest win you can get on a slot machine: the combination of symbols that pays you back for all your time and effort.

For example, if you need to line up three gold 7s on one payline to win the jackpot, it's likely that each reel has only one gold 7 on it. On a three-reel machine with a total of 20 symbols on each reel, your chances of lining up all three gold 7s are:

Number of gold 7s per reel: 1–1–1

Possible symbol combinations on all three reels: 20×20×20 = **8,000**

Odds of hitting three 1/20×1/20×1/20 = gold 7s on three reels: **1 in 8,000**

Diminishing Returns

If there happen to be 120 symbols (instead of 20) on each reel, but still only one gold 7, your odds or chances of hitting the jackpot are reduced to

$1/120 \times 1/120 \times 1/120$, or **1 in 1,728,000**!

It gets even worse when you play a five-reel machine with just 20 symbols each:

$1/20 \times 1/20 \times 1/20 \times 1/20 \times 1/20 =$ **1 in 3,200,000**.

(That's less than one chance in three million!)

The number of reels and the number of symbols on each reel greatly affect your chances of winning. It's certainly not a case of "the more the merrier" in slots!

Sweating the Small Stuff

The payout table on the front of a slot machine tells you what the winning combinations of symbols are for that machine and what each combination pays based on the number of coins you put in for the spin. You have a much greater chance of hitting any of the lower-paying combinations (the small stuff) simply because there are many more of those symbols programmed on each reel. That shouldn't discourage you, though, because those small wins keep you in the action long enough to hit the big one!

Here's how to figure your chances of lining up three cherries on a hypothetical three-reel machine with 20 symbols on each: If there are four cherries on one reel, three on another, and two on the third reel, you have 24 ways ($1/4 \times 1/3 \times 1/2$) to line up three cherries across all three reels. Out of 8,000 possible combinations, you have 24 ways to hit three cherries, or 1 in 333 (which is 8,000 divided by 24). The odds against you are stated as 332 to 1, which means you have 332 ways to lose and only 1 way to win.

Some machines will pay you if you line up just one special symbol on any of the reels. For the probability of getting just one cherry, for example, the math gets a little more complicated—but the odds get better! You need to multiply the chance of getting a cherry on one reel by the chance of not getting a cherry on the other reels. Then repeat this for all the reels and add up the results. Here's how to do it for our hypothetical three-reel machine:

$1/4 \times 1/17 \times 1/18$) + ($1/16 \div$ **1/3** $\times 1/18$) + ($1/16 \times 1/17 \times$ **1/2**) = **2,632** ways to hit exactly **1** cherry.

Another quick calculation (2,632/8,000) shows that you have approximately 1 in 3 chances of hitting a cherry. In plain English, that means you should get exactly one cherry on this hypothetical machine in every three spins—which makes the odds only 2 to 1 against you!

What Makes the Jackpots So *Big?*

You already know that the odds against you on the old-time mechanical slot machines were limited by how many symbols could be squished onto each reel and how many reels could be jammed into a slot-machine cabinet. But did you know that on today's computerized models, the number of symbols on each reel is programmed into the computer that operates the slot machine? And the actual number of symbols (which you no longer see) depends on the size of the jackpot that the machine offers. For example, on two similarly configured machines (say, three-coin quarter machines with three reels), the machine that offers the higher jackpot generally has a greater number of symbols programmed on each reel.

The reason for all the "programmed" symbols is to make the jackpot rare enough that the machine generates enough money to pay for the jackpot and yield a profit for the casino. The higher the jackpot, the more symbols are programmed on each reel, making it harder for anyone to hit the winning combination. With computer technology, modern one-armed bandits can be programmed to respond as though they had hundreds or even thousands of symbols on a reel, making the odds against hitting the jackpot astronomical. And you thought this was gonna be easy!

Bet You Didn't Know ...

When slot machine manufacturers first attempted to replace mechanical spinning reels with video displays because they couldn't fit hundreds of symbols on one mechanical reel, the gambling public voted their discontent by ignoring those machines. To gain greater acceptance, many manufacturers replaced the newfangled video displays with the old style, 20-symbol mechanical reels, so that slot machine aficionados could still continue to enjoy watching them spin; even though the spin doesn't control the outcome— the computer program does!

Nanoseconds to Wealth

If you did happen to know that the odds of hitting a jackpot on a particular machine were 1 in 8,000 spins, then you could logically conclude that the machine would start its *pay cycle* over every 8,000 plays. In those 8,000 plays, you should theoretically be able to hit all the other possible combinations of payouts at least once. Right?

Wrong! The concept of a pay cycle helps explain what happens in the long run, but in the short run, things don't always work out that way. The reason is simple: Each possible combination of symbols (both winning and losing) on a modern slot machine is assigned a number in the computer program that controls the machine. One of the functions of the program is to continuously generate random numbers that correspond to the symbol combinations. The random number generator works faster than you do and never stops. When you press the SPIN button or pull the slot handle, the number generator pauses briefly to display the symbol combination that corresponds to the random number that was just selected when you activated the spin. However, even while you watch the reels rotate to find out whether you won, the random

Gamb-lingo

A **pay cycle** is a theoretical expression—the number of plays required for the machine to cycle through all possible winning and losing combinations. But payouts are randomized. In the short run, a machine doesn't actually hit each possible combination exactly the number of times specified in the pay cycle.

Best Bet

Dwight and Louise Crevelt offer an insider's view of how modern slot machines are programmed in their book, *Slot Mania*. If you want to know what makes a slot machine tick, this is a good place to start!

number generator continues to generate numbers, waiting for your next spin.

Because of the way symbol combinations are selected by the random number generator, a modern slot machine can hit another jackpot in only eight more spins, or it can take another 80,000. All you know for sure is that over the life of the machine, it *will* average out to one jackpot in approximately 8,000 spins, *and*, if luck is with you, you'll be sitting there for at least one of them!

Playing the Payback Percentages

Not only are the odds stacked against you, the house also has the percentages on its side. For every complete pay cycle (let's say, 8,000 spins on our 3-reel, 20-symbol favorite) the machine is set to keep a percentage of coins played. Most machines are set to pay out anywhere from 80 to 98 percent of the coins played in the course of a pay cycle (which also includes paying out the jackpot!).

Many casinos compete by advertising high payouts—some as high as 97.4 percent or more. That's a pretty fair shake, although it means that in the long run, you will lose at the rate of 2.6 percent. Unfortunately, it doesn't mean that every machine in the casino will give back 97.4 percent, nor does it mean that everyone who plays one of those machines will lose only 2.6 percent. What it does mean is that over a long enough period, the machine will pay back an average of 97.4 percent of the money it takes in.

Gamb-lingo

A **flat top** slot machine's jackpot is always a fixed amount. A **progressive** slot machine's jackpot keeps increasing each time a coin is played. It resets when the jackpot finally hits.

So Many Machines, So Little Time

All this talk about randomization, odds, and percentage payouts can be pretty boring when all you want to do is get out there and play, but you may find it comes in handy when you're standing in the middle of an oasis trying to decide which machine to try first.

There are basically two kinds of slot machines: *flat tops* and *progressives*. They are virtually identical, except for one distinguishing feature: The progressives have a jackpot (and sometimes two jackpots) that keeps growing and *growing* with each coin that's played. You can identify a progressive machine by the flashing electronic payout sign at either the top of an individual machine or suspended above a group of machines that share the same jackpot.

When a progressive jackpot covers many machines, it grows as each machine is fed coins. Any machine in the group can win. Progressive jackpots can be tied to all the same machines in a casino or, like the Megabucks in Las Vegas that paid one hungry student $10.9 million after five minutes of play, all the same machines in a whole state. These multi-machine progressives are the ones that offer the largest jackpots and, consequently, the worst odds.

Gamb-lingo

A **carousel** is a group of slot machines arranged in a circle. A **change** stands in the center and changes your hundred-dollar bills quicker than you can blink an eye! A **bank** is also a group of slot machines, but they are arranged back-to-back, with no room for a change person in between.

Flat tops, on the other hand, have fixed jackpots that remain the same no matter how many coins you feed them or how long you play. Because they operate independently, they don't need to be placed on *carousels*, or banks, of the same type of machine, although sometimes they are. Because their jackpots are smaller and less enticing than the progressives, most people think they pay more often. If you read the past few sections about odds, you'll understand why that's probably true.

Bet You Didn't Know ...

Many of today's video machine games, like video poker, video blackjack, and video keno, are derived from slot machines and actually operate using the same microprocessor technology and randomization sequences. Because they give the player real options and choices, however, they require an element of skill and knowledge of the underlying games that regular slot machines don't. For that reason, we've chosen to cover them on their own in Chapters 16 and 25.

Variety Is the Spice of Life

As we said before, the "theme" of your slot machine, like Blazing 7s, Signs of the Zodiac, Fruit Salad, Red White and Blue, 5X, and so on, doesn't matter at all. What's most important is how your machine is set up. Choose a machine according to your *budget* and your *risk tolerance*. There's a huge variety of machines out there, designed to accommodate everyone from the timid to the wild and crazy (and those of us in between).

You'll be faced with these decisions whether you elect to play a simple standalone flat top or a progressive machine:

- ◆ What denomination of coin to play?

- ◆ How many reels and how many coins?

- ◆ Single or multiple paylines?

- ◆ One, two, three, or more coins?

The Price of Admission

Most modern casinos and slot palaces have an abundance of quarter and dollar machines, with a few nickel machines scattered around the outer edges. It's getting harder to find half-dollar machines anymore, but keep looking if that's what you enjoy.

To accommodate the more daring among us (or should we say, "high rollers" or "whales"?), larger casinos have installed $5, $25, $100, and even $500 machines in special VIP areas. Of course, these machines require the use of custom coin tokens or cash bills, and when you fire one up, there's a drum roll.

Lucky for me, I can still get simple pleasure in finding a lonely quarter machine to pass the time when my luck runs out, but many less fortunate souls believe that graduating to a higher denomination machine will help them get their money back. Theoretically, they're right—as long as they win. Unfortunately, these high-dollar machines usually have the very same adverse odds as all the other slots. Call me a wimp, but I still believe that if your personal pot of gold isn't endless, you're not ready for the drum roll yet!

Denominations and Payouts

Generally, nickel machines have poorer payouts than quarters, and quarters seem to pay out less than dollars. The reason is that the casino's cost of operating a slot machine does not depend much on the denomination of the coin accepted, but rather on the amount of floor space required, the number of change people, maintenance, and so on. All things being equal, for a machine to yield a targeted number of dollars or winnings for the casino, a higher percentage must be kept if the machine accepts smaller coins. Consequently, the nickel machines are said to have among the lowest payout percentages and $5 and $25 machines are among the highest. To find the denomination video poker or slot machines you want to play in a crowded casino, look at the color of the light, or candle, on top of each machine. The bottom of the candle is color-coded according to the denomination of the machine so that technicians, floor people, and players can find them more easily.

As you can see in the following figure, the top of the candle is a plain white light that lights up when you hit a jackpot or your machine needs servicing. The bottom part is colored according to this code:

- Nickel machines are red.

- Quarter machines are yellow.

- Half dollar machines are orange/gold.

- Dollar machines are blue.

- Five-dollar machines are purple.

Reels of Fortune

It's not too tough to line up one symbol on a payline. That's why they don't make any one- or two-reel machines. The most common machines these days have three reels with a two- or three-coin maximum.

When you start playing the progressives, you find more four- and five-reel machines, which are harder to hit. Remember, the more symbols on a reel and the more reels a machine has, the greater the odds *against* you getting the jackpot symbol on every reel on the payline. The mega-jackpots almost always come on four- or five-reel machines that can take as many as five coins. As casinos continue to up the jackpot ante in an effort to outdo each other, I'm sure more reels (with more losing symbols on each reel) will be added to the big progressives.

How Many Ways Does It Pay?

The standard slot machine has one payline, and three paylines are not that uncommon. When a machine has three paylines, as shown in the following figure, that means you get paid for lining up the right combination of symbols on each line. However, you don't get paid unless you have one coin in to activate each payline.

Here's how it works: You get paid for the first coin you play when you hit a winning combination on the center payline. For the second coin you play, you get paid for combinations on the upper payline, and for the third coin you play you get paid for combinations on the bottom payline. The bottom line is if you don't load these puppies up with the maximum coins, you're not taking advantage of all the possibilities the machine has to offer. Occasionally, you'll find machines with eight or more paylines. Watch out!

Fortunately, this instant millionaire had three coins in!

If you play a second coin, a winning combination will win on either the top or the center payline.

With only one coin in, you have to line the symbols up on this center payline.

When you play three coins, a winning combination on any payline wins!

Know When to Load 'Em

As you'll soon learn, there are many subtle variations among machines. You will find many two-coin, three-reel machines (with only one payline) that pay twice as much on every winning combination hit with two coins played as it does with only one coin in—just as you would expect. On those machines, it doesn't make much difference whether you prefer to play one or two coins.

Other slots, however, more than double the jackpot on a two-coin win compared with a one-coin win and more than triple the three-coin jackpot. Some three-coin machines don't even offer a jackpot on one coin, and the three-coin jackpot often pays more than one and a half times (150 percent) a two-coin win. When you're playing one of these machines, your best bet is to load it up.

If you don't want to play the maximum coins in a machine, read the payout table at the top or bottom of the machine carefully to make sure it isn't one in which the number of coins played makes more than a *proportional* difference in the size of your payoff.

Know *Where* to Go

Where you play can be just as important as what machines you play. As we mentioned before, machines can be set to return a percentage of all the money played, over time. If a machine is set to pay back 80 percent of the money you put in, you lose at a rate of 20 percent, on the average. Your challenge, if you think that is a reasonable price to pay for the enjoyment of playing slots, is to find the machines that pay the most. Nevada offers the most liberal slots overall. There are good slot machines in many other states, but you have to know where to find them.

You'll find big differences between slot payoffs from casino to casino in any city. Because slot players seem to gravitate toward the loosest ones, it's a good idea to shop around and play where the slot machines seem to be the busiest. Also, look for slot machines placed near the busiest entrances. Casinos often place their most liberal machines where they're likely to draw the most customers.

The Least You Need to Know

- Slot machines were invented in the late 1800s, became popular in the 1940s, and downright addictive in the 1990s. Computer chips control modern slot machines.

- Your odds of hitting a jackpot on the old machines with three reels were 1 in 8,000. The odds on today's new improved machines are not only exponentially worse, they're almost impossible to figure out.

- Most machines are set to give you back 75 to 97 percent of the coins you put in, meaning the casino keeps 3 to 25 percent. Because of the randomness designed into the machines, your short-term results will vary substantially from play to play.

- If a machine has more than one payline, you probably need to put in an additional coin for each additional payline.

- If you choose to play a machine with multiple paylines, a progressive, or a flat top with a large difference in payouts for the number of coins played, don't forget to load it up!

Chapter 6

More on Slots (A Sensible Strategy)

In This Chapter

- What a real loser looks like
- Choosing which slots to play based on your bankroll
- A simple strategy that won't make you rich, but won't kill you either!
- Keeping your winnings from finding their way back into the same machine
- When to take the progressive plunge, and how to do it

In the previous chapter, we told you a little about the history of slot machines and a lot about your chances of winning. The good news is that the same technology that makes today's slot machines so hard to hit also allows your favorite casino to offer extraordinary, millionaire-making jackpots! Aside from the fact that playing them *is* downright fun, that's probably why slot machines have become the odds-on favorite in any gaming capital.

In this chapter, we'll provide a simple, logical strategy that may help you hold on to your money longer as you single-handedly wage the all-out battle between man and machine. We'll also help you figure out how much money you should start with to give different-denomination machines your best shot, and we'll explain why some machines are better to play than others, depending on your tolerance for risk and appetite for riches. We've even thrown in a little advice about entering slot tournaments as a way to really enjoy yourself and maybe even come away a big winner!

Be Good

You can read all the books you want about playing slots and it still comes down to one word: *luck!* If you've angered any gods, killed any flies, hit little children, or walked under a ladder within the past 24 hours (or however long it takes to clear *your* karma), don't even play. Slots can be one of the most dehumanizing, demoralizing, and devastating games out there, and your spirits, biorhythms, and positive vibrations need to be *way* high to win. Having a winning attitude is almost as important as having the vast sums of money needed to stake your claim. If you're still determined to find entertainment this way, keep reading.

How Much *Is* Enough?

First, you must decide how much you are going to play with. What's your bankroll? The size of your "wad" will help you figure out a strategy. *Never play with more than you can afford to lose.* The numbers in the following table show you what it would cost per hour to play a typical three-reel slot machine—and *lose* every spin (assuming *only* 10 spins per minute).

Cost Per Hour to Play (and Lose) at a Three-Reel Slot Machine

Denomination	One Coin	Two Coins	Three Coins
Cost per Hour, Based on the Number of Coins Bet			
Nickel ($.05)	$30	$60	$90
Quarter ($.25)	$150	$300	$450
One dollar ($1.00)	$600	$1,200	$1,800
Five dollars ($5.00)	$3,000	$6,000	$9,000
Twenty-five dollars ($25.00)	$15,000	$30,000	$45,000

Fortunately, losing on *every* spin is nearly as improbable as winning on every spin—but it can happen! In reality, you should be able to retain at least 80 to 98 percent of your payments, depending on the overall percentage payout of the machine you select and how long you play. If you seem to be losing all your money as quickly as the preceding figure would indicate, *run*—don't walk—to the nearest exit!

Great Expectations

Now that you've seen the worst-case scenario, let's take a look at what's more likely to occur. Let's say a casino advertises 90 percent payout on their slots, and you're lucky enough to find one that is currently running pretty true to a 90 percent return. To figure out what you can expect to lose on that machine, take 10 percent of every cost per hour number listed in the preceding figure. For example, if you were playing three quarters per spin, you should more realistically expect to lose $45.00 per hour, instead of $450.00. Remember, of course, that this is an *average*; in real play, you might get back less than 50 percent in one hour, 85 percent in another, and hopefully 150 percent in the next.

Best Bet _____

In Nevada and Atlantic City (places where gambling is carefully regulated), slot machines are required by law to pay back a certain percentage. In Las Vegas, for example, the minimum payback allowed is 75 percent. Knowing that they must compete with other casinos for your business, most casino operators in regulated cities set their machines to pay back in the 90 percent range. *Strictly Slots* magazine, which you can find in many of your favorite casinos, lists the payback percentages for different denomination slot machines in all of the major gaming centers in the country.

How Long Are You *In* For?

Another factor in determining what type of machine to play is the amount of time you'd like to spend playing. There's a big difference between playing for an hour or two every other week at your local casino, and "staying alive" (in the money) for a week in Las Vegas. Before deciding on a level of play, do this:

◆ Divide your total bankroll for the trip by the number of days you plan to play.

◆ Divide your daily allowance by the number of hours of play you'd like to enjoy per day. Be sure to take into account all the playing sessions you want to enjoy per day (for example, one between breakfast and lunch, one after dinner, and so on) and calculate the amount of time to give yourself for each.

◆ Use the preceding table and the information in the previous two sections to get a rough idea of the machines you should be playing. For example, if you want $1,000 to last for four days of five hours of play (20 hours total), that means you can afford to lose $50 per hour. With average results (approximately 90 percent payback) and expected losses, you should be playing quarter machines at three quarters per spin.

◆ If you come up nickels in your calculations but want to play dollars, give up some of your playing *time* (play fewer hours) to up the ante. Then do as you promised and quit playing when the money runs out!

The *Risk* Factor

Some of you might have the money but not the stomach to pour large sums of cash into high-priced machines. You are truly the lucky ones. There's no shame in playing way *below* your means as long as you continue to be entertained. That's the key to this whole adventure. When slot playing ceases to be entertainment and becomes the center of your life, you're either in too deep or just dreaming.

If you play *way beyond* your means, remember: There are more promising and lucrative ways for you to invest your time and money. Perhaps you should consider telling the boss to "take this job," and use your unspent energy and resources to start your own business or a new career. Dumping your savings into a slot machine may feel exciting and daring at the moment. However, it will not resolve inner conflict, dissatisfaction with your present situation, or any other business or personal problem that might be temporarily numbed by the mindless exchange of coins. Set realistic financial limits, and *don't* play Russian roulette with your future.

Preserving Your Capital

Once you decide whether to play nickel, quarter, dollar, or *VIP machines*, start out slow and then up the ante as you begin to collect your winnings. You may find this approach contrary to the way you're used to playing (that is, putting your *big* money up first, and then backing down to a lower denomination or simpler machines when things don't go your way), but it makes more sense to use only your *winnings* on the riskier (progressive) or more expensive machines. The key is to start collecting the house's money early, or stop playing. Risk the house's money, not your own!

Playing by the Magazine

Every month *Strictly Slots* magazine helps you become an "informed" player by listing the past month's payout percentages for each denomination machine—by casino. In the table at the beginning of this chapter, I took an average of the *Strictly Slots* information for June 2002 to give you an idea of the payout percentages you can expect from different denomination slot machines in different parts of the country.

Location	Percentage Payback by Slot Machine Denomination					
	$.05	*$.25*	*$.50*	*$1.00*	*$5.00*	*$25.00*
Atlantic City	91.2	92.6	93.2	93.2	96.3	102.0
Nevada	93.1	96.8	97.0	96.8	98.3	106.7
Connecticut	n/a	91.01	90.9	92.0	94.9	97.0
Louisiana	92.1	93.0	94.1	94.6	96.5	100.6
Mississippi	91.7	92.8	94.3	95.5	95.3	95.4
Missouri	91.1	94.3	95.2	95.6	97.7	102.6
Illinois	92.6	94.8	95.4	95.9	97.7	98.3
Indiana	94.3	92.6	94.4	95.2	99.5	97.9
Iowa	92.8	93.8	n/a	95.9	97.9	106.4
Colorado	93.5	95.2	95.4	n/a	n/a	n/a

First, look for the two-coin, three-reel flat tops; they're known to be more benevolent (easier to win at) than similarly configured progressives. Some of these machines include Wild Cherries, Double Wild Cherries, and Home Runs. Other good choices include Crazy Doublers, Double Diamonds, and some Red White and Blues because they offer either wild cards or double-up symbols, which increase your payouts. Be sure to read the fine print on the machine's payout table first; casinos know these machines are favorites, and sometimes put look-alikes right next to them.

Gamb-lingo

A slot machine that requires $5 or more per spin is often referred to as a **VIP machine** because those who play them are Very Important Players to the house. VIP machines are often located in special, roped-off areas of the casino.

A winning flat top.

Three winners lined up on the payline!

Right-Sizing Your Investment

Regular slot players advise you to always *load up* your slot machine. And they're right: Playing the extra coins more than doubles your winnings on a two-coin machine, or more than triples your winnings on a three-coin machine (that means the third coin pays you more than *150 percent* of your two-coin winnings). It's also the soundest advice when playing flat tops with multiple playlines or *any* type of progressive.

In plenty of other machines, including the Wild Cherries and some Red White and Blues, your two-coin winnings are exactly twice the amount of your one-coin winnings, and your three-coin winnings are always triple. If you don't like to play the maximum number of coins, these are the only machines you should play.

Gamb-lingo

When you **load up** a slot machine, you play the maximum number of coins the slot machine or video game machine allows on each spin.

The reason many people believe you should always load up a machine is that, like buying a home with a small down payment, the extra coins played allow you to leverage a small investment (that extra coin or two) to win *the extra money that only a maximum bet wins*. What they don't tell you is that playing the extra coins also increases your level of risk (the amount of money you wager is what is at risk), which in the long run can wind up costing you plenty of money. On those few machines where your extra coin doesn't matter, play at a level that you feel most comfortable with and don't worry about the "experts." If you absolutely don't want to play the maximum number of coins and can't find the machines that will let you get away with less, consider dropping down to a smaller coin so that you can load up the machine.

Know When to Walk Away

The bottom line is to play the denomination of coin you're most comfortable with and switch to another similarly configured machine if the one you're on won't pay. The objective is to *hit and run*. Most winners tell you, and I've often experienced this myself (Stanford doesn't play slot machines, but I do!), that if a machine is going to give you a big one, it does so when you first start playing. One roll of coins or a few ten or twenty dollar bills is enough to tell whether you've found a winning machine. Understanding this can save you hundreds or thousands of dollars! Don't keep feeding stubborn machines. There are good machines waiting to be found.

Best Bet

The change people on the slot floor have to hang around the casino when you don't, so they usually know which machines are better, meaning they might have a higher payback percentage, or they've been paying out recently and might still be hot. If you ask nicely and offer a token of appreciation when they're right, you may find it pays!

If you search and search and still can't find a good machine, nothing should stop you from leaving. If you're on vacation and still want to play, pick up a local newspaper or magazine and find out which casinos in the area advertise the 95 percent and higher slot payouts. Then take yourself to one of those.

If you're really serious about your slot money, spend some time learning about slot machines by playing penny or nickel machines before raising the stakes to a higher denomination. Take notice of the kind of machine you are playing, how often you get a win, which symbols come up more often, which symbols don't come up at all, etc. Try different machines out so you can pick up the nuances that distinguish a "good" machine from a "bad" one, i.e., more small wins, money returned on every other spin, lose one in four spins, etc.

I'm always trying to psychoanalyze slot machines—I want to believe there's more to them than just random numbers—and some day I'll crack the code! Recently I found a bank of three-coin, three-reel, Red White and Blue nickel machines that offered a new Mercedes as the jackpot. At 15 cents per pull, I had a great time analyzing the play by watching my credits (a.k.a money) go up and down. All the time wondering when it would finally hit and how much my car insurance would cost!

Bet You Didn't Know ...

Many casinos offer special promotions and clubs to entice slot players. If you're a regular player or tend to stay in one hotel/casino while you're gambling, joining a slot club can save you hundreds of dollars in room and board expenses. To cash in on these deals, speak with the casino's slot host or hostess on your next visit, and read Chapter 30 to find out more.

As a club member, every dollar you drop into a machine earns you special discount credits and sometimes even cash back. The only catch is that you might have to play a higher denomination of coin or spend more time playing than you ordinarily would to qualify. Because each club is different, check around until you find one that fits your budget and playing style. After you join a slot club or two, you'll get free-room offers in the mail. You may never have to pay for a vacation room again!

Taking It with You

Slot machines aren't entirely the mercenary machines we've made them out to be. Any regular player will tell you that one of the main reasons slot players lose is because *they don't leave when they're winning!*

Today you'll find more and more casinos converting their coin-in slot machines to coinless ones. Coinless machines make it easier for you to keep track of your winnings because they accept bills ($1, $5, $20, and $100s) rather than coins, and spit out printed tickets that serve as both a receipt for your money and a record of how much money you have left. If your casino's slot machines have been converted to the coinless ones you no longer have to wait for a "fill" when your machine runs out of coins. Nor do you have to scoop up all your coins and haul buckets to the cashier cage to get an official count of your money. Coinless machines keep track of your money by way of machine "credits." If you are playing a quarter machine ($.25), each credit counted is equal to $.25. You accumulate credits with each jackpot and spend credits with each spin. The credit meter will always show you how you're doing as you play. To cash out, all you have to do is press the Collect button and a built-in printer will print you a ticket for the dollar amount of your machine credits. This system makes it a lot easier to cash-out and leave a bad machine!

Bet You Didn't Know ...

Bill feeders are another modern convenience that casinos have installed in order to part you from your money quicker. You no longer have to wait for the change person to arrive, you don't have to take time to drop coins into the machine, and with the credit meter, you don't even have to wait for your winnings to drop into the basket because a credit ticket is printed.

To make life even easier, casinos are now contemplating "cashless" machines that will enable you to insert a credit card-size "smart card" into a machine instead of cash. All you'll have to do before playing is to go to the cage, or cashier's desk, and deposit the money you want to use. Then, insert the card into the slot machine or video games you want to play and your credits and debits will be applied as you play. When you run out of credits on the card, just go back to the cage and deposit more money.

Hot and Cold Running Money

Once you find a good machine, credits can help you keep track of the machine's highs and lows. Most experienced slot players will tell you that slot machines run in hot and cold cycles. When you play the credits on a hot machine, you can watch how high it lets your credits mount up before it starts to take them away as you continue to play. You can also see how far down it takes the credits before it lets you build them back up with more winnings. When your most recent high doesn't get you above the previous high, or the dips are starting to get lower, that probably a sign that the joyride is over for now.

The problem with tracking a machine's highs and lows or hot and cold cycles is that what you're looking at is history. Even if you think you've got a hot machine, you have no way of knowing whether it will stay hot if you keep playing, nor do you have any way to predict when a cold machine will warm up. Your safest bet is to cash out any winnings before you lose them all and walk away from a machine that doesn't return enough coins or credits for the amount of money you've put in.

Best Bet

Casinos often put "loose" machines right in the middle of, or next to, a group of machines set with lower payouts (that is, "tight" ones). If you think the one you're on is tight, check out the machines on either side. They might be looser!

Moving On Up!

After you start cashing in some of the house's money (that means you've been stashing it away), you can in good conscience decide to climb the next mountain. Or you can remain content in the knowledge that the gods are smiling on you *right where you are*, and just keep playing at the same level.

> ### Bet You Didn't Know ...
>
> Back in Psych 101 I had a white rat named Elmo who didn't get fed until he learned to press a bar in his cage. Whenever he pressed it, a pellet fell into his dish. Elmo quickly learned to press the bar when he got hungry.
>
> Then one day we (the professor and the rest of us budding psychologists) changed the rules. Sometimes we gave Elmo dinner when he pressed the bar—and sometimes we didn't. Poor Elmo no longer knew when to expect his food. So you know what he did? He pounded that bar relentlessly until the food finally came. Sound familiar?
>
> The biggest lesson we learned from Elmo (and B. F. Skinner) was that if you want to make behavior stick, *don't* reward it all the time; reward it now and then. This strategy is called *random reinforcement,* and it's the same principle at work on us when we play slot machines.

Best Bet

Another way to win at slots is to casually look for abandoned machines with credits on them. Sometimes players forget to cash out before they leave!

If you elect to get your adrenaline flowing a little faster by taking the climb, you can move up to a higher denomination machine or stay with the same coinage but switch to a progressive. Remember from the previous chapter that progressives carry higher jackpots (often *much* higher), but don't pay out as many of the small wins that keep you in the running longer. Once you move up, play with the same hit-and-run attitude you had before: Dip your toe in to see if a machine's hot or cold, and move on when you have to.

Proceed With Caution

There's no mistaking that progressives offer the glamour and dream of windfall profits that most flat tops don't. It's the progressives that people are playing when you read about them winning $50,000 on a quarter machine, or a million or more on a three-dollar bet. But invariably, either those people *hit* and *ran* and are now seriously grateful, or the windfall may have been just enough to even them out over the course of their "chronic" playing life.

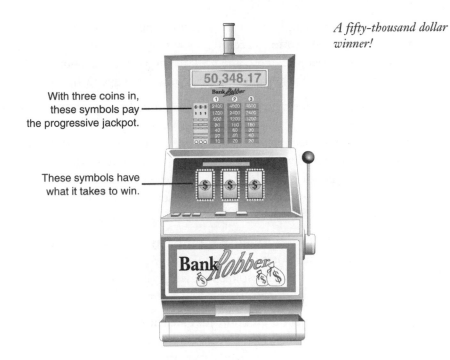

A fifty-thousand dollar winner!

With three coins in, these symbols pay the progressive jackpot.

These symbols have what it takes to win.

Either way, there's no disputing that a big jackpot's nice, but it's not going to happen to most of us. So, if you enjoy the challenge, the adrenaline rush, the isolation, whatever, be content in that enjoyment and leave the checkbook at home! Progressives have a way of killing you softly with their song.

Progressing Nicely

Here's some advice that may help keep you alive while you're progressing:

Always **load up a progressive machine.** As we said before, progressives don't pay as often or as many of the small winning combinations that simple machines do, so you're actually playing for the jackpot only. In that case, you have to load them up to get the jackpot. *Read the payout table!*

Pay attention to the sound of the casino. Notice which machines are hitting and which aren't. Often there will seem to be "hot" carousels and cold ones. Follow like sheep to the hot ones.

Play the progressives with the highest jackpots. It makes sense to seek the greatest reward if you're willing to take the progressive risk. Ask the change person for help in locating top jackpots.

Stake out a seemingly hot carousel and spend an evening (between dinner and second show time) watching how the machines do. After you've seen enough, go to sleep. Then come back in the very early hours of the morning and hit the ones that have been played hard but haven't hit yet!

If you happen to see a group of machines linked to a large progressive jackpot (in a carousel) and all the machines are being played, it could be the jackpot is so high that the machines are paying back over 100 percent. Come back when you're likely to find an available machine—probably in the morning. Of course, be sure the jackpot is still high. If it was recently hit, the players are gone because none of the machines on the carousel are worth playing anymore. (In that case, all bets are off!)

Resist the temptation to move up the pay scale when you're losing. Because slots have the worst odds, increasing your level of play can be the worst bet in the house! If you must keep playing, get off the progressives and find some simple nonprogressive (flat top) machines.

When you finally hit a jackpot, just sit there. Take a deep breath. Don't mistakenly pull the handle again or touch a button. Most jackpots, especially those that are $1,000 or more, are paid by an attendant who will come over to verify your win and pay you off in cash.

Bet You Didn't Know ...

Another common myth or misconception about slot machines is that those on the aisles often pay better. The reason end machines appear to be better is because they're played more often. Machines that get more play are often set to pay back more generously.

For example, suppose a machine needs to win $1,000 for the casino to cover the expense of each machine. If $10,000 of play is expected, that machine will be set to pay back 90 percent ($10,000 − $1,000 in cost = $9,000 or 90 percent). If $20,000 of play is expected, the machine will pay back 95 percent ($20,000 − $1,000 in cost = $19,000 or 95 percent). The important point to remember is to play the machines that seem to get the most action.

Your Own Personal Piggy Bank

One of the common misconceptions about slot machines, and progressives in particular, is that if you keep feeding one machine, it's got to pay off sooner or later. Well, you can feed the machine so much money that even winning the big one won't pay back what you fed in. This is especially true on many of the one dollar progressives, where the jackpot starts at around $1,000. I have personally witnessed many players feverishly throwing what appears to be much more than $1,000 in coins into a machine to win a $1,065 jackpot. Even many experienced players have given a jackpot or two *back* trying to recapture the moment! Machines have minds of their own, and you can't buy them. *Hit* and *run!*

Tournaments Pay!

One way to almost guarantee yourself a good time whether you win or lose is to enter a slot tournament. Many casinos now offer promotional slot tournaments for a fixed entry fee, which entitles you to participate in a multi-day tournament event, enjoy free room and board at the casino hotel while the tournament is in progress, and be wined, dined, and treated like the valued customer you are by casino personnel. Not only that, your participation gives you the opportunity to compete against other enthusiasts to win thousands—even *hundreds* of thousands—of dollars in tournament prize money.

Most slot tournaments have a number of rounds in which contestants are given the same amount of machine credits and told to play them until the time is up or their machine credits run out. The contestant with the most credits at the end of each round wins a substantial prize and a spot in the final round. The top prizes are usually awarded to the top three finalists.

If you enjoy the thrill and excitement of playing slot machines, slot tournaments may offer just the advantage you need to come out ahead. Because slot playing relies solely on luck, all you really need to do to get an edge in a tournament is 1) Press the **SPIN** button quickly (to get as many chances as you can to hit the jackpot in a limited amount of time), and 2) Find tournaments that return the greatest share of your entrance fee in prize money and room and board comps. To find out more about slot tournaments, inquire at the slot club desk at your favorite casino.

Some Rules to *Win* By

We've tried to give you some insight into the best strategies for keeping your head above water long enough to win at slots. But no one truly knows how to beat today's computerized slot machines. You can only hope for a few hours of fun and the possibility that luck will rain down on you. The best advice to leave you with are these tips:

- ◆ Join a slot club so you, too, can reap the benefits of playing.
- ◆ Participate in slot tournaments for a chance to win big money while you enjoy free hotel room and board.

◆ Keep your eyes open for defective machines that might pay out more than the posted amount for a winning combination. Machines that need refilling are often good candidates.

◆ When cruising the slot areas, check around for machines that might have credits on them. It happens!

◆ *Don't* play with any more money than you can afford to lose. Plan your limit, and stick to it.

◆ *Do* leave home without it! Don't bring your credit cards, ATM card, or checkbook to the casino. (You need only one credit card to pay for the room, so make sure a responsible person in your party is in charge of it!)

◆ *Don't* play when you feel like someone the Statue of Liberty would welcome. ("Give us your poor, your tired …" You get the picture.) Keep yourself well-rested and well-fed. The combination of hunger, fatigue, and slots can wreak havoc on your common sense, willpower, and control.

◆ *Don't* play when you're upset, angry, or bothered by the player next to you. There's plenty of time, and plenty of other machines to play.

◆ *Don't* push it—or chase it! If you're ahead but still haven't hit the big one, give it a rest. Winners sleep better.

◆ *Hit* and *run!*

◆ Never forget: There's always tomorrow!

Sue's Views on Slots

These are some of the most important lessons *I've* learned from my years playing slots. They might not be statistically significant but if they can save you the money I spent learning them, then they're worth sharing:

◆ It seems to me that most of my biggest and best wins happen when I first start playing a machine. If a machine takes too much of your money when you first start to play, chances are it's not going to warm up. Find another machine. (No matter what the experts say, machines DO run hot and cold.) Why bother losing on a cold one when you can spend your money looking for a hot one?

◆ If a machine gives you a jackpot right off the bat, give it a little bit more money and if nothing happens—take your money while you still have it!

♦ A machine is never "due." Just because you keep stuffing money in it doesn't mean it's going to hit. But the next one you try might.

♦ When keeping a record of your daily gambling winnings write down the *day* of the week, too, so you can see if you win more often on some days than others. You could have a guardian angel who's only available on Fridays.

Risky Business

When you win $1,199 or more on any type of slot machine, the house must report your name, Social Security Number (SSN), and the amount you won to the IRS. If you play slots and plan on winning, bring a picture ID and have your SSN memorized or written down somewhere handy.

♦ Be a good sportsman and be happy for another player who hits a jackpot on a machine you were just playing. You'll feel better about yourself and you might even get some karma points out of it.

♦ Like the song says "You can't hurry luck, you just have to wait." Be a patient and responsible player and sooner or later it will be your turn.

The Least You Need to Know

♦ Determine which machines to play not by which are rumored to be paying out the most, but by what you can afford to play.

♦ Start out on simple, two-coin, three-reel flat tops. Let the winnings start piling up before you move on to deadlier progressives. If you lose, go back to the simpler machines and start over, or go home!

♦ *When* you play a progressive can be as important as *how much* you play. Stalk the progressive carousels first, and find the ones that are being played a lot. Then come back in the early morning hours when everyone else is sleeping, and give it your best shot!

♦ Enjoy yourself. If you set your limits and are playing at a machine you can afford, you're *not* playing with anything you can't afford to lose!

7

Twenty-First Century Slots

In This Chapter

- ◆ How technology has changed the face of slot machines
- ◆ What's the difference between electronic slot machines and video slot machines
- ◆ What all those wavy lines mean on a video slot machine
- ◆ What to expect in mega-jackpot play

You don't have to look any further than your nearest casino to see how technology has changed our way of life. In the few short years between our first edition of this book (1996) and now, slot machines have evolved from simple three-reel videos and progressives into multi-line video and mega-progressive money machines! In this chapter, I'll report on what's new in the world of slots, and what's in store for the future.

The Ambiance

As you learned in Chapter 5, slot machines are no longer simple machines with mechanical spinning reels. They are complex, state-of-the-art computer programs that offer endless possibilities in terms of outcomes, jackpots, and entertainment.

Machine manufacturers such as Bally Inc., International Game Technology (IGT), SEGA (the video game people) and others, have spent a fortune gathering market information about the games you like to play, the music you listen to, your favorite television shows, and more. And what have they done with all of this knowledge? They've developed entertainment machines for slot enthusiasts. Your listening pleasure is no longer limited to the rhythmic drone of handles being pulled and coins clanking into metal coin baskets. To fill the sound void left by coinless machines and push buttons, slot machines have been outfitted with their own pre-programmed music piped through individual stereo speakers, flashing lights, and full-featured video screens that display bonus animations and video clips. There are even machines with small-screen television sets. This I know because I played one once while watching the evening news. I wasn't even concerned with what game I was playing. I just wanted to watch the news!

All of these new features are just the tip of the iceberg when it comes to finding new and better ways to make you want to stay and play (not that a continuously *hot* machine wouldn't do it for me!). Manufacturers are experimenting with slot machines that emanate aromas designed to calm and soothe while enticing you to spend. Perhaps they'll incorporate reclining chairs with handheld buttons and built-in beverage centers so you no longer have to wait to get a drink. And what about that inevitable restroom break? A flashing "occupied" sign would be a nice enhancement to make it perfectly clear that this little entertainment center is busy right now!

The good news is that slot machines are certainly undergoing a customer-focused evolution. The bad news is, if your machine is so comfortable and inviting that you don't want to leave, you could go broke sitting there. That's why you need to arm yourself by learning about the games and machines you're no doubt going to play. In the rest of this chapter we'll go over some of today's more popular (and elaborate) slot machines and video slots.

Technology Updates (Decisions, Decisions, Decisions)

Breakthroughs in computer technology have enabled manufacturers to change slot machines in many ways. As we mentioned earlier, slot machine and video gaming machines have become coinless, which means that you now need cash instead of coins to play. That's good because you no longer have to get your hands dirty scooping up your winnings and you get to keep track of your wins and losses easier. It's bad because you now need $1, $5, $10, $20, or $100 bills and they seem to go quicker because the games play faster without coins.

Freedom from coins has enabled video slot manufacturers to offer you "choice." Some video slot machines offer a choice of denominations to play, i.e. $.05, $.25, $.50, $1.00, etc. Some machines even offer a variety of games to choose from. To make your selection now on any of these multi-"choice" video slot games, you just touch the screen to select the denomination or logo of the game you want to play. Gone are the days when you have to physically move from machine to machine to play a different game or change the size of your bet.

Best Bet

I've found that when I play multi-game machines, I can win on one game but when I switch to another game I lose. This leads me to believe that each game is controlled by a different computer chip so it might be worth it for you to try them all out before giving up on that machine entirely. Or before you sink all of your money into one losing game.

The Latest Rage is Video Slots

If you haven't been in a casino in a few years, don't be surprised if it takes you a while to find the standard three-reel machines you're used to playing. They still exist and people still love to play them but they seem to be playing second fiddle to the popularity of today's video slots.

Video slots are actually video games, much like the games your kids play on your home computer or PlayStation 2. The reels don't really spin because they're not really reels. They're just pictures of spinning reels. Other than that everything else about video slots is the same as electronic slots; they're programmed by a computer chip that predefines the probability of each winning combination, a random number generator is constantly generating random numbers that determine where the reels will stop, and it takes luck to win!

The real value of video slots vs. traditional electronic slots is that manufacturers can be more creative with them, offering you more entertainment and options. Video slots games can use video clips of movies and television shows to make you feel like you're part of a show, or animations of famous cartoon characters like Blondie and Dagwood, Popeye, and Betty Boop. And, because the video screens are touch screens, you can interact with games in ways that you couldn't with electronic slot machines. Under certain conditions, for example, some video slots game will ask if you want to play a "bonus" round. You reply by touching the screen to start the action. With video slots the possibilities are endless so you'll be seeing many different kinds of games in the future. Right now, the must popular video slots are multi-line games and bonus games. Who knows what the future will bring?

So Many Lines—How Do You Win?

Well, have no fear. I've stopped to ask a number of avid players and for the most part, they don't really know why they win other than that a certain symbol appears on a specific line at exactly the right moment when the moon is in the seventh house and Jupiter aligns with Mars. Hmmmmm …

Fortunately, the manufacturers of some of these games have given me some hints, and I'll share them with you.

Most video reel games have five reels that display three rows of symbols and as many as 45 different paylines. Paylines correspond to lines on the screen on which you can place a bet. Paylines aren't always straight lines. Symbols must line up in certain patterns on the paylines for you to win. Fortunately, you don't have to remember all of the winning patterns or symbol combinations. The machine tallies how much you've won on each payline at the end of each spin. But, remember, you only win money on the paylines that you've activated with a bet. Each time you press the Credit button on to place a bet, an additional payline is activated and it will light up on the screen so you can see which one has been activated by the credit. If you want to bet all paylines, press the Max Bet button.

Some games have scatter symbols, which are special symbols that pay when they appear on any payline, regardless of whether you've bet on that payline.

Best Bet

To check your machine's paylines and what it takes to win on each, press the See Pays or Payouts button on the machine.

Risky Business

Games with bonus rounds are exciting and fun to play but the payouts in the primary game are often smaller or less frequent than in similar nonbonus games. So, you actually pay for the chance to win more in the bonus round by having a lower payback percentage in the nonbonus rounds.

Some games have multipliers, which are symbols that multiply the amount of a winning combination if it appears on the same payline as the winning combination. So, if you have a 10-credit combination and a 15 times multiplier symbol on the same payline, you win 150 credits in stead of 10.

To make it even more interesting, some games launch bonus rounds when special symbol combinations line up. Bonus games are very popular lures because they're fun and they give you the opportunity to win lots of extra money! There are too many different types of bonus games to cover, but most are interactive and easy to play. You can easily recognize games that offer bonus rounds because they often have extra video screens on top to launch cartoons or movies, or have stereo speakers that let you know in no uncertain terms that you've just qualified for the bonus round! When the bonus round starts, follow the directions on the screen and hope for the best.

Mega Mania!

Mega-jackpots are another rage in slots and video slots these days. As you learned in Chapter 6, casinos can offer huge jackpots without jeopardizing their business because of technology and the marvels of computerization. Payouts are no longer related to the number of symbols you can count on each reel, but rather the number of symbols and combinations programmed into the computer chip that runs the game. Consequently, your odds of hitting one of these mega-jackpots are infinitely smaller. Casinos collect enormous amounts of money between jackpots as thousands of players try their luck.

In addition, your local casino isn't responsible for paying out mega-jackpots won on their Wheel of Fortune, MegaBucks, Thrillions, or similar machines. These really big jackpots are actually owned and operated by machine manufacturers like IGT and Bally who lease the games to casinos. The manufacturers are responsible for certifying the win and paying it!

Machine manufacturers link most mega-jackpot games on computer networks that cover many casinos. In the case of MegaBucks and Wheel of Fortune, the network is usually national, although it can be set up to include all of the same machines in a local area or state. So, when you are playing a mega-jackpot machine you are not only in competition with the person sitting next to you, but with hundreds and possibly thousands of players in casinos throughout the country.

Best Bet

Some mega-jackpots pay the lucky winner in annual installments over 20 years. Others give you a choice of annual installments or a lump sum payment. When given the choice, a lump sum payment is usually better. But it's always a good idea to consult your legal and accounting advisors before making your decision.

Want to be a Thrillionairre?

Bally Gaming rolled out Thrillions in 1998 as a "multi-area" progressive system that links machines in Nevada, Atlantic City, Mississippi, and most Native American casinos. Most Thrillions machines are multi-denominational, which means that nickel, quarter and dollar players all compete for and contribute to the same jackpots. There are currently four different games in the Thrillions series: Betty Boop, Blondie, Millionaire Sevens, and Popeye. Each of these four games has its own mega-jackpot that goes up each time players in Nevada, Mississippi, Atlantic City, or Native American Casinos play that game. In addition to the mega-jackpot, most of the games offer a much smaller quick-hit jackpot.

The MegaBucks Stop Here

International Game Technology (IGT) is the owner of MegaBucks games, and a host of other mega-jackpot progressives including Wheel of Fortune, Quartermania, Elvis, Jeopardy, and The Price is Right. Much of their success is based on the excitement of history's favorite television game shows.

As of this writing, IGT machines are not multi-denominational, so nickel players do not compete with quarter and dollar players for the same jackpots. While they have too many mega-jackpot games to describe, the following table presents a list of their biggest jackpots on record as of August 2002.

Denomination	Machine Type	JACKPOT!!!	Location
.05	Fabulous Fiftys	$6,716,646.07	Trump Plaza, Atlantic City, NJ
.05	Wheel of Fortune	$3,058,385.10	Menominee Nation, Keshena, WI
.05	Jeopardy! Video	$2,188,462.23	Trump Taj Mahal, Atlantic City, NJ
.05	Nickels Deluxe	$1,655,988.24	Harvey's Resort Casino, Stateline, NV
.05	Addams Family	$1,239,413.31	Fremont Hotel, Las Vegas, NV
.05	Nevada Nickels	$957,035.35	Cactus Pete's, Jackpot, NV
.05	I Dream of Jeannie	$876,664.10	Trump Marina, Atlantic City, NJ
.05	Diamond Cinema	$765,813.92	Harrah's Rincon, Valley Center, CA
.25	Jeopardy!	$8,152,574.75	Hollywood Casino, Shreveport, LA
.25	Wheel of Fortune	$7,691,929.55	Grand Casino, Gulfport, MS
.25	Quartermania	$3,778,205.71	Harrah's, Las Vegas, NV
.25	Quarters Deluxe	$2,504,989.24	Golden Nugget, Laughlin, NV
.25	Wheel of Gold	$1,498,917.42	Ameristar Queen, Kansas City, MO

Denomination	Machine Type	JACKPOT!!!	Location
.25	Totem Pole	$1,212,786.77	Ballys Park Place, Atlantic City, NJ
.25	Party Time	$1,197,633.86	Isle of Capri, Vicksburg, MS
.50	Fabulous 50s	$6,716,646.07	Trump Plaza, Atlantic City, NJ
.50	Wheel of Fortune	$4,725,5065.46	Lake Tahoe Horizon Resort, Stateline, NV
.50	Jeopardy!	$1,348,030.69	Trump Taj Mahal, Atlantic City, NJ
1.00	Megabucks	$34,955,489.56	Sheraton Desert Inn, Las Vegas, NV
1.00	Wheel of Fortune	$10,295,956.63	Fitzgerald's, Tunica, MS
1.00	Jeopardy!	$6,104,120.50	Showboat, Atlantic City, NJ
1.00	Dollars Deluxe	$4,516,364.90	Golden Eagle Casino, Horton, KS
1.00	Elvis	$544,285.31	Stratosphere Tower, Las Vegas, NV
5.00	High Rollers	$2,326,142.80	Caesars, Atlantic City, NJ
5.00	Wheel of Fortune	$3,999,163.54	New York, New York Casino, Las Vegas, NV

A sample of IGT's record-setting jackpots as of August 2002

The Least You Need to Know

◆ Video slot machines come in an ever-changing variety of themes, offering new sights and sounds to enrich your gaming experience.

◆ Video slot machines can offer multiple play lines, but it's hard to tell what you need to win. A row of sevens no longer does the trick. Always check the machine's rules and payout table.

◆ Games that offer bonus rounds sometimes have reduced payout schedules when compared to machines that don't have bonus rounds—simply because they pay a bonus.

◆ Today's mega-jackpots are huge and they can be linked to all of the same type slot machines locally, nationally, or even worldwide.

◆ When playing a progressive mega-jackpot machine, always play MAX coins or you won't get the chance a millionaire.

◆ When confronted with the choice between two different progressive mega-jackpots of the same denomination, play the machine(s) with the bigger jackpot.

Chapter 8

Roulette—American Style

In This Chapter

◆ The difference between European and American roulette

◆ How many ways are there to bet on the outcome of a spin?

◆ The best roulette bet in the house

On one of my visits to the Garden State, my parents were hoping to keep me entertained by showing me Atlantic City. Because I was anxious to share with them my newfound gambling prowess, I went willingly and headed straight for the blackjack tables. In no time at all, against Atlantic City's multiple-deck games—using a strategy my father prescribed instead of the one I had practiced so faithfully in Las Vegas—I was down to my last two $5 chips.

Leaving the table, chips in hand, I set off to find Dad and seek some consolation. In a sequence that I'll never forget, he left the crap tables and slowly walked me around the casino floor.

Stopping right in front of the roulette table, he took my last remaining chips and put them down on number 36 in a fatherly fashion. As the *croupier* exchanged them for roulette chips, I stood there pondering the wisdom of my father's action. And then he won! It was good to be home.

Just Another Game of Chance?

Roulette (like baccarat) conjures up romantic images of the world's most beautiful people, whiling away balmy evenings in Monte Carlo, sipping champagne, exchanging witticisms (and whatever else one cares to exchange on balmy evenings in Monte Carlo), undaunted by the small fortunes they let ride on the spin of a wheel. How satisfying to know that roulette's American counterpart has descended gracefully from the elegance of Europe's finest casinos. (Did we say "descended gracefully"? Well, not quite!)

The game of roulette did originate in France, but its descent into America's gambling mainstream has been less than graceful. In fact, it's been downright tough! You see, roulette is played with a spinning wheel on which the numbers 1 through 36 are marked. In European casinos, the typical roulette wheel also has a zero, giving the player a total of 37 numbers from which to choose. The American roulette wheel includes a double zero (00) in addition to the European single zero (0), giving American players no less than 38 numbers on which to stake their fortunes. Although that may not seem like a big deal, that little extra 00 makes the American game more expensive. We'll show you how to play the extra 00, and explain why it's in your best interest to find a European wheel.

Gamb-lingo

The French word for dealer is *croupier,* which in roulette is the person who spins the wheel and sells you chips.

Whichever version you decide to play, roulette is a simple game of chance that, unlike slot machines, provides the opportunity to test your luck among the company of strangers.

Follow the Bouncing Ball

When you sit down to play roulette, you exchange your cash or gaming chips for special roulette chips that are all the same color. Each player is given his or her own color so it's easy to distinguish one player's bet, or multiple bets, from another player's.

Roulette is an easy game. The objective is to select the one number that will be randomly chosen out of 37 (European) or 38 (American) numbers on a roulette wheel. You place your bet on a roulette table layout that corresponds to the different possibilities on the wheel. A typical roulette table is arranged like the one shown next, with the wheel on one side and the table layout where the bets are placed on the other. Sometimes you find the wheel placed in the center of two layouts.

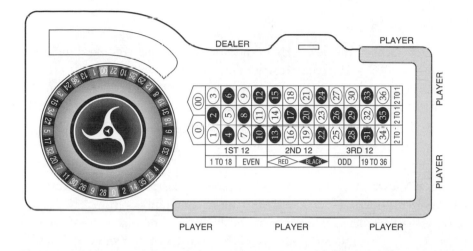

The roulette wheel is kept spinning all the time, but once a game is about to begin, it speeds up and a small ball is released along the outer edge and spun in the opposite direction. Bettors can place their bets right up until the time the wheel slows down and the ball falls onto the wheel. Eventually, the ball randomly drops into one of the 37 or 38 numbered slots on the wheel, thus designating the winning number. (To make things easier on all of us, let's just discuss the American version with 38 numbers and point out the European differences when it's important.)

As the Wheel Turns

The roulette wheel, the device that randomly selects the winning number in each game, is actually a very precise instrument, and sometimes you see it enclosed in a plastic case. The slightest scratch or movement can upset the balance and skew the outcome of the number selection, making it somewhat less than random. If the wheel is defective so that one or a few numbers win too frequently, customers notice and bet those numbers, which costs the casino money. That's why roulette wheels are inspected routinely, and you are reminded not to lean on or near one.

The wheel shown in the following figure represents the American version, which includes 38 numbers: 1–36, 0, and 00. Half of the numbers from 1 to 36 are red and the other half are black. The zeros are always green and placed opposite each other on the wheel. The numbers 1–36 are placed in pairs of odd and even numbers all around the wheel in what seems to be no *apparent* logical sequence. In actuality, they are arranged quite methodically so that high, low, odd, and even numbers are mathematically balanced as much as possible.

The "danger" sign, warning you that this is an American wheel.

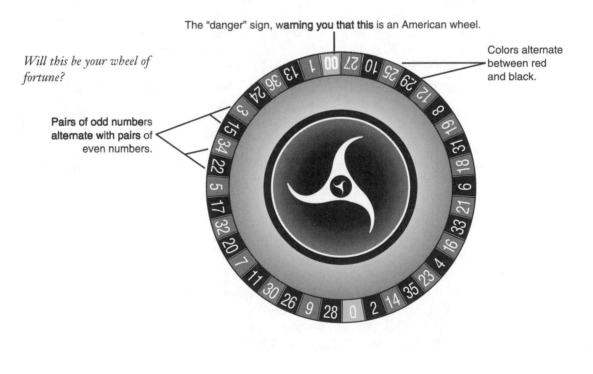

Will this be your wheel of fortune?

Colors alternate between red and black.

Pairs of odd numbers alternate with pairs of even numbers.

Bet You Didn't Know ...

Another popular method professional gamblers use to try to beat roulette is to spot a *biased* wheel. A wheel bias is a mechanical flaw that makes a particular number, say 14, come up every 20 or 30 spins on the average, instead of every 38 spins as mathematical probability would dictate.

Finding a biased wheel isn't an easy proposition. You have to methodically watch and record the outcome of thousands of spins of the same wheel, looking for those numbers that win considerably more often than could be due to chance.

This painstaking method of charting the numbers to locate those that come up frequently is tedious work and generally isn't worth the trouble. You'll rarely find a biased wheel these days because they are inspected and maintained routinely.

The Betting Table

As many as six players can sit along the edge of a roulette table and place their bets. All the possible outcomes of a spin are clearly marked on the table layout, along with different betting options. As you can see in the next illustration, the numbers 1–36 are arranged in three columns of 12 rows each. The numbers are laid out across the rows in numerical sequence. Each number is colored red or black, corresponding to the same color used on the wheel for that number.

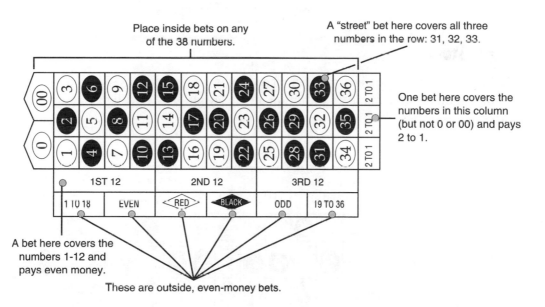

Place inside bets on any of the 38 numbers.

A "street" bet here covers all three numbers in the row: 31, 32, 33.

One bet here covers the numbers in this column (but not 0 or 00) and pays 2 to 1.

A bet here covers the numbers 1-12 and pays even money.

These are outside, even-money bets.

A roulette table in action.

Bettor Business

You can make nine types of roulette bets: six different kinds of *inside bets* and three different *outside bets*. The house sets the *betting limits* separately for inside and outside bets. If they are not posted on a plastic placard near the wheel, ask the croupier (or dealer) for the minimum and maximum betting limits when you sit down.

Gamb-lingo

Each casino game has **betting limits** that establish the minimum and maximum amounts of money you can wager on one bet. You can't wager less than the minimum or more than the maximum amount posted at a gaming table. The betting limits vary from game to game and often from table to table in the same game.

There are very specific rules about how to place your bets in roulette, and we'll explain those rules later. Because your odds (chances of winning) increase or decrease depending on the type of bet you make, your payouts vary, too. You can place as many different bets as you'd like as long as each bet is within the table's minimum and maximum bet limits. Bets can be placed right up until the time the ball is dropped onto the wheel. As a matter of fact, Stanford once saw a woman scatter so many bets around the roulette table that by the time the dealer called "No more bets," she had a bet on every number! She was sure of getting a pile of chips pushed to her no matter which number came up, but she also virtually assured herself of losing, as you'll see.

The Inside Story

Inside bets involve all the bets you can place on any number from 1–36, 0, or 00, or a combination of these numbers within the inside layout. The next figure shows how to place an inside bet.

When you have "inside" information, bet these!

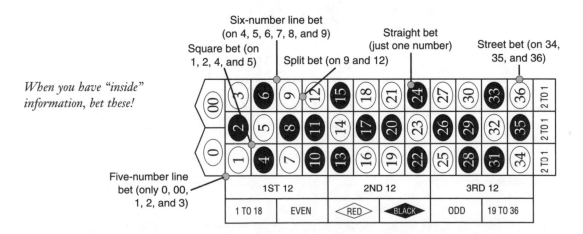

Six-number line bet (on 4, 5, 6, 7, 8, and 9)

Square bet (on 1, 2, 4, and 5)

Split bet (on 9 and 12)

Straight bet (just one number)

Street bet (on 34, 35, and 36)

Five-number line bet (only 0, 00, 1, 2, and 3)

The simplest inside bet is a *straight*, single-number bet. When you want to pick only one number to win (1–36, 0, or 00), place your roulette chip squarely in the center of that number. If your number wins, you'll be paid 35 to 1. A $1 bet on 7 wins $35 if 7 shows up; you keep the money you bet with, so your $1 turns into $36.

A *split bet*, or two-number bet, allows you to cover two numbers with one bet, and pays 17 to 1 if either number comes up. You can place a split bet only on numbers that are right next to each other on the table layout. To indicate a split bet, place your chip on the line that separates the numbers. A split bet is the same as betting half as much on each of two straight bets. For example, $2 split between numbers 7 and 8 turns into $36 if one of the numbers shows, which is what would happen had you placed $1 on 7 and $1 on 8.

Gamb-lingo

When you place a bet on any roulette number or combination of numbers from 1–36 and 0 or 00, it's an **inside bet**. The three different types of roulette bets that let you bet on a bigger group of numbers, at a lower payout, are **outside bets**.

A *street bet*, or three-number bet, lets you cover three numbers in a row with one bet and pays 11 to 1 if any of them win. To place a street bet, place your chip on the outside line at the start of the row. A street bet is the same as betting one third as much on each of three straight bets. You wager $3 to win $33 if one of your numbers hits. (Your $3 turns into $36.) A *square bet*, *quarter bet*, *corner bet*, or *four-number bet* (you can call it what you will!) lets you bet on any four numbers that converge. It pays 8 to 1 if one of the numbers wins. To place a four number bet, place your chip on the spot in the center of your four numbers. A square bet is the same as betting one fourth as much on each of four straight bets. You wager $4 to win $32 if one of your numbers hits. (Your $4 turns into $36.)

There's only one kind of *five-number line bet* you can make, and it pays 6 to 1. To place the five-number line bet (00, 0, 1, 2, and 3), place your chip on the intersection of the dividing lines between 0 and 1. We'll tell you why this is the worst bet in the roulette house shortly.

The *six-number line bet* pays 5 to 1, and there are 11 possible ways to make it. You can place a six-number bet only on two rows of three numbers that are right next to each other. Just place your chip on the line above the dozens bet(s) so that it rests in between the two rows you want to cover.

Outside Looking In

Outside bets cover the areas on the table layout that we haven't covered so far. These bets, which are outside the 00, 0, and 1–36 playing area, include *even-money*, *column*, and *dozen bets*.

There are three different *even-money bets*, which as the name implies, pay 1 to 1:

◆ You can place a *high-low bet* to cover the numbers 19–36 (high) by placing a chip on the 19 to 36 spot. To cover 1–18 (low), place your chip on the 1 to 18 spot.

◆ If you happen to be more of a color person, you can bet on red or black by placing your chip on either of these spots.

◆ If most of your lucky numbers happen to be odd or even, bet on all the odd numbers or all the even numbers by placing your bet on one of these spots. Zero (0) and double zero (00) are not included as odd or even numbers.

A *column bet* is a bet wagered on 12 numbers contained in any one of the three long columns of numbers. Column bets pay 2 to 1 and you just place your chip on the "2 to 1" spot at the end of the column you want to select.

Risky Business

Even-money bets pay 1 to 1, but they are not 50-50 chances. Because there are 38 possible numbers, including the zeros, but only 18 winners for an even-money bet, your odds of winning are actually 18 to 20.

A way to bet a different set of 12 numbers is to place a *dozen bet*. Dozen bets, located just above the even-money bets, divide the roulette table into the first (1–12), second (13–24), and third (25–36) sets of numbers, grouped in dozens. Like column bets, dozen bets pay 2 to 1. To place a dozen bet, place your chip on the spot of choice: 1st 12, 2nd 12, or 3rd 12.

Bet You Didn't Know ...

Numbers are laid out nonsequentially on a roulette wheel. Some players believe they can predict the *area* of the wheel where the ball will drop based on previous spins and the way the croupier spins the wheel and drops the ball. To accommodate these players, charts are available to help you locate the numbers as they are grouped in different sectors of the wheel. This makes it easier for a player to place multiple bets (for numbers in the same area on the wheel) quickly. Some players make big killings by betting sectors in casinos with inadequate maintenance (where the ball may end up in one area more often than in other areas), which sometimes is the case overseas, particularly in Asia.

The "Cutting" Edge

Now that you know how to place a bet, let's see what happens when you do. In the American game, the wheel spins and the ball can fall into any one of 38 spots. That means each number has a 1/38 probability of coming up next. But it does not mean that in 38 spins, each number should come up exactly once. Each spin is independent. A particular number can come up two times in a row, and another number might not show for hundreds of spins.

The odds of hitting your number is 1/38, which can be stated as 1 to 37. If you were paid according to the true odds, you would keep the original bet *and* win $37 for every $1 that you wagered. If your number were to finally come in on the 38th spin, you would get back all the money you spent trying to hit your number.

But we know from the previous section that a straight single-number bet pays only 35 to 1. The house payout is $2 short of the amount you would need to be paid if you were given true odds on the bet. That $2 per 38 spins is called the *house edge*, and it amounts to 5.26 percent (or 5.26 cents) of every dollar wagered on a straight bet. In fact, the house edge on all bets wagered in American roulette is 5.26 percent, unless you place a five-number bet, which at 7.29 percent is the worst bet on the table! The house edge shouldn't keep you from playing roulette if the game intrigues you, but it should make you think twice about playing too long. Put enough of those 5.26 percent together and you've got … nothing!

Why the Dollar Is Up in Europe

The European game, with no 00 on the wheel, is more advantageous to the player. Because there are only 37 numbers played in the European version (compared with 38 in the American), the true odds of hitting your number are reduced to 1 in 37, but the house still pays 35 to 1. This means they're taking in only $1 more than what the true odds would dictate, reducing the house edge to only 2.63 percent. This is true for all bets because they pay the same in the European version as in the American. Because there is only one 0 and no 00, you can't place a five-number bet, which, as you remember, is the worst bet on the American table.

Best Bet

Many casinos offer both the American and European versions of roulette. A European game won't have the 00 on the roulette wheel. When you have a choice between the two, *always* play the European version.

Waving the White Flag

A betting option from European roulette has also found its way into some of the American roulette games, depending on where you play. The option is called *Surrender* (or *en prison*, in French), and you can do it on even-money bets only, when either the 0 or 00 come up. It is the equivalent of losing only half your bet immediately.

For example, if you bet on Odd and the 0 comes up, without Surrender you would automatically lose. When Surrender is available (and you should ask the croupier if it's allowed before you start playing), your bet remains on Odd for the next spin, which gives you an extra chance on the same bet. (They call this option *en prison* because your bet is temporarily captured until the outcome of the next spin.) If an odd number comes up on the next spin, you don't get paid for the win, but at least you get to take your original bet back. (If an even number comes up, you lose the bet.) The Surrender option cuts the house edge on even money bets to approximately 2.63 percent in the American game and 1.35 percent in the European game.

It's Play Time

We've covered almost every aspect of roulette that you need to be aware of to start playing. Any time you're not sure how to place your bet, or not sure you've been paid-off correctly, ask the croupier.

We could tell you about different "systems" and betting strategies that supposedly help you beat the game, but basically none of them work. Roulette is another risky proposition that makes you feel like a million when you're hot—and like you can't hit the broad side of a barn when you're not! Here are some sensible betting options:

- When given the choice, *always* play the single-zero European version instead of the double-zero American game.

- *Don't* place a five-number bet; it's the worst odds on the table!

- If you see someone betting big and winning, follow their lead and bet the same numbers. Who knows—they may know something you don't know!

- For maximum excitement, put your whole bet straight up on one number (the way my father did), instead of scattering them all around the table.

- If you have plenty of time on your hands, station yourself for days at a time recording the outcomes of one wheel. Look for numbers that come up more frequently. Do this repeatedly at different wheels until you find one that happens to be biased. Then lay your money down before they fix it!

- When you've had enough excitement or lost your limit, it's time to leave. Don't press your luck at roulette!

- If you think roulette is really your game, save your money and go to Europe to play.

The Least You Need to Know

- The European roulette wheel doesn't have a double zero (00), which makes it much more favorable for the player than the American wheel.

- The best bet in the roulette house is an even-money outside bet when Surrender is offered.

- Avoid the five-number bet. It's got the worst odds on the table!

Mini-Baccarat—A Small Game with a BIG Heart

In This Chapter

◆ How to distinguish between baccarat and mini-baccarat

◆ Why you probably won't find an easier table game in any casino

◆ What's your best bet?

If you ever wondered what those people are doing writing things down at what looks like a blackjack table, they're probably playing mini-baccarat. It may seem strange to see people taking notes in a casino, but they're keeping track of who won each hand. They've got nothing else to do besides sip their drinks, laugh, and keep score while the dealer plays all the cards for them! You'll see why in this chapter.

The *t* in *baccarat* is silent (bah-cah-rah), and remembering to say it this way is the only difficult part of the game. Baccarat is played in a relaxed, friendly atmosphere and is enjoyable because 1) It makes no difference how other players are betting—their actions in no way affect the outcome of your bet, and 2) The house edge is among the lowest you'll find, so you're more likely to win baccarat than almost any other casino game.

One Size Doesn't Always Fit All

Baccarat is a game of chance from the glamorous casinos of Europe. Perhaps Americans are intimidated by the ambience and regal air that surrounds the game or the more formal attire sometimes required in the baccarat *pit*. For whatever reason, players are missing the opportunity to enjoy a game with a very low house edge.

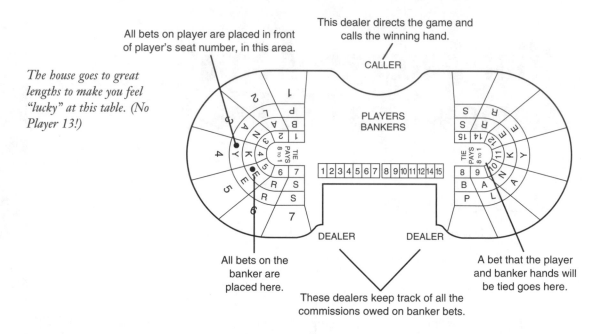

All bets on player are placed in front of player's seat number, in this area.

This dealer directs the game and calls the winning hand.

CALLER

The house goes to great lengths to make you feel "lucky" at this table. (No Player 13!)

PLAYERS
BANKERS

DEALER   DEALER

All bets on the banker are placed here.

These dealers keep track of all the commissions owed on banker bets.

A bet that the player and banker hands will be tied goes here.

Two styles of baccarat are played in American casinos: the more formal full-pit version (shown in the preceding figure), which is played on a long table with 12 to 14 players and a courtly team of house personnel, and its unpretentious little brother, "mini," which is played on a standard blackjack-sized gaming table (shown in the next figure) with six players, one dealer, and less formality.

Best Bet

In Las Vegas, "dressing up a bit" can mean anything from keeping the jeans but ditching the sneakers to dusting off the dinner jacket and buying a new evening gown. It always depends on where you're playing (or dining), so ask if you're not sure!

American-style baccarat is an adaptation of a French card game, sometimes referred to as *Nevada-style baccarat*, or *punto banco*. The baccarat *pit* is a casino area set aside for one or more baccarat tables. Mini-baccarat is a scaled-down, lower-limit version of American baccarat, played with fewer players and dealers but following the same rules.

Because casinos give little or no thought to who wears what when they play mini-baccarat, and usually impose a lower table limit (which is good for novice players), we'll focus on the mini-baccarat game. But we'll also point out the subtle differences you'll encounter when you decide to dress up a bit and go for the gold at the full-scale tables.

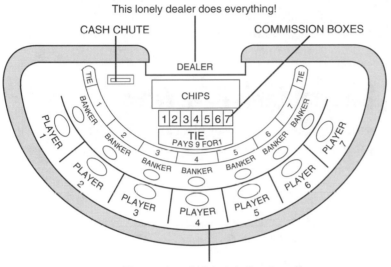

Cutting baccarat down to size. (This is mini-baccarat.)

What's the Object of the Game?

No matter how many players are seated at a baccarat table, only two hands are dealt: one for the player and one for the banker. Each hand initially receives two cards. Your mission is to wager with chips before the cards are dealt on which of the two hands will come closest to a total of nine. You can bet on the banker, the player, or a tie. All the playing decisions are made, according to rules of play, by the baccarat dealer, or *croupier*.

The minimum and maximum betting limits are posted at the baccarat or mini-baccarat table. Generally, the betting limits at full-scale baccarat tables are higher than at the mini-baccarat tables and may range from a $5 or $20 minimum bet to as much as a $4,000 maximum bet. You can bet any amount within the range posted. At a mini-baccarat table, you're likely to find a $2 or $3 minimum bet requirement with up to a $1,000 bet limit.

Like Fine Crystal, Baccarat Cards Have Value

Mini-baccarat is played with six decks of cards dealt from a *shoe*. Full-scale American baccarat uses eight decks that are also dealt from a shoe. Each card in the deck has a numerical value, as shown in the following table.

Card Values in American Baccarat

Card (Any Suit)	Card Value (Points)
Ace	One
2	Two
3	Three
4	Four
5	Five
6	Six
7	Seven
8	Eight
9	Nine
10, Jack, Queen, King	Zero

As you can see, *face cards* (kings, queens, and jacks) and 10s have no value, or 0 points, and all other cards (ace, 2 through 9) are worth their face value.

If the total value of the cards in a hand is greater than 10, you drop the first digit. For example, two 8s would total 16, giving you a point value of six. A three-card hand of a 9, 2, and 7 would total 18, giving you a point value of eight.

Whenever a two-card total of either eight or nine is dealt, the hand is called a *natural*, and neither hand gets a third card. An eight is *le petit* natural, and a nine is *le grande* natural. *Le grande* natural always beats *le petit* natural because nine is higher than eight.

Playing on Cruise Control

After the first two cards are dealt to each hand, strict rules dictate how the cards are played; nobody makes any decisions. Whether you're playing full-scale baccarat or mini-baccarat, the rules of the game are the same. Oddly enough, you don't need to know the rules to play the game, but knowing them helps you understand what's going on.

First, the croupier checks both hands to see if there is an immediate winner:

- ◆ If either the player or banker hands total eight or nine, the *natural* hand wins and the game is over.

- ◆ If both hands total eight or nine, *le grande* natural wins. If they are both equal in value, it is considered a tie and the game ends in a tie.

If neither hand has a natural, both hands are played out as follows: The player hand is always the first to be played, regardless of what's in the banker hand. It is played according to the rules in the following table.

When the banker hand totals eight or nine, the player does not draw a card. If the banker hand totals less than eight, the player with a low total draws one card, as follows:

Rules for Completing the Player Hand

If the Player's First Two Cards Total	The Player's Hand Must
Zero through five	Draw another card
Six or seven	Stand
Eight or nine	Natural—no cards drawn

The banker hand is always played last, depending on how the player hand was played. If the player hand did not draw a third card, the banker hand always follows the following table:

Rules for Completing the Banker Hand When the Player Hand Totals Six or Seven and the Player Did Not Draw a Third Card

When the Banker's First Two Cards Total	The Banker Will
Five or less	Draw
Six or more	Stand

When the player hand totals eight or nine and the player did not draw a third card, the banker does not draw a card.

When the player hand draws a third card, the banker hand is always played according to the rules in the following table:

Rules for the Banker Hand When the Player Hand Receives Three Cards

When the Banker's First Two Cards Total	The Banker *Draws* Only When the Player's *Third* Card Is	The Banker *Stands* Only When the Player's *Third* Card Is
Two or less	1-2-3-4-5-6-7-8-9-10	
Three	1-2-3-4-5-6-7-9-10	8
Four	2-3-4-5-6-7	1-8-9-10
Five	4-5-6-7	1-2-3-8-9-10
Six	6-7	1-2-3-4-5-8-9-10
Seven		1-2-3-4-5-6-7-8-9-10

No more than a total of three cards can be drawn for either hand. When both hands have been played out, the hand closest to nine wins. The dealer pays those who bet on the winning hand. In the event of a tie, all bets on banker and on player are pushes, neither winning nor losing. Banker and player bets are paid even money (1 to 1), although a 5 percent commission taken from winning banker bets drops the actual payoff ratio down to 19:20. Tie bets are usually paid 8 to 1, which sounds good, but really isn't.

Playing for Keeps

Now that you know what the rules are, we'll take you through a quick game. After seating yourself at the baccarat or mini-baccarat table, you'll find three spots in front of you labeled player, banker, and tie. These are where you place your baccarat bets. You'll notice that the dealer deals the cards out of a shoe.

At the beginning of the game, six or eight decks are shuffled and a player is asked to *cut the cards*. After cutting, the decks are placed into the shoe. The *cut card* is inserted near the end of the deck so the dealer knows when it's time to reshuffle. Before the dealer starts the game, he or she removes the first card from the shoe and turns it over to determine how many cards will be *burned*, or removed from play.

When the shuffle is complete, the game begins with all the players placing their betting chips in either the player, banker, or tie spots. The minimum and maximum betting limits should be posted on the table, but if they're not, don't be embarrassed to ask. After all bets are placed, the dealer begins to deal the two-card hands for the player and the banker.

If you're playing "big" baccarat rather than mini, you may find the game tended by no less than three croupiers: two to handle the payoffs and one to handle and call the cards. You might also find that as a player you are offered the option of drawing the cards from the shoe and passing them to the caller. This has absolutely no effect on the game, and the caller will tell you exactly what to do. However, if you don't want to draw the cards, you don't have to; the deal will go on to another player. In mini, one dealer does everything, and players are not asked to participate. In either version, the dealer makes all the card-drawing decisions for each hand, according to the rules discussed earlier.

Gamb-lingo

Part of the card-shuffling ritual, **cutting the cards** divides the card decks in two so they can be reassembled in a different order. **Burn cards** are removed from the top of the deck and not played. The dealer inserts a **cut card** at the end of the deck as a reshuffling reminder so that the last hand doesn't run out of cards.

Bet You Didn't Know ...

Full-scale baccarat (not mini) may be the only game in which the casino regularly employs *shills*, people who are paid to pretend to be players. Baccarat shills generally are expensively dressed, attractive women. A lone customer need not play alone. A person who wants to sit next to an attractive woman for an evening can do so.

High rollers at full-scale baccarat may also be able to have sumptuous meals brought to them at the table so they don't miss a turn of a card. They are also usually allowed to bend the cards all they want to—an option that's not allowed at other casino card games.

After a third card is drawn for each hand as needed, the hand that is closest in value to nine wins. Players are paid off 1 to 1 for winning wagers on player or banker. Tie bets pay either 8 to 1 or 9 to 1, depending on where you play. After the bets are paid, all played cards are discarded, the next bets are placed, and the cycle repeats until the shoe is over.

Playing a Vigorish Game

The rules of baccarat are such that the player hand is always played out first, giving the banker hand a slight edge over the player hand. As a result, existing rules enable the banker hands to win approximately 50.7 percent of the time and player hands approximately 49.3 percent of the time, when tie bets are excluded.

Gamb-lingo

The **vigorish** (a.k.a. **vig**) is the fee, or commission, taken by the house on winning bets on the banker hand.

Risky Business

When you play, play to win! Betting on a tie between banker and player is a long shot and the worst bet in baccarat. If your goal is to make money faster, put more money on banker or player.

There would be nothing to stop a smart player from betting the banker all the time and enjoying an approximate 1.4 percent advantage and positive expectation, were it not that all winning bets on the banker are taxed at the rate of 5 percent. That means whenever you bet the banker and win, you're paid off at 1 to 1, but a 5 percent commission is charged on your winnings. You don't pay the tax, or *vigorish* (a.k.a. *vig*), as it's called, immediately because it would be time-consuming for the dealer to make such small change, and it would cut into your available playing chips. But the dealer does keep track of the vig you owe from each winning banker hand and will ask you to settle up either at the end of the shoe or when you leave the table.

As a result of the vigorish, the house enjoys a 1.17 percent edge on all banker bets and a 1.36 percent edge over all player bets when ties are included in the count.

Not Like Getting a "Tie" for Christmas

Betting on a tie between the player and banker hands usually pays 8 to 1 since it rarely happens because of the way baccarat rules are set up. The odds of any hand resulting in a tie are actually 9.5 to 1, but because the house pays only 8 to 1, the payback is 85.5 percent. If you're lucky enough to find a casino that pays 9 to 1 on ties, the payback is 95.5 percent.

What's So Hard About Baccarat?

The thing about baccarat is that there's nothing hard about it. You can't make a mistake that will give the house a greater edge. There are no complicated strategies to follow, rules to learn, or cards to count. Baccarat remains a game of chance that's very easy to play. The simplest strategy is to stick with banker and player bets and avoid tie bets like the plague.

You'll often find electronic posts rising high above a mini-baccarat table showing you which hands have won in the past 30 or so plays. These posts certainly heighten the anticipation and allow you to spot trends, but they are not a reliable way for you to select the next winning hand (nor are the baccarat score cards that casinos provide for you to keep track of winning hands when electronic posts aren't available).

Many players believe that tracking the outcome of previous hands helps them predict which hand will win next, based on whether one particular hand is "hot" or whether one is "due" to win. Unfortunately, there's no way to know whether a trend will continue or end on the next hand, so a trend is not useful information. It's just history; a record of things that have occurred.

Bet You Didn't Know ...

Counting cards means keeping track of the cards that have been played from a deck so that the player knows which cards will be dealt. When good cards remain in a deck, an astute player bets more. When most of the favorable cards have already been dealt, the player decreases the bet. In blackjack, the ability to count cards can be profitable.

Counting cards in baccarat, however, only earns you pennies per hour if the shoe is dealt way to the end and if you can get away with betting zero (0, nothing!) most of the time and $1,000 on the occasional last hand before the shuffle. But casinos don't deal out enough cards anymore, and even if a casino did deal out almost all of the cards, it certainly wouldn't let someone make the bets required to beat the game. If you want more information on the subject of counting cards in baccarat, read Peter Griffin's book, *Theory of Blackjack*, pages 216-223.

If you've had success spotting trends and betting accordingly in the past, by all means keep it up! But don't be disappointed if you can't. Most of us don't have much luck spotting trends or determining how long they will last.

For the most part, selecting the winner of each successive hand is a guess. But it's a guess that can be both fun and profitable, and that's what gambling is all about. With the relatively small house edge, baccarat gives high-rolling patrons the opportunity to win (and lose!) large sums of money. It can also afford low-rolling novices the opportunity to hang in there for quite a long time.

For the dedicated baccarat player, many books are available that outline different betting strategies. Most of these systems are variations of the Martingale system, which in a nutshell tells you to double up after each losing bet. Doubling up means that if you bet $5 on player and lose, you should bet $10 on the next hand, and so on. Unfortunately, this system doesn't work, nor do any other betting systems. Your best bet in baccarat, as in any game of chance, is to wager only what you can afford to lose on any single hand. And have fun!

The Least You Need to Know

- There are two forms of American baccarat: the more formal, full-scale baccarat and mini-baccarat. Except for the table limits and protocols, bets in both games are decided by the same rules.

- The only decision a player has to make is what and how much to wager. Both hands (player and banker) are played out according to the rules of the game.

- The house enjoys a very small edge in baccarat; only 1.17 percent on banker bets and 1.36 percent on player bets.

Part 3

The Competitive Edge (Games of Skill)

Everybody loves a winner. And who doesn't want to win? That's why we've devoted this section to games that give you more of a chance. With a little skill and a lot of practice, you can actually wind up winning more often than not when you play some of these games.

We spend two chapters (Chapters 10 and 11) on teaching the most popular table game, blackjack. You'll learn the rules of blackjack as well as Stanford's Basic Strategy, so be prepared to pay attention. Chapter 12 covers the basics for staying afloat at the crap table. In Chapter 13, we'll keep you on the edge of your seat at the race track. If you'd rather bet on sports than horses, we'll show you how in Chapter 14.

Chapter 10

Blackjack—The Most Popular Game You Can Beat

In This Chapter

- Recognizing a blackjack table in a crowded casino
- Why you *should* learn to play blackjack
- The object of the game and how it's played

I once played blackjack for 22 hours straight while on a "free" 24-hour turnaround junket to Las Vegas. I'm a small bettor and was perfecting my basic strategy while gaining confidence in my as-yet "unreliable" card-count. But I still didn't have the nerve to do what the experts, like Stanford, tell you to do when the count gets good. So I kept my bet at an even $5 a hand (the junket minimum) for a day straight.

By the time I left that table, not only did I feel like ENIAC—counting 0s and 1s like a computer—I was probably up about $100. Not much for what amounted to three days' work, but I was learning! Besides, the last pit boss (I went through a couple that day) so marveled at my stamina and perseverance that he treated me to the best shrimp cocktail and filet mignon breakfast I ever had!

Blackjack is a game of chance and *skill*—it's one casino game in which your ability to understand the rules and make the right playing decisions almost ensures that over time, you, too, can come out a winner! Luckily for us, Stanford wrote the book(s) on it. The playing strategy and tips we'll share in this chapter are not difficult to learn. All it takes is a little thought, discipline, patience, and *practice*! Did I mention that it also happens to be fun? You don't think I'd sit there that long if it weren't, do you?

A Game by Any Other Name

Known the world over as vingt-et-un, 21, pontoon, even California Aces, it's all the same: variations of the good old American game of blackjack. Although it originated in France—hence *vingt-et-un* (French for twenty-one)—it's been one of the most popular casino table games in America for decades. Today you'll find slight variations in blackjack rules depending on the city, state, and even casino in which you play, but the game is basically the same. We'll cover many of these variations as well as a basic strategy (in Chapter 11) that will suit just about any style of blackjack you're likely to encounter.

Gamb-lingo

Chips are used on casino gaming tables in lieu of cash. You buy chips, or "checks" as they're sometimes called, when you enter a game. To **bust** is to go over 21. If you bust, you lose. If the dealer busts and you don't, you win. If both you and the dealer bust, you lose anyway.

Casino blackjack is a card game played with all 52 cards in a standard deck. From one to seven players can play against a dealer, who is in charge of everything from changing your cash into *chips*, dealing the cards, playing the house's hand, and even summoning a waitress for cocktails. Each player, including the dealer, is dealt two cards. Your goal is to beat the dealer by: accumulating a higher-scoring hand than the dealer, without going over 21, or holding a low hand when the dealer's hand goes over 21 (*busts*). In the next chapter, we'll describe strategy after we get the details—table layout, card values, and game rules—out of the way.

Environmental Issues

In most casinos, an area is set aside strictly for table games, which, as the name implies, require special tables. You'll find many blackjack tables in these areas because it's such a popular game. A typical blackjack table is semicircular and seats anywhere from five to seven players, as shown in the following figure. Four or more tables are grouped in a circular fashion, one dealer behind each table. All dealers stand in the center area, called the blackjack *pit*, which can be easily supervised by someone who is commonly referred to as a *pit boss*. (In black-jack discussions on the Internet, the common term is *pit critter*.)

The table has important information on it. It tells you what the house pays you when you're dealt a blackjack, or *natural*, and the point total at which a dealer must stop taking additional cards. This simple statement alerts sophisticated players to the appropriate strategy for this game, because the likelihood of a dealer busting changes depending on what point total she or he must *stand* on. Finally, the third message tells you if you can take *insurance* against a dealer's potential natural. (We'll analyze insurance later.)

Gamb-lingo

Insurance is a side bet that the dealer has a natural, or blackjack. It is offered only when the dealer's up card is an ace. If the dealer has a natural, the insurance bet wins double. If the dealer doesn't have a natural, the insurance bet loses. When a player **stands**, he or she refrains from taking another card.

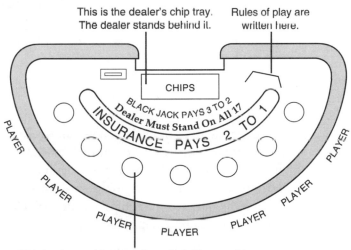

This is the dealer's chip tray. The dealer stands behind it.

Rules of play are written here.

This is where a player places a bet. Players sit in front of their betting circles, or spots.

A typical blackjack table can tell you a lot about the game.

The Seating Arrangements

Below these messages on the blackjack table are the five, six, or seven circles that indicate how many players are welcome in the game. Each circle is accompanied by a seat—make yourself comfortable.

You'll often hear the seat at the far left of the table (as viewed from the player's side) referred to as *third base* because it's the last seat to receive a card before the dealer does. Many people believe this is a critical place to sit because the plays the third baseman makes can influence the outcome of the dealer's hand. For example, if everyone knows that the dealer has to take a hit because the *up card* (the dealer's card that is face up) is a low card, many players refrain from hitting their own hands in anticipation of the dealer busting. If the player at third base hits and causes the dealer to wind up with a good hand instead of busting, the other players may blame their losses on the third baseman. Whether or not you believe that the third baseman's actions affect your overall chances of winning depends on your own experience and belief system.

Gamb-lingo

You're at **first base** if you're nearest the dealer's left hand; your hand will be played first, before the dealer moves on to the next player. You're at **third base** if you're nearest the dealer's right hand; your hand will be played last before the dealer plays his or her hand.

Gamb-lingo

A player who has established credit with the casino can write a **marker**, which is essentially a check, at the gaming tables. This is the casino's way of accommodating players who want to bet really big; they can buy a tall stack of large-denomination chips without having to bring a pocketful of hundred-dollar bills to the table.

Of course, the third baseman cannot really affect the game. But the seat *does* give the player who's sitting there the advantage of seeing more of the cards before playing her or his hand, and for that reason it's probably the best seat in the blackjack house—provided you can stand the heat!

The seat on the far right of the table, by the way, is often referred to as *first base*, because it's the first seat to receive a card. Unlike third base, there's nothing controversial or mysterious about this position.

The Money Pit

The table's bank account sits in front of the dealer. These are the rows of chips you're aiming for—the ones your winnings are paid out of. The dealer sells you some of these chips when you buy in or use a *marker*. Don't worry about going on a hot streak and running the dealer out of chips; the dealer's chip tray is replenished as necessary.

If a dealer's chip tray is running low on any denomination of chip, the pit boss calls for more chips. The dealer signs for them and then drops the paperwork into the cash *drop box* built into the table. That box also serves as the repository for any cash you may have exchanged for chips. The drop box is replaced with an empty one at the end of every shift.

More Table Decor

You'll find a few other essential items on a blackjack table to help you size up the game before deciding whether to sit down. The first of these is a plastic placard showing the table limits and the minimum and maximum bets you can wager on each hand. The table limits vary from casino to casino— and often from table to table within the same casino. It's not unusual for the house to change the table limits on any particular blackjack game depending on the day of the week, time of day, and overall crowd level.

The table limits can be changed by simply replacing the plastic sign with another one. If the limits at the table you're sitting at get raised above the level at which you were playing, it's customary for you to be *grandfathered* at the original level. This means you can continue to play at your lower minimum bet level until you leave the game.

Gamb-lingo

A **pack** refers to a group of card decks that are used in a multiple-deck game. The **discard tray** is a tray on the dealer's right that holds all the cards that have already been played; it's brought back into use at the next shuffle. The **drop box** is a secure box underneath the table in which the dealer stashes your bills or markers when you buy chips.

Another important clue to the nature of the game is the presence, or lack, of a *shoe*, which is a wooden or plastic box designed to hold four, six, or eight decks of cards. The appearance of one on your blackjack table indicates that a multiple-deck game is in progress. With experience, you might be able to determine how many decks they're using by the size of the *pack*, but when you're a beginner, it doesn't hurt to ask!

In most places, six decks is the norm in a multiple-deck game. If there's no shoe on the table, you can assume that either a single- or double-deck game is being played. You can generally determine whether there are one or two decks just by looking at how many cards the dealer is holding and how many have been stashed in the *discard tray*.

While the skilled player is slightly better off with single- and double-deck games, you'll see in Chapter 11 how you can successfully use basic strategy no matter how many decks are in play.

What Makes the Game So Inviting?

As Stanford points out in his book *Basic Blackjack*, dealing blackjack is more boring than playing it. If you've ever stood on the edge of a blackjack pit and watched the blank faces of the dealing troops, you know exactly what he means. A dealer makes no decisions; she or he simply follows house rules. Every procedure the dealer uses is cut-and-dried, uniform for the whole casino. For example, if your dealer cuts the pack into six equal stacks at the beginning of the shuffle, it's because every dealer in the casino must cut the pack into six equal stacks.

Although the dealer's job is mechanical, yours is filled with choices. You make meaningful decisions on each hand you play. Using basic strategy as your guide helps you minimize the advantage the house holds over the player. Perfecting your use of basic strategy can actually tip the scales in your favor, if the house rules are kind enough.

The chance to enjoy the excitement and entertainment that casinos offer *and* have an expectation of winning is what makes blackjack such an inviting and rewarding game. This is not to say that anyone who reads this chapter and the next will automatically walk away a winner at blackjack. As with any other worthwhile endeavor, there are many other books to read and hours of practice to endure before you can expect to become proficient. With blackjack, at least, you have a chance to get the better of the casino!

The Value of Your Cards

All face cards (jacks, queens, and kings) are worth ten points. An ace is worth either one or eleven, depending on how you want to use it in your hand. The remaining cards are worth their face value. For example, a 3 is worth three points and a 10 is worth ten. The suits (clubs, spades, diamonds, and hearts) make no difference in determining the value of a hand. Your objective, as we mentioned before, is to beat the dealer without going over 21.

Gamb-lingo

When you **cut** a deck, you divide it into two parts. The dealer then inverts the order of the two parts. After a shuffle and cut, one card is placed on the bottom of the deck or in the discard tray. This procedure is called **burning a card**, and the card temporarily removed from play is called the **burn card**. When the blackjack dealer gets a card face-up and a card face-down, the **hole** card is the card that is face-down.

It's *How* You Play the Game

To get started, select your seat at a blackjack table and place your bet in the betting circle in front of you. If the game is already in progress, the dealer will deal you in on the next round, or you might have to wait for a shuffle before you are allowed to start playing. After the cards are shuffled, the dealer obligingly places the pack in front of a player. That player's duty is to cut the deck.

After the cards are cut, the dealer inserts the *cut card* near the end of the pack so that he or she isn't tempted to deal down to the bottom. The first card is always *burned*, or discarded. Then the dealer begins to deal, starting again with the player at first base and working clockwise around the table. Each player is dealt two cards, and it makes little difference whether they are face-up or face-down. At least one of the dealer's cards is dealt face-up (the up card) so that all can see part of the dealer's hand; the card dealt face-down to the dealer is called the *hole card*. After the dealer receives a second card, the game begins. (A variation used in Europe: The dealer takes only an up card and no hole card.)

Starting Out Naturally

If the dealer's up card is an ace, players are usually asked whether they would like to take *insurance*, which is a bet that the dealer has a *natural*. A player takes insurance by putting up a side bet of up to half the amount of the original bet. Without turning the hole card over completely, the dealer discreetly checks to see if it is worth 10 (remember—in blackjack, there are 16 cards in each deck that are worth ten points: four 10s, four jacks, four queens, and four kings). If it is, all insurance bets are paid 2 to 1, and all original bets are removed from the table. Even if you took insurance for the full amount allowed, you lose your original bet, but the insurance payoff reimburses you for the loss. The net effect is that you come out even if you take insurance and the dealer has a natural.

If the dealer doesn't have a 10 tucked under the ace, the insurance money is swept from the table, like term life that expired, unused and unneeded, and the game continues.

If you're fortunate enough to be dealt an ace and a 10, you have a natural and should immediately turn both cards face up to let the dealer know you won. In most casinos, you are paid 3 to 2 for a natural, as is written on the table. This really means you get one and one-half times your bet.

If the dealer also has a natural, you *push*—which means you don't get paid for your natural unless the dealer has an ace up and you elect to take *even money*. Accepting even money when you have a natural and the dealer has an ace up is the same thing as taking insurance, and it

Gamb-lingo

A **natural** is a two-card hand of 21 points. The only way to make a 21 in two cards is to be dealt an ace and a 10 or face card. Sometimes a natural is referred to as a *blackjack*. To **hit** a hand is to take another card. The card you receive is also called a **hit**.

Gamb-lingo

A **push** is a tie hand between a dealer and a player, and no money changes hands. A push occurs when both you and the dealer have unbusted hands with the same total points. If you bust, you cannot push.

Risky Business

Many people believe that insurance is a good bet. It isn't. The dealer will not have a natural often enough to make insurance look like a smart purchase. If you have a natural, taking even money is the same thing as taking insurance, and again, you are better off not taking it, and possibly winning 3 to 2 or pushing. We'll explain this point in more detail in Chapter 11.

means you are paid 1 to 1 instead of 3 to 2 on your natural, before the dealer checks the hole card. (You'll learn in the next chapter why taking even money and placing insurance bets are not good strategies.)

In some casinos, the dealer may check the hole card under a 10 to see if there is an ace tucked under to make the hand a natural. If the dealer does have an ace under, you automatically lose your bet unless you have a tying natural. If you happen to have a natural and the dealer does not check under a 10, you are paid for your natural after the dealer gets around to checking the hole card.

Playing It Out

Most of the time, neither you nor the dealer has a natural, and the game continues with players making their "informed" playing decisions based on basic strategy, which you'll learn about in the next chapter. In a nutshell, you may be required to make these decisions as you play each hand:

- ◆ Should I surrender my hand?

- ◆ Do I have a "splittable" pair of cards?

- ◆ Is this a "double down" opportunity?

- ◆ Should I take a hit or should I stand?

Gamb-lingo

To **surrender** is to give up half your bet for the privilege of not playing out your hand. You keep the other half of your bet. A **stiff** is a hand that is not *pat* and that could bust if hit once. Stiffs include hard twelves through sixteens. A **pat** hand is an unbusted hand worth at least seventeen points.

"I Give Up!"

Some casinos offer you the option to *surrender* a *stiff*, or bad hand. This means you are allowed to turn in a hand without playing it for the cost of half your original bet. Obviously, you would consider surrendering only a hand of little hope. In essence, you save half the money you think you're going to lose anyway.

There are two types of surrender sometimes offered: early and late. *Early surrender* means it's allowed before the dealer checks for a natural, and *late surrender* means it's allowed only after the dealer checks for a natural. Early surrender is more advantageous because it allows you to occasionally save half of your bet when the dealer has a natural. When you want to surrender and the option is available, just tell the dealer you give up. The dealer will gladly pick up your cards and half of your bet and go on to the next player.

Breaking Up Is Fun to Do (Splitting Pairs)

A pair is any two cards that have the same face value, such as two 3s, or two 10s. Technically, you can split any pair dealt to you in the first two cards, but you'd never want to break up a perfectly good twenty to split a pair of 10s. When you get into basic strategy in the next chapter, you'll see which pairs are the best for you to split, depending on the dealer's up card.

When you split a pair, you turn your hand into two separate hands. When you split, you must put up another wager of the same amount as your original bet. You must bet the same amount of money riding on each of your two hands as you bet on your original hand. Tell the dealer you're splitting your pair by separating both cards face up and placing the extra wager by one of them. When it's your turn to act, you play out the first split card by drawing as many cards as you want for it, before playing out the other. If you happen to be dealt a third identical card for either hand, you may be allowed to re-split, depending on the house rules. Each re-split requires an additional bet. When you split aces, you are usually allowed to draw only one card for each ace.

Gamb-lingo

A **pair** is any two cards that have the same value, like 3 and 3 or 10 and 10. Whether two unlike 10s (such as a queen and a king) is a pair is up to the casino management. Generally, a pair may be split and played as two hands.

Double Your Pleasure by Doubling Down

Doubling down means you are doubling your wager on the chance that you will win with just one more card dealt to you. The advantage of doubling down is that you are allowed to increase your bet after you see your hand and the dealer's up card. The disadvantage is that you are entitled to take only one more card.

In many casinos, you can double down for less by putting up less than you originally wagered. Many casinos allow you to double down on any two cards, but some restrict you from doubling down on anything but ten or eleven. Some casinos permit you to double down after splitting a pair.

When you want to double down, lay your cards down in front of your original bet and place the additional wager next to (not on top of) your original bet.

The Sadistic Side of Blackjack: Hitting

When you want another card because your first two cards aren't close enough to 21 to win, you indicate to the dealer that you'd like another card by scratching the surface of the table lightly with your cards. This is called *taking a hit*. Each time you scratch, the dealer gives an additional card face-up. If your original cards were dealt to you face-up, you might not be allowed to touch your cards. In this case, just motion that you want a hit by tapping the table in front of your cards or by scratching the surface of the table lightly with a finger. The dealer will get the idea. If a hit makes your hand bust, turn your cards face up and watch the dealer take them (and your bet) away.

When you think you have a good enough hand, let the dealer know that you want to *stand* by placing your cards under your original bet, or waving your fingers as if waving the dealer away. Do this with one hand only, and without touching your bet. Handling your bet while it's in action and touching your cards with both hands are two things that make a dealer nervous.

How the Game Ends

After all players are done, the dealer's hand is played out according to the rules of the house. As the pressure mounts, the dealer turns over the hole card, so now both cards are exposed. If you're lucky, the dealer's hand will total sixteen or less and everyone will breathe a collective sigh of relief; the dealer will take a hit and continue hitting until the hand totals seventeen or more. Unlike players, the dealer is not allowed to split, double down, or surrender. Whether the dealer is required to hit or stand on a soft seventeen is up to the casino, and is usually indicated right on the table.

Gamb-lingo

Any hand that contains an ace that can be counted as eleven is called a **soft hand**. An ace and a 6, for example, is called a *soft* seventeen. Any hand that does not contain an ace is a **hard hand**; for example, a 6 and a 7 is a hard 13. A hand with an ace can be hard, too, if every ace in the hand counts as one point.

After the dealer's hand reaches seventeen or more, the dealer turns to each player's hand and compares totals. If the dealer busted and your hand didn't, you automatically win no matter how weak your hand is. If the dealer does not bust but has a lower total than your hand, you win and are paid even money (1 to 1). If the dealer does not bust and has a higher total than your hand, you lose and your bet is placed in the chip tray. If you and the dealer have the same total, you *push*, and no money is exchanged.

After settling up with each of the players, the dealer picks up all the played cards and places them in the discard tray to await the next shuffle.

The Least You Need to Know

- ◆ The object of blackjack is to beat the dealer without going over 21. You can learn what the house rules are in blackjack games by reading the table or asking the dealer.

- ◆ The dealer has to play according to the house rules—you don't. Therein lies your advantage!

- ◆ If you are dealt a natural, turn your cards over (face-up) for the dealer to see, and smile!

- ◆ Taking insurance, or even money, enables you to insure your natural against a dealer's possible natural. It is not considered a good bet to make.

- ◆ When you split a pair, you are turning your existing hand into two separate hands, each with a bet equal to your original bet.

- ◆ When you double down, you are doubling your wager and your hand gets one (and only one) more card.

Chapter 11

Playing Blackjack with a Strategy

In This Chapter

◆ Why everyone needs to use basic strategy

◆ What to look for in a game of blackjack

◆ How to use basic strategy to help you win

◆ How anyone can get an advantage playing blackjack

It's unlikely that an inexperienced player could sit down at a blackjack table and start playing the game to his or her advantage. Many of the plays are just not obvious. How many of you, for instance, would look at a sixteen and think that the best way to play that hand against a 7 is to stand? If you raised your hand on that one, keep reading. The average player makes mistakes about 15 percent of the time, and they cost dearly. The proper way to play that particular hand is to take a hit because a six-teen won't do you any good against a dealer's seventeen or higher, and you have to assume that the dealer has a 10 buried under the 7. You might not know how many different ways that dealer's hand could possibly have

Gamb-lingo

The **expected win rate** is a percentage of the total amount of money wagered that you can expect to win (+ percent) or lose (– percent) over time.

been played out—but Stanford does, and that's the kind of information he used to develop basic strategy.

To play blackjack to win, you should at least know the basic strategy in this chapter. It also helps if you know your *expected win rate* and what casino rules are most favorable. You'll learn all that and more when you read this chapter.

Putting Time on Your Side

One thing that makes blackjack unique is that the *house edge*, or *advantage*, differs for every player and is based on level of skill. A novice who's never heard of basic strategy and just sits down and plays is up against a house edge of approximately –2 to –3 percent, depending on the playing conditions. That means the novice can expect to *lose* $2 to $3 for every $100 wagered.

The house starts out with an advantage over the players because the players finish their hands before the dealer does. If a player and the dealer both bust, the dealer wins.

Loaded with information and an understanding of the playing conditions, a card-counting blackjack player can actually eliminate the house edge and tip the scales in his or her favor. Using basic strategy, a novice can expect to almost break even and, blessed with favorable house rules, conceivably come out ahead in the long run.

This doesn't mean you'll win every time or that you'll win tons of money. (That depends on how well and under what conditions you play and how much you bet.) But it does mean that as you continue to play and practice basic strategy, and learn even more by mastering the material in other books (including Stanford's *Basic Blackjack, Blackjack Secrets,* and *Professional Blackjack*), you can gain a certain amount of control or "edge" over the house and wind up a winner over time. Not a bad proposition for someone who enjoys casino gambling!

What Conditions Are Favorable?

While we're on the subject of house edge, you should understand how the variations in the game that you find from casino to casino can affect what's called your *expected win rate*. The expected win rate is the flip side of the house edge—it's what you, the player, can expect to win (or lose). Your expected win rate using basic strategy depends on the rules of the game and how many decks are shuffled together.

Some rule variations are favorable to the player, and others are favorable to the house. For example, you're 0.3 percent better off playing a single-deck game than playing a double-deck game. You're 0.2 percent better off playing a double deck than playing against four or more decks. Compared to a single deck—everything else being equal—you are at a 0.5 percent disadvantage playing a four-deck game. Playing against more than four decks is only marginally worse than playing against four decks.

Best Bet

When you're learning, you might want to play against dealers who deal their cards slowly—like dealer trainees who are *also* learning. Find out which casinos are known for hiring trainees and what time of day those trainees work. Then practice your basic strategy on them!

Under the following conditions, basic strategy can put you even with the house: If the game is single deck, the dealer stands on soft seventeen, you're allowed to double down on any two cards but not after splitting a pair, your naturals win 3 to 2, and surrender is not offered. In a game that offers these baseline conditions, using basic strategy levels the playing field between you and the house so that the house edge and your expected win rate are both equal to 0.0 percent.

To tip the scales in your favor when you use basic strategy, you can seek out games in which any of the rule variations discussed in the following table are offered in addition to the baseline conditions.

Conditions That Improve Your Expected Win Rate with Basic Strategy

Look for These Rule Variations	To *Increase* Your Expected Win Rate by
Natural pays 2 to 1	+2.30%
Early Surrender	+0.70%
Player paid for tied natural that pays 3 to 2	+0.30%
Double down on any number of cards	+0.24%
Double down after splitting pairs	+0.14%
Late surrender	+0.06%

The most common game you can beat with basic strategy alone (no card counting) is promotions involving 2 to 1 payoffs on naturals. Receiving 2 to 1 on naturals is worth 2.3 percent, which is a lot more than what you lose going from single deck to multiple decks, so jump on any 2 to 1 games you find, no matter how many decks are being used. Jump quickly, because they do not happen very often and don't last long; the casino loses money too quickly.

What Conditions Are *Un*favorable?

Although it's getting more and more difficult to find a single-deck game and any of the most favorable blackjack conditions listed in the preceding table, basic strategy can still help you increase your expected win rate even when less favorable conditions, like the ones listed in the following table, apply.

Gamb-lingo

Any hand that doesn't contain an ace is a **hard hand** (6 and 7 is a hard thirteen). A hand with an ace can be hard, too, if the hand totals twelve or more and each ace in the hand counts as one (for example, 5, 10, and ace is a hard sixteen). The term *hard* is not used with hands of eleven or less.

If you can't find a game that offers the baseline conditions, subtract the percentages listed below from your 0.0 percent expected win rate to find out how damaging an unfavorable condition can be. Try to avoid games with so many unfavorable conditions that the odds are too heavily stacked against you. To keep your playing field as level as possible, try to avoid playing under too many of the conditions listed in the following table.

Unfavorable Conditions and How They Affect Your Win Rate When You Use Basic Strategy

Avoid These Rule Variations	That Change Your Expected Win Rate by
Six or eight decks	–0.56%
Four decks	–0.48%
Two decks	–0.30%
Dealer hits soft seventeen	–0.20%
Can't double down on nine	–0.13%
Can't double down on soft hands	–0.13%

Introducing Basic Strategy

Stanford developed a generic basic strategy for the most common blackjack rules and situations you're likely to encounter in the majority of casinos in the United States. The strategy, which is explained in the following chart, is a set of playing rules that you should commit to following on *every* play of your cards. Although it may seem to you that standing on a *hard* sixteen against a dealer's 7 is the practical thing to do, the fact is you're better off hitting, by between 8 percent and 14 percent. You are more likely to lose than to win whenever you're dealt a hard sixteen against a dealer's 7, but you lose less often if you hit.

Each play recommended in the strategy has been tested in both computer simulation and live play and proved to give you the greatest expected win for that hand. Whether an action turns out to win or lose on one isolated hand doesn't determine whether the decision is correct or incorrect. What matters is what the average outcome over thousands of such decisions has proved to be.

Generic basic strategy is designed for use against the baseline rules and is applicable against any number of decks. In other words, the strategy works just as well whether you're playing a single-deck game or multiple decks dealt from a shoe. (The number of decks used still affects your expected win rate, of course.)

If you've located a casino and blackjack game where you're allowed to double down after splitting a pair, we offer a modified splitting strategy, too, to help you take advantage of this favorable condition.

Using the Basic Strategy Chart

To be successful, you must learn this strategy inside out. Memorize it and use it every time you play! Here's a good way to start:

◆ First, learn what the strategy symbols mean:

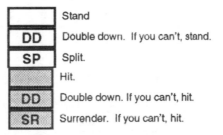

	Stand
DD	Double down. If you can't, stand.
SP	Split.
	Hit.
DD	Double down. If you can't, hit.
SR	Surrender. If you can't, hit.

Notice that an unshaded box indicates you *should not* take another card (stand), and a shaded box means you *should* take another card (hit). When you see the symbol for double down (DD) in an unshaded box, that means you should double down if the house rules allow you to do so and stand if they don't. The same is true of splitting a pair (SP). When you see the symbol SP in an unshaded box, split the pair when you're allowed to and stand if you can't.

When you see the symbol for double down (DD) in a shaded box, that means you should double down if the house rules allow you to and take an additional card (hit) if they don't. The same is true for surrendering a hand (SR): If surrender is an option, do it when you see SR in a shaded box; when you can't surrender, take a hit.

◆ Look for the correct way to play any hand on the basic strategy chart, shown on the next page.

Find the row that shows your hand and then run your finger across until you locate the column that shows the dealer's up card at the top. Remember that rows go left and right and columns go up and down. Player's hands are listed in the order of splits, soft hands, hard twelve through twenty-one, and five through eleven. (Anything lower than a five is either a pair or a soft hand.) The next figure shows how to figure out what to do with a pair of 7s against a dealer's 8.

◆ Each time you take an additional card (hit), check the basic strategy chart again to see what to do with your new total. Keep checking the basic strategy chart after each hit until the strategy tells you to stand on that total against the dealer's up card. (Now you've got a "hand" to stand on!)

◆ If you split your first two cards, you play the first hand out according to the strategy before playing the second hand.

Then, find the dealer's up card
in one of these columns.

How to use the Basic Strategy Chart.

Dealer's Upcard										
Player's Hand	**2**	**3**	**4**	**5**	**6**	**7**	**8**	**9**	**10**	**A**
A-A	SP	SP	SP	SP	SP	SP	SP	SP	SP	SP
10-10										
9-9	SP	SP	SP	SP	SP		SP	SP		
8-8	SP	SP	SP	SP	SP	SP	SP	SP	SP	SP
7-7	SP	SP	SP	SP	SP	SP				
6-6		SP	SP	SP	SP					
5-5	DD	DD	DD	DD	DD	DD	DD	DD		

First, look for your hand
in these rows.

Find the proper strategy for this hand in
the intersection of the row and column.
In this case, HIT—don't split!

Basic Strategy
(Double Down NOT Allowed After Splitting)

Player's Hand	Dealer's Upcard									
	2	3	4	5	6	7	8	9	10	A
A-A	SP	SP	SP	SP	SP	SP	SP	SP	SP	SP
10-10										
9-9	SP	SP	SP	SP	SP		SP	SP		
8-8	SP	SP	SP	SP	SP	SP	SP	SP	SP	SP
7-7	SP	SP	SP	SP	SP	SP				
6-6		SP	SP	SP	SP					
5-5	DD	DD	DD	DD	DD	DD	DD	DD		
4-4										
3-3			SP	SP	SP	SP				
2-2			SP	SP	SP	SP				
soft 19 - 21										
soft 18		DD	DD	DD	DD					
soft 17		DD	DD	DD	DD					
soft 16			DD	DD	DD					
soft 15			DD	DD	DD					
soft 14				DD	DD					
soft 13					DD					
hard 17 - 21										
hard 16								SR	SR	SR
hard 15										
hard 14										
hard 13										
hard 12										
11	DD	DD	DD	DD	DD	DD	DD	DD	DD	
10	DD	DD	DD	DD	DD	DD	DD	DD		
9		DD	DD	DD	DD					
8										
7										
6										
5										

Key

	Stand		Hit.
DD	Double down. If you can't, stand.	DD	Double down. If you can't, hit.
SP	Split.	SR	Surrender. If you can't, hit.

◆ *Practice, practice, practice!* Before you go up against a real casino, make sure you *know* the basics. Practice playing blackjack with a friend using the strategy chart as a guide until you've memorized it. Another good way to practice is to use one of the many blackjack computer games available at your local software store. Be sure you get a program that alerts you if you stray from correct play. Many programs allow you to change the conditions and rules. If you want a good program that has lots of options and is used by many professionals to test their own strategies and modifications, get Stanford's *Blackjack Count Analyzer* software or the version of it that uses basic strategy only and no card counting: *Blackjack Analyzer*.

◆ When you're finally ready to play against the casino, bring the tear-out card in the front of this book (which also shows the basic strategy chart) with you in case your memory lapses in live action. You may be able to use the basic strategy card at the table, as long as you don't slow the game down. Don't be concerned if a pit boss comes over and asks to look at it; he or she is making sure you're not hiding any playing cards with it. The card is likely to start a lively debate about strategy, and you'll probably wind up as the center of attention. Good luck!

Basic Strategy When Doubling Down *Is* Allowed After Splitting

If you're allowed to double down after splitting, you'll find that you win more on splits, so you should split a few more pairs than you would otherwise. Doubling down after splitting helps a player who uses the basic strategy modifications presented here by +0.14 percent. If the casino where you are playing allows you to double down after splitting a pair, use these rules in addition to the basic strategy:

When the Dealer's Up Card Is	Split a Pair of	Instead of
2	6s, 3s, and 2s	Hitting
3	3s and 2s	Hitting
5	4s	Hitting
6	4s	Hitting

(An important reminder: Doubling after splits changes basic strategy only on splits. Continue to make the rest of your decisions according to the basic strategy presented earlier.)

Basic Truths About the Dealer's Up Card

Besides the cards in your own hand, you are also allowed to see one of the dealer's cards. Don't ignore it because it's often important information for the play of your own hand.

Basic strategy is built on the premise that the dealer's up card provides enough information for you to make reliable predictions about the most likely outcome of his or her hand. A deck of 52 playing cards contains a total of 16 cards that are worth ten in blackjack scoring (10, king, queen, and jack in all four suits), which accounts for a little more than 30 percent of the deck.

A dealer with an up card of 2, 3, 4, 5, or 6 is more likely to bust, and a dealer with an up card of 7, 8, 9, 10, or ace is more likely to have a pat hand. When the dealer is likely to bust, your best bet is to avoid busting your own hand, and be aggressive on splitting and doubling down, as shown in the basic strategy chart.

Conversely, whenever the dealer has a 7, 8, 9, 10, or ace up, basic strategy tells you that the dealer is less likely to bust. That means hitting your own stiffs, less doubling down, and less splitting. Here again, the basic strategy chart tells you what to do, so use it!

Gamb-lingo

The **up card** is the card in the dealer's hand that is face up for all the players to see before they play their hands. When the dealer gets a card face up and a card face down, the **hole card** is the card that's face down. You're not supposed to know the value of the hole card until after you play your hand.

Basic Truths About *Your* Hand

For some of your hands, the dealer's up card doesn't matter. In the following situations, play your hand according to these simple rules of basic strategy:

♦ *Never* ruin a hard seventeen or higher or a soft nineteen or higher by hitting. Although it may not always win, it's not worth the risk. There's little chance of improving a good hand!

♦ *Always* split aces. A pair of aces is either two or twelve. When you split them, each ace automatically counts as 11 and you have a very good chance of catching a 10. Although you are entitled to receive only

Bet You Didn't Know ...

A dealer can be expected to:

♦ Bust about 28 percent of the time

♦ Stand with 17–21 about 67 percent of the time

♦ Catch a natural almost 5 percent of the time

one card on each ace, and if you get a 10 you won't get paid 3 to 2, you will probably win more than you would if you hit, double down, or stand.

◆ *Always* split 8s. When you split 8s, you're breaking up sixteen, which is the worst possible hand you can get. You're more likely to wind up with at least one winning hand by splitting than if you were to try to win by hitting or standing on your sixteen. When playing out each of the split hands, let basic strategy be your guide.

Is Insurance Worth It?

The basic strategy chart doesn't say a word about *insurance* or *even money*, but Stanford does. The word is: *Don't take it!* Here's why:

Suppose you have a natural and the dealer shows an ace in a single-deck game. If you remove your 10–ace and the dealer's ace from the deck, 49 cards are left. There are 15 10s left in the deck to give the dealer a natural, and 34 other cards that won't. If you don't insure your natural, you will win 3 to 2, or 150 percent of your bet, 34 times, and push 15 times, out of the 49 possible outcomes. This averages out to winning 104 percent of your bet by not insuring, as opposed to only 100 percent of your bet by taking insurance, or even money. Similar arithmetic will yield the same advice for multiple decks and for you having hands other than a natural. The smart player takes a chance *only* when the odds favor it. In this case the odds favor *not* taking insurance, 104 to 100.

Counting Cards: Not Quite as Easy as 1-2-3

As a novice, you're in no position to think about card counting, but it's a skill you will want to learn if you enjoy the game. Here's how it works:

Gamb-lingo

Card counting means keeping track of a statistic that describes the cards that have been played since the shuffle (not just the current hand). Card counters generally vary bet size and playing strategy using what they know about the cards that have not yet been dealt.

In blackjack, if cards are not shuffled between rounds, cards used in one round of play are out of commission until the next shuffle. Each successive hand must be composed of cards that have not been used since the last shuffle. A *card counter* keeps track of each card that's been played in order to make bets and play hands according to the makeup of the cards that remain to be dealt.

A card counter looks for situations where there is a higher percentage of 10s and aces left than normal, because this is the opportune time to increase the bet. A card counter even knows when insurance might be a good bet—when more than one third of the remaining cards are 10s. (If exactly one third of the remaining cards are 10s, insurance is a break-even bet.) In general, a pack that is rich in 10s and aces favors the player, and a pack that is rich in low cards (2, 3, 4, 5, and 6) favors the dealer (because the dealer is less likely to bust).

A more simple but still powerful card-counting system is the high-low system; it assigns the value of +1 to each low card, –1 to each 10 and ace, and zero to each 7, 8 and 9. Card counting can give a player a positive expected-win rate, but requires a great deal of skill and practice. You should master basic strategy before you attempt to count cards. When you're ready to move on, read Stanford's book *Professional Blackjack* for all the details!

Reality Check

By now, some of you might be wondering why you're playing blackjack in the first place! Sure, blackjack is a beatable game if you play correctly under the right conditions. But I (Susan, that is; not Stanford) don't play to get rich or even to win all the time. I play because I happen to enjoy Las Vegas! I like the food, the excitement, the shows, the swimming pools—I even like the heat! And blackjack happens to be a delightful game of both chance and skill that's not only fun—it allows me to play longer on my meager bankroll than any other game!

Think about it. You get to sit there sipping all the exotic beverages you desire, sample those high-priced waters that people like me are too cheap to buy at home, and watch hundreds of people in all shapes and sizes having a good time—or going down trying! Not only that, you meet all kinds of interesting people you'd probably never have the time or inclination to talk to if they weren't sitting at your blackjack table.

Then you get to go upstairs or home, with enough money left over to play again tomorrow. Not to mention, as Stanford so eloquently pointed out in the baccarat chapter, enjoying the attractive casino personnel parading before us: "Is it my imagination, or is that great-looking guy in the Armani suit a pit boss?" When I play slots, all I get to see is my own bleak reflection staring back at me.

 Best Bet

How much fun you have at blackjack is determined more by the other players at your table than anything else. So look for a table having fun or people whose company you'll enjoy! If the fun goes away, you should go, too.

Taking As Much Advantage As You Can!

An astute player knows how to take advantage of opportunities that present themselves. Besides looking for the most favorable blackjack conditions and sticking with basic strategy, you can sometimes sway the odds in your favor just by keeping your eyes open … and your mouth closed!

All's Fair in Love and Blackjack

An example Stanford describes in *Basic Blackjack* is a moral dilemma every blackjack player faces now and then: an incorrect payoff in your favor. Whenever it happens to me, I ask myself, "Should I say something so the dealer won't get in trouble, or should I just keep quiet and reap the benefits of the mistake?" By the time I finish pondering the basic meaning of life (which is something I tend to segue into when faced with moral dilemmas of any dimension), I've invariably picked up my "take" and moved on to the next hand.

When the same thing happens for everyone at a crowded table, (like the dealer paying everyone for a six-card 21 as if it were a bust!), the group dynamic is powerful. You can almost see the wheels turning in everyone's head as they try to figure out

Gamb-lingo

To **toke** a dealer is to give him or her money or chips as a tip.

"who will break the bond" or whether the dealer will suddenly re-count. Ordinarily, no one dares speak up against the solidarity of the group, and when it's all over and we've all been paid safely, the table breathes a collective sigh of relief. (At which point a self-appointed Karma-tist generally *tokes* the dealer for a job well done!)

Anyway, the point Stanford makes is that the casino owner is the one responsible for procedures, not you or me. There's no reason for us to take on this extra burden of morality or gamesmanship. A smart player will take an edge wherever it can be gotten legally. There are enough procedures, pit bosses, and security cameras in place to protect casinos from the simple mistakes (or blatant incompetence) of their employees, and we are under no ethical obligation to point out the error of their ways unless we want to—or if it is to our advantage, of course! So the rule of thumb is this: If the dealer makes a mistake in the casino's favor, raise your hand and speak up. If it's in your favor, let your raised consciousness be your guide.

By the way (Stanford would like me to add), he doesn't apply this morality to a clerk ringing up a purchase; in a store or restaurant, any error he catches he corrects. But casinos are different. A bet at blackjack is not lost until the dealer picks it up. If the dealer does not pick it up, it is not lost; if the dealer pays it, it's a winner.

Casinos are always looking for subtle ways to get or keep a slight advantage over players. (That's one reason it's harder to find a single-deck game anymore.) So when you find a dealer who makes mistakes in your favor, stick around! Errors in payoffs tend to run in bunches for the simple reason that dealers are human. Perhaps your dealer had a bad night last night or has had to work double shifts three days in a row. Maybe the dealer doesn't feel well, but can't take the day off and is loaded up with cold medication.

Don't feel like you're taking unfair advantage. You're within the rules, which is what every red-blooded sportsman who plays to win is trained to do. Remember, the mistakes would be made whether you were there to benefit from them or not!

This is probably a good time to warn against cheating. Overlooking a dealer's unintentional mistakes is not a crime, but such things as marking the cards and colluding with the dealer are felonies that could win you free room and board in a state institution.

Best Bet _____

It's easy to get *comps* when playing blackjack. Comps are free meals, free tickets to shows, and more. Ask and maybe you will receive. One way to earn more than your fair share of comps is to bet bigger when the pit boss is watching.

Sticking to the Basics (Strategy, That Is)

As a beginner, your play will be slower than average when you first start out, and it's perfectly all right to ask the dealer for help when you need it. For example, if you just took a number of little hits on a soft hand and are having a hard time counting the points, don't hesitate to ask the dealer to count them for you. However, don't rely on anyone else's advice to play out your hand; stick with basic strategy.

Most blackjack players do not know basic strategy. They are happy to give you advice on playing your cards, but if they play their own cards differently from basic strategy, they won't give you good advice on blackjack. Basic strategy works better than playing hunches, but it works only if you use it faithfully. Don't use it for one hand and not for another because it didn't work the last time. There's no guarantee that any one hand will work out right every time. In fact, if there were, we'd all be putting up our own hotels on Boardwalk. In the long run, however, the strategy you've been given will work out more times than not.

Don't let the dealer play your cards for you. For example, if you have a hand on which most people stand but you don't want to stand, don't let the dealer pass you by. If you want to hit, split, or double down, make sure to have your hand or chips out there before the dealer gets to you. When you win a hand, make sure the payout is correct. If it's not, ask the dealer to check the payout before you touch the chips.

Right now you probably feel like there's a lot to learn, but after a few hours of action, you'll get the hang of things and start to have some real fun. And fun is what you're really here for!

Bet You Didn't Know ...

A bit of history that's worth repeating: In the old days when a dealer had to peek under a 10 to see if the hand was a natural, the dealer would have hole-card information that was potentially valuable to the player. You could sometimes spot a dealer who inadvertently divulged that information through body language; this is known as a *tell*. If the dealer showed a 10 and you had a stiff, basic strategy was to hit; if you were sensitive to the dealer's body language, however, you could occasionally read a sign that correctly said to stand.

For example, a dealer who found a 6 under the 10 and wanted you to stand might hold the deck away from your cards or might turn slightly toward the next player. Now most casinos no longer have their dealers peek under 10s, but if you get the opportunity to play at a blackjack table where dealers still do, look out for telltale signs that can work in your favor!

The Least You Need to Know

◆ Basic strategy levels the playing field between you and the casino, particularly when you're playing a single-deck game. If multiple decks are used, the house still has a slight advantage over you.

◆ An average player who doesn't use a basic strategy gives the house a 2 to 3 percent advantage.

◆ Smart players take advantage of all kinds of favorable playing conditions and avoid unfavorable ones.

◆ Even if you play under all of the most favorable conditions, you'll still lose sometimes.

◆ Above all, enjoy the game. You probably won't break the bank, but you can have fun trying!

Baby Needs a New Pair of Shoes

In This Chapter

♦ What's going on at the crap tables

♦ Who's doing what to whom

♦ Which are the best bets to make, whether you're right or wrong

♦ How to place a bet and know whether it's time to take your winnings

Craps flourished during World War II, probably because it was always easy to make room for a "floating" crap game and not too hard to hide the evidence. Today, you'll find old salts huddled around crap tables trying to pass on ancient wisdom to the younger generations.

Craps happens to be one of the fastest and most exciting games in the casino. Although dice are tossed by only one player at a time, wagering on the outcome is a group activity. It's not unusual to find a hot roller leading a group prayer before each toss. If she's got a streak going and everyone's betting on her, the excitement can be deafening.

Just Another Day in Pair-A-Dice

Craps is played with a pair of six-sided *dice* (as shown in the next figure), a crap table, and a crew of up to four casino employees who run the game, as we'll explain in greater detail later. The layout of the table and the seemingly endless array of bets you can place make the game somewhat intimidating and confusing for the beginner. But the objective is really quite simple: to bet whether a *shooter* throwing a pair of dice will be able to *roll* a winning combination.

Setting the Crap Table

Perhaps a good place to start is to explain the crap table. You could walk through a crowded casino and miss the crap game entirely if not for the throngs standing around it. That's not to say a crap table isn't big—it is! But its profile is low, and you can't actually see the game part of the table or how it's laid out, until you get right up next to one and look down.

Gamb-lingo

A **die** is a cube with a number from one to six marked on each side. A *pair* are called **dice** and are used in a crap game by a **shooter** who, holding the dice and the fate of the entire crap table in the palm of his or her hand, **rolls** (tosses) the dice.

The table is designed to accommodate up to 12 players who stand along its top rail and lean over to place their bets on the sunken table layout below. The next figure shows the standard crap table layout.

As you can see, the table layout *is* complex because the player has so many betting options. But if you divide the table into sections—left, right, and center—the game is not as intimidating as it looks. First, notice that the left and right sides are the same. (There goes one third of the confusion.) Now, look at the center markings. These are the very risky bets (called *center bets*) that give the casino a higher percentage. We'll tell you what these bets are, but we'll also show you how to play without ever placing a center bet. (How's that for chipping away another third of the confusion?)

Because each of the number markings on the table corresponds to a bet that you can make, you may want to refer back to this figure as we explain each bet and show you how to play.

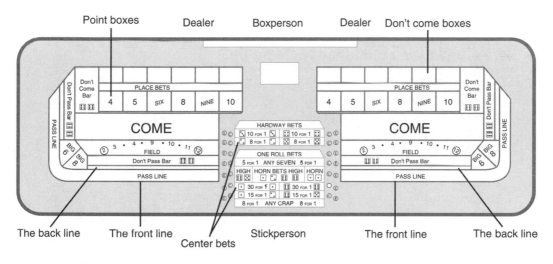

It's only half *as bad as it looks!*

Let It Roll

Crap players bet on the roll of the dice. Just in case there's anyone who doesn't know this, each die has six sides. A number from one to six is marked in tiny dots on each

side. In a perfectly balanced die, each of the six sides has an equal chance (1 out of 6) of landing face-up when the die is rolled.

When you roll a pair of dice, the numbers shown on the two sides facing up are added together. Because the smallest number on each die is 1, the lowest total you can roll with a pair of dice is two. The highest total you can get is twelve, by rolling two 6s, or *boxcars*.

Gamb-lingo

When you roll a two in craps, it's called **snake eyes**— *eyes* because they look like eyes, *snake* because they're bad news (for the shooter). Two 6s rolled in a craps game are called **box-cars** (boxcars are the last cars on a train).

Many Ways to "Roll with It"

Because each die has six sides, there are 36 possible results from rolling them (6 × 6 = 36). For instance, there is only one way to roll a two or a twelve, as we just explained. But there are two ways to get a three: 1 and 2 or 2 and 1. Imagine rolling a red die and a green die. Three can appear two ways: with a red 1 and a green 2 or with a green 1 and a red 2. The following table shows all the possible combinations when rolling a pair of dice.

Here's How the 36 Combinations Stack Up

Number Rolled	How Many Ways to Roll the Number?	True Odds	Winning Combinations
Two	1	35 to 1	
Three	2	17 to 1	
Four	3	11 to 1	
Five	4	8 to 1	
Six	5	6.2 to 1	
Seven	6	5 to 1	
Eight	5	6.2 to 1	
Nine	4	8 to 1	
Ten	3	11 to 1	
Eleven	2	17 to 1	
Twelve	1	35 to 1	

As you can see, you can roll a seven in six different ways: 1 and 6, 2 and 5, 3 and 4, 6 and 1, 2 and 5, or 4 and 3. You are more likely to roll a seven than any other number.

You can calculate your chances (odds) of rolling a particular number in craps based on the number of possible ways you can roll the number, as shown in the preceding table.

Figuring Your Odds

To figure your chances (or "true" odds) of rolling any number, divide 36 by the number of possible ways to roll the number, as listed in the preceding table. For example, to determine your odds of rolling a three, divide 36 by 2 (two is the number of possible ways to roll a three), and get 18. That means you have a 1 in 18 chance of rolling a three. Expressed as odds, that's 17 to 1 *against* rolling a three because for every eighteen rolls, you expect to get something other than 3 seventeen times, and to get three once. The odds of rolling each number are posted in the preceding table along with the amount of possible combinations for each number. You'll want to refer back to this table as we talk about different bets and how the house edge can eat away at your profits.

Generally, the *house edge* is the difference between the *true odds*, as listed in the preceding table, and what the casino actually pays for rolling a winner. If, for example, you bet $1 on three and a three is rolled, your dollar turns into $15. It would have turned into $18 if the casino wasn't trying to make money on the game. You get 16.67 percent less than the true-odds payoff, so if you make this bet frequently, over time you should lose 16.67 percent of your money. No wonder when you stay too long at a game like craps (or any other game that has a large house edge), you begin to feel like even when you win, you lose!

In the rest of this chapter, we'll focus on the bets that won't gobble up your profits as quickly as center bets. Making the bets we recommend will mark you as an experienced player.

Who's Running This Game?

It takes a *crew* of casino employees to run a hearty game of craps. When things get rolling, you'll generally find four friendly faces ready, willing, and able to take your money and help you place your bets. At prime time (the hours between dinner and a little after midnight, depending on the night of the week), you'll find a *boxperson* sitting between two dealers, directly across from a *stickperson*. The boxperson's job is to supervise the box, the area in the center of the table where center bets are placed. The boxperson tells the dealers who and how much to pay on winning *center bets* and to officiate, or settle any disputes that might arise.

A dealer stands on each side of the boxperson and handles all the money and chips. The dealer changes your cash into chips when you enter the game, pays off all your winning bets, and quickly clears the chips from the table when you lose. The dealer also marks the *point*, which you'll learn about when we start playing, and helps you place bets on those hard-to-reach numbers.

Because a casino can lose hundreds of thousands of dollars quickly if bad, or *crooked*, dice are brought into a game, the stickperson's primary job is the security of the dice. He or she also calls the outcome of each roll of the dice, setting the tone and making the game exciting.

Best Bet

A proper roll requires that the dice bounce off the far (or side) wall of the crap table before coming to rest. Bouncing off a wall helps the casino ensure that the winning numbers are random.

To start each game, the stickperson passes a handful of dice to a new shooter. The shooter selects two and rolls. After calling the total rolled, the stickperson uses a long, curved stick to retrieve the dice from the opposite end of the table and moves them to the middle of the table. After all bets are placed for the next roll, he or she passes them back to the shooter. If a die or pair of dice happen to be thrown off the table, it's the stickperson's responsibility to retrieve them and make sure they weren't altered before putting them back in play. The stickperson also stands near those risky center bets and is the one to motion to when you feel the urge to place one.

When you play in the wee hours of the morning or anytime other than prime time, you may find a crew of only two handling the whole table; that's all they need to handle the lighter *action*.

Gamb-lingo

The amount of money wagered is defined as the **action** a game is getting at any given time. The **box** is the center section of the crap table layout where center bets are placed. The **point** is a rolled number (four, five, six, eight, nine, or ten) that causes pass line bets to win.

Being a Team Player (Whether It's Right or Wrong)

Craps is a team sport: a game of right vs. wrong, do's vs. don'ts. Large numbers of players either win together or lose together. It's a noisy, back-slapping, drink-spilling game! If you're lucky enough to find a "hot" table—one where points are being made—chips pile up quickly in front of the "right" bettors.

When you enter a craps game, you quickly become a member of either the "right" team or the "wrong" team, depending on how you place your bets. *Right bettors* tend to be optimists who stand behind their leaders and go with the flow. Consequently, they bet on the shooter to *win*. *Wrong bettors*, on the other hand, are generally contrarian and pessimistic by nature. (Maybe their experience has been that if you want something done right, you have to do it yourself!) They bet *against* the shooter, convinced that he or she will lose.

Gamb-lingo

A **right bettor** in craps bets on the shooter to win by making pass and come bets. A **wrong bettor** in craps bets on the shooter to lose by making don't pass and don't come bets. **Sequence bets** are decided on one or many rolls of the dice, as opposed to **one-roll** bets that are always decided on the very next roll of the dice.

You can make a whole series of *sequence bets* as either a right bettor or a wrong bettor, and we'll cover those first. If you just want to sit on the fence in a craps game and make your own fun by betting whatever numbers pop into your brain, we'll explain how to do that too, but you'll be missing out on a lot of commotion—and the opportunity to make the most favorable bets. You'll see why as you keep reading.

Getting In on the Action

If you can, inch your way up to the table, find an empty spot along the rail and rest your drink on the lower shelf. Have the dealer change your cash into chips. When you're ready to make a bet, reach down and set the chips you want to bet on a line, not in one of the betting spaces. That signals the dealer that you want to make a bet. The dealer will ask you what you want to bet. Some bets (such as place bets and buy bets) must be moved to the proper spot by the dealer, and even experienced players make those bets by setting their chips on a line instead of handing them directly to the dealer. Other bets, such as pass and don't pass, you can put in the proper place yourself and the dealer will show you where, but you might have to wait a few rolls before you can make the bet.

Starting Out on the Right Side

When the dice are passed to a new shooter, players start their wagering by making pass-line bets, also called line bets. *Line bets* are even money (1 to 1) bets that actually pay back 98.6 percent because they win 49.3 percent of the time. (This means that the house edge on a line bet is 1.4 percent.) *Right bettors* bet on the pass line, wagering that the shooter will win.

For a pass-line bet to *win*, a shooter has to:

♦ Roll either a seven or an eleven on the first roll, which is called the *come-out* roll, or

♦ Establish a *point* by rolling a four, five, six, eight, nine, or ten on the come-out roll, and then roll the point number again before rolling a seven.

Once a point is established, pass-line bets are in limbo and cannot be removed. Players are allowed to make pass-line bets at this point, but you'd be foolish to do so because you've missed the opportunity to be paid if a seven or an eleven is rolled. In fact, once the point is established, a pass-line bet loses when a seven is rolled.

Gamb-lingo

The **come-out roll** is a shooter's attempt to win a line bet by rolling seven or eleven. Line bets lose if the come-out roll is two, three, or twelve. After rolling seven, eleven, two, three, or twelve, the same shooter comes out again. Any other roll **establishes a point.** Once a point is established, **making** the point (re-rolling the point number) wins, seven loses, and any other roll does not affect the pass-line bets.

Risky Business

The casino allows you to make a bet on the pass line after a point has been established. If you're foolish enough to do it, your bet will win even money if the point is rolled and lose if a seven is rolled. If you want to bet that the point number will be rolled, you're better off making a place bet, which is explained later in this chapter.

If, after establishing a point, the shooter rolls any other number except the point number or seven, the line bet is kept in limbo and the shooter must keep rolling until the point number or a seven is rolled. Rolling the point number causes line bets to win, and rolling a seven causes line bets to lose.

If the point is made, all pass-line bettors are paid. At this point, the money on the pass line has no strings attached, and bettors can pick up their chips or place new bets by leaving their chips on the line. The same shooter comes out again with the next roll. For example, if the sequence of rolls is ten, eight, ten, six, then the first roll would establish the point as ten; the eight would have no effect on pass-line bets; the second ten would win for the pass line, and the same shooter would now be coming out for a new point; and the six would be the new point. Now pass-line bets need a six to win; a seven would lose, and any other roll would be no decision.

Gamb-lingo

A shooter **craps out** when he or she rolls "craps," which is a two, three, or twelve on the come-out roll. When a shooter rolls a seven after establishing a point, he or she has **sevened out**, and the dice are passed to the next shooter.

Risky Business

Whenever you win a come bet, your original wager and the payoff are placed on the come box part of the layout, so you must stay alert to retrieve your chips or they will remain in action for the next roll.

A pass-line bet *loses* when a shooter:

♦ Rolls a two, three, or twelve on the come-out roll, which is called *crapping out*. The shooter can crap out on the come-out roll and still continue to shoot. The casino usually requires a shooter to have a bet in action someplace on the table, so losing a line bet on a craps roll might mean the shooter must make another bet.

♦ Rolls a seven after the point is established, which is called *sevening out*. After a shooter sevens out, the dice pass to the next potential hero. (Eventually, everyone gets the opportunity to shoot.)

To show you how this works, let's say you've been hanging around the fringes of a fast game, and you finally want to get in on the action. Because you're relatively new at it, you're going to make things easy on yourself and wait for a come-out roll. Finally, your moment arrives, and you're in. You make a minimum bet on the pass line while the dice are in the middle of the table awaiting a come-out roll. The come-out roll is a lucky seven! You've made money already!

Now, quickly grab your spoils and leave your original bet on the pass line. The next roll is six, your new lucky number. Don't touch your pass-line bet unless you want the roof to fall in on you. Come on, six! No, it's a four. No problem—your money's still out there, even though you still can't touch it. The point is still six. Next roll, nine.

Still nothing. Yes! Lucky six rolled again! Now you can do one of three things: Take the money and run, grab your profit but keep the original bet out there while the shooter comes out for a new point, or keep reading to see what's on the rest of the table.

Taking Odds

After a point has been established, smart bettors back up their pass-line bet by *taking odds*. Taking odds is a way of making a wager that pays off at the true odds when the shooter makes the point. Taking single odds lowers the overall house edge on your total action from 1.4 percent to just 0.8 percent.

Some casinos offer double odds, which means they allow you to make an odds bet that's twice as large as your original pass-line bet. Taking double odds lowers the house edge to just 0.6 percent of your total action. Some casinos offer more than double odds—10 times odds is the highest we've seen. Most knowledgeable players take as much odds as they can get. You should, too.

Plan on betting odds, and reduce your initial bet accordingly. If, for example, you want about $10 in action on the front line (if you have $10 to bet) and you're playing in a casino that allows double odds, make your original line bet $3 or $4. With $3 on the line and $6 odds, you'll have a total of $9 in action, just a little under your $10 target. With $4 on the line and $8 odds, you'll have $12 in action, which is just a little over your target. Taking double odds gives you a payback of 99.4 percent, which is better than the 98.6 percent you'd have with a $10 line bet and no odds.

Bet You Didn't Know ...

To figure the true odds of making the point before rolling a seven, compare the number of ways of rolling a seven (six ways) to the number of ways of making the point. For example, there are three ways to roll a four, so the odds of doing so before rolling a seven are six to three, or 2 to 1. You're paid 2 to 1 when you win an odds bet on four. You are also paid 2 to 1 when you win an odds bet on ten. When the point is either five or nine, the odds are six to four, or 3 to 2. If the point is either six or eight, the odds are 6 to 5.

After a point has been established and you want to take odds, you simply place your odds wager outside the pass line. The dealer knows by the position of your chips that you're taking odds and checks to be sure you're not taking more odds than the casino allows.

If at any time you want to increase or reduce your odds bet, just do it (unless the dice are rolling, of course).

Bet You Didn't Know ...

A $4 double-odds bet on six should pay off 6 to 5, which amounts to $4.80. But because most crap tables don't have dimes, you'd likely receive only $4.00 or $4.50. But don't despair. Most casinos that allow double odds allow you to take 2.5 times odds if the point is six or eight. For example, they allow you to take $5 odds on a $2 bet, which if the point is made pays off a nice round $6. If you have trouble figuring out how much to wager on an odds bet, ask the dealer. Dealers know this stuff inside out!

Pressing Your Luck

Each time your bet wins, the dealer stacks your winnings next to your original wager. At that point, you can decide to take your winnings and run, reduce the amount of your chips but keep a bet on the table, or stack the new chips on your original pile and let the whole stack ride! When you let your winnings or a portion of them ride like this, it's called *pressing* your bet. Many lucky gamblers have amassed tons of money by pressing their bets (and their luck) on one shooter's hot roll! By the same token, many others have lost small fortunes doing the same.

Gamb-lingo

A bettor who lets winnings ride by wagering them along with the original bet is **pressing** the bet—and his luck!

Come All Ye Faithful

A *come bet* is another even-money bet that right bettors often make. Think of a come bet as being like a pass-line bet, except you make it when the shooter already has a point. The major difference between a come bet and a pass-line bet is that you can make a come bet on every roll of the dice *only after a shooter has established a point*. If you're not sure whether a point has been established yet, look for the *puck* placed on top of the point number on the table layout. If you don't see the puck with its white side up, or if you see it off to the side with its black side up, the point hasn't been established yet. To make a come bet, put your chips in the come section of the table layout.

Gamb-lingo

A **puck** is a marker (white on one side and black on the other) used to indicate the point that has been established.

Once the shooter has established a point, a bet in the large come box:

◆ *Wins* when a shooter rolls a seven or eleven on the first roll after the come bet is made.

◆ *Loses* when a shooter rolls a two, three, or twelve on the first roll after the come bet is made.

◆ Remains in limbo if the shooter rolls any other number (four, five, six, eight, nine, or ten). When any of these numbers are rolled, all come bets are moved from the large come box to the smaller box with the appropriate number on it. Come bets that have been moved to a number are in limbo, just as line bets are after a point has been established. After your come bet has been moved to a number, it's still your money, but you can't have it unless you win the bet.

Once a come bet has been moved to a number:

◆ The bet *wins* when a shooter rolls that number again before rolling a seven.

◆ The bet *loses* when a shooter rolls a seven.

◆ The bet stays frozen in limbo when the shooter rolls any other number, waiting for the appropriate number or a seven to be rolled.

After the dealer moves your come bet from the come box to the smaller box appropriate to the number just rolled, you can make another come bet if you wish.

If the shooter rolls a number that has a come bet riding on it (a come bet that has already been moved to that number's part of the table layout), that bet wins. The dealer pays winning come bets by moving them back to the come box and matching them with an equal stack of chips. Once the dealer pays a winning come bet, those chips can be removed from the layout. If they belong to you, you'd better grab them before some other player claims them.

A bettor who wants a lot of action can keep making come bets on each roll and, if no seven appears, wind up covering every number (meaning four, five, six, eight, nine, and ten).

Taking Odds on Come Bets

Odds on come bets pay according to the number needed to win, just like odds on pass-line bets. The only difference is that you move the chips for odds bets on your pass-line bet, but the dealer moves the chips for odds bets on come bets.

To take odds on a come bet, set your chips on a line on the table and tell the dealer what you want to do with it. Any line will do; putting your money on a line tells the dealer that you need assistance making your bet. If you put your intended odds bet in the come box, for example, the dealer and everyone else will think you meant to make a come bet; if the dice roll before you make your wishes known, your money might be in action as a come bet instead of as an odds bet.

After you place your chips on a line, the dealer picks them up and puts them in the appropriate spot. The dealer never takes money or chips directly from your hand or puts chips directly in your hand—a casino rule that prevents theft.

By making come bets and taking as much odds as possible, you can make a lot of money when the shooter's on a roll. (Of course, you lose all your come bets and the odds on them when the fateful seven is rolled, but that's what makes it gambling!)

Turning the Odds On and Off

When you want to remove the odds on come bets, tell the dealer to take your odds *down*, which means to remove the odds bets from the layout. If you want to only temporarily not have action on the odds on a come bet, tell the dealer, "Odds off." The dealer will mark the odds bet with an off marker. When you're ready to reinstate the odds, ask the dealer to put the odds back on by saying, "Odds working." Come-bet odds are always temporarily off during a come-out roll and are automatically put back in action once a point is established—unless you instruct the dealer to do otherwise.

Gamb-lingo

Taking a bet **down** means removing it from the table. Not all bets can be taken down. Specifically, after a point is established, a line bet cannot be taken down, and a come bet that has been moved to a number cannot be taken down. Any other bet can be taken down.

If a bet is *off*, it's still on the table layout and looks like a working bet, but both the player and the dealer know it's off and won't be at risk (won or lost) until the player declares it working again. Only odds and *place* bets (which we'll cover later) can be temporarily off. When a bet is *working*, it's at risk on the next roll of the dice. If you've taken off an odds or place bet, you can turn it back on by telling the dealer that it is working again.

Easy Come, Easy Go?

To show you how things can really heat up with just the four bets we've covered so far, let's say you're the same guy we met earlier, but you've been taking the odds on the pass line and now you're loaded. It's time to start spreading that money around!

You start by making another pass-line bet. The dice roll eight, so the point is eight. You take odds and decide to make a come bet, too.

The dice roll six. Your come bet is moved to the number six along with come bets made by a couple of other people. But don't worry—the dealer knows which bet is yours. While the dealer is moving your money, you decide to take odds on the come bet and make another come bet as well. You now have five bets on the table: a line bet, odds on the line bet, a come bet on the number six, odds on that bet, and a new come bet.

The next roll is ten. The dealer moves your new come bet to the number ten. You toss out chips for odds on that bet and you now have six bets riding: line and odds, six and odds, and ten and odds. Maybe you better hold off making another come bet for a while.

The next roll is eight. Your pass-line bet wins and your pass-line odds bet wins 6 to 5. Pick up that money and make another pass-line bet!

Now it's time for a new come-out roll. Your come bets on six and ten are working, but it's your choice whether you want your odds working on the come-out roll. Most people don't want them working, figuring they need a seven to win their pass-line bet. You think that logic's ridiculous, so you tell the dealer odds are working on the come-out roll.

The shooter rolls a four. This is your point. Put your odds bet down on the table. Now you have six bets working again: line bet and odds, come bet on six and odds, and come bet on ten and odds.

Next roll is eight. Nothing. Ah, go ahead and make another come bet. That's seven bets riding.

The next roll is three. Your come bet loses. Now you're back to six bets again.

The next roll is lucky ten! Your second come bet wins and your odds bet on it wins 2 to 1! Maybe you should pocket those chips for a while and have four bets riding.

Next roll is two. That's okay; you've got plenty of time. But maybe you ought to make another come bet while you wait for the six or four to roll?

Next roll: seven. Oh, no! That come bet you just made won, but the other four bets have just become the property of the casino.

Nobody's Right If Everybody's Wrong

You've seen how easy it is to be a team player and bet with the crowd. But what if you're tired of diversity, think teams are the last communist plot, and would rather not be part of one for business or pleasure? Well, there's still hope for you at the craps tables! Being a *wrong bettor* means you probably won't get a slap on the back when the shooter rolls a three on the come-out roll—but you will get chips! If that's fine with you, bet wrong!

Actually, betting "wrong" isn't a bad way to bet, especially if nobody's hot. You just won't enjoy much camaraderie if you bet against every shooter. (Some people take things so personally!)

Instead of betting the pass line, you start out by betting the don't pass. Then, after a point is established, you give odds instead of taking them, and you bet the don't come instead of the come. We'll review each of the wrong-way bets, one by one.

Gamb-lingo

In craps, when you make a **don't pass** or **don't come** bet, you can back it up by **giving odds** after the point has been established, which reduces the house edge on (and increases the overall payback percentage of) your action.

The Flip Side of Pass: Don't Pass

When a new game starts and everyone else is betting the pass line, wrong bettors bet the don't pass. Don't pass is an even-money bet that the shooter will do the following:

◆ Crap out on the come-out roll by rolling a two or a three. (Although rolling a twelve loses for pass-line bettors, it's only a tie for don't pass bettors.)

◆ Roll a seven before repeating the point number once a point has been established.

Gamb-lingo

When the house **bars the twelve** in a craps game, that means a twelve is a tie bet for don't pass on the come-out roll, and on the first roll for a don't come bet. In some casinos it is "Bar the two," in which case the two is a tie. If the casino *really* wants to stack the odds against you, it'll bar the three.

Don't pass bets lose when the shooter:

◆ Rolls a seven or eleven on the come-out roll.

◆ Repeats the point number before rolling a seven after the point has been established.

The reason don't pass bettors tie instead of win when a shooter rolls a twelve on the come-out roll is that winning this bet gives don't pass bettors a slight advantage over the house, and the house likes to have an edge! In some casinos, the roll of a two is *barred* instead of the twelve, which means that instead of a twelve being a tie to don't pass bettors, the roll of a two is a tie. You'll find the rule that applies written in the area of the table marked "Don't Pass Bar" and "Don't Come Bar."

Unlike pass bets, don't pass bets can be taken *down* after a point has been established. Removing your don't pass bet from the table is allowed after the shooter has a point because the shooter is more likely to roll a seven than any other number. But, removing a don't pass bet at that time is a foolish thing to do.

Giving Odds

In the same way that a pass-line bettor can reduce the house edge to 0.8 percent or 0.6 percent by taking odds after a point has been established on the come-out roll, the don't pass bettor can *give*, or *lay odds*. Giving odds is the opposite of taking odds, and it reduces the overall house edge on a single-odds bet by 0.5 percent, and a double-odds bet by 0.7 percent. When a player gives odds on a don't pass bet, he or she is betting that a seven will be rolled *before* the point number (just to review, taking odds on a pass bet is a bet that the shooter will roll the point number before rolling a seven).

After a point is established, a don't pass bettor is more likely to win because there are more ways to roll a seven than any other number. Because the odds are in your favor, the payout is less than 1 to 1. For example, if the point is six, the don't pass bettor who lays odds has to bet $6 to win $5 (5 to 6 odds). The maximum bet for laying odds is determined by the payoff. For example, if the point is ten and you have $10 riding on the don't pass and you are allowed double odds, you can lay $40 of odds to win $20 if a seven is rolled before a ten. As always, if you're unsure about the maximum odds you can lay for your bet and the point, ask the dealer. Don't hesitate to ask for information you should have—not asking puts you at a disadvantage!

The odds of rolling a seven before the point number is repeated are shown in the following table:

Point Number	Correct Odds and House Payoff When Giving Odds
4 or 10	1 to 2
5 or 9	2 to 3
6 or 8	5 to 6

To give odds, put your money next to your original don't pass bet, offsetting the bottom chip slightly to identify the stack as an odds bet. The dealer will show you how. You can change or remove your odds bet after any roll.

The Flip Side of Come: Don't Come

Don't come is another even-money bet that wrong bettors often make. Think of a don't come bet as being like a don't pass bet, except you make it when the shooter already has a point. To make a don't come bet, put your chips in the Don't Come section of the table layout. The major difference between a don't come bet and a don't pass bet is that a don't come bet can be made on every roll of the dice *only after a shooter has established a point*. Therefore, a wrong bettor can cover the table in don't come bets in the same way a come bettor can cover the table in come bets.

Risky Business

Whenever you win a don't come bet, your original wager and the payoff are placed on the don't come part of the layout, so you must stay alert to retrieve your chips or they will remain in action for the next roll.

Don't come bettors are paid *even money* when the shooter:

 ◆ Rolls two or three on the first roll after the bet is made. A twelve is a tie for don't come bettors. (In some casinos, a two is a tie instead of a twelve.)

 ◆ Rolls a four, five, six, eight, nine, or ten, and then rolls a seven before repeating that number.

Don't come bets *lose* when the shooter:

 ◆ Rolls a seven or eleven on the first roll after the don't come bet is made.

 ◆ Rolls a four, five, six, eight, nine, or ten, and then rolls that number again before rolling a seven.

To make a don't come bet, put your chips in the don't come section of the table layout. If the dice roll four, five, six, eight, nine, or ten, the dealer will move the chips behind the appropriate number on the layout. Then you can make another don't come bet, if you want.

Giving Odds on Don't Come Bets

After the don't come bet is behind a number, the best bet for the wrong bettor is to give odds on that bet. Giving odds on a don't come bet gives wrong bettors the same advantage as giving odds on a don't pass bet. To give odds on a don't come bet, set your chips on a line on the table and tell the dealer what you want to do. The dealer will pick up your chips and put them in the appropriate spot.

Other Sequence Bets

We mentioned earlier that there are other sequence bets you can make as either a right bettor or a wrong bettor, besides pass and come or don't pass and don't come bets. As you'll remember, sequence bets are a general category of bets that aren't always decided by the very next roll of the dice.

Place Bets

A *place bet* is a bet that a particular number will be rolled before the shooter rolls a seven. You can place the four, five, six, eight, nine, or ten. You make a place bet by putting your chips down on the table and telling the dealer "place" and the number. Some numbers are harder to roll than others, as you learned before, so the payoffs on place bets differ from number to number. Casinos make a profit on place bets by paying off winning bets at slightly less than true odds. Here's how the place bets stack up:

Best Bet _____

If you're a right bettor and want to make place bets, the numbers 6 and 8 offer the best payback (98.5 percent). But don't make the mistake of confusing either place bet with a bet on big 6 or big 8, which give very poor paybacks.

Number	True Odds	Place Bet Payoff	Payback
4 or 10	2:1	9:5	93.3%
5 or 9	3:2	7:5	96.0%
6 or 8	6:5	7:6	98.5%

Like the odds bets, place bets are automatically *off* on the come-out roll, unless you tell the dealer specifically that you want them to remain *on*, or *working*. Place bets are never in limbo; you can bail out, increase, or reduce a place bet at any time.

Buy Bets

An alternative to making a place bet is a buy bet. Like the place bet, a *buy bet* is a wager that the number you bet on (four, five, six, eight, nine, or ten) will be rolled before the seven. But instead of taking its profit out of the payoff, the house pays buy bets at the true odds, and takes a 5 percent commission, or *vigorish*, out of all buy bets you make. That means that if you want to buy a particular number for $100, the price is $105. If that number rolls, you're paid off at true odds on the $100. If the buy bet wins and you want to repeat it, you must pay a new commission. If you take down a buy bet, your commission is returned to you.

Lay Bets

Lay bets are to buy bets as don't pass is to pass. Laying a number, also called *buying behind* a number, is attractive to a wrong bettor who is rooting for a seven. You can buy behind the four, five, six, eight, nine, or ten, receiving true odds on your bet and giving the casino a 5 percent commission. As you remember from laying odds, the seven *is* more likely to be rolled than any other number, so you have to bet more money than you will receive if you win. The 5 percent vig on a lay bet is paid when you make the bet and is figured on the amount you can win, not on the size of your bet.

Gamb-lingo

In craps, **vigorish** (a.k.a. **vig**) is the fee (or commission) taken by the house when a player buys a number. In any casino game, the vig is a fee charged by the house for a bet that pays the true odds (without the vig, the house would not expect to make a profit).

Here's an example: If you give the dealer $205 with the instructions "$200 on four," the dealer will put $5 in the rack and $200 behind the four. You will win $100 if a seven rolls before a four—actually, your net win would be $95 (the $100 you won minus the $5 commission you paid).

If you look at the commission as a percent of the wager instead of a percentage of the payoff, the cost of laying a number ranges from 2.5 percent (behind four or ten) to 4.2 percent (behind six or eight).

Best Bet

Buying the four and ten is cheaper than placing them, but placing the other numbers is cheaper than buying them.

Big 6 and 8 Bets

The big 6 and big 8 bets are similar to, but less attractive than, placing the six and eight. Big 6 and big 8 bets pay even money. Why bet $6 on the big 6 to try to win $6, when you can place the six with that same $6 and try to win $7? The big numbers have a big 9 percent house edge! Place bets are a better bargain, so don't bother making these big bets.

The Hard Way Bets

Any of the center, or proposition, bets we warned you about earlier are the worst bets on the table.

A *hard way* is one kind of center bet. To win a hard-way bet, your number not only has to be rolled before a seven, it has to be rolled with two dice of equal value; if your number is rolled "the easy way" (with two dice of different values), you lose. For example, if you're betting on hard four, it has to be rolled as 2 and 2 for the bet to win; if it comes in as 3 and 1 or 1 and 3, you lose, and if a seven rolls, the hard-way bet loses.

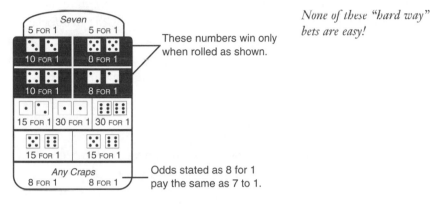

These numbers win only when rolled as shown.

None of these "hard way" bets are easy!

Odds stated as 8 for 1 pay the same as 7 to 1.

You can make a hard-way bet at any time by throwing your bet on the table and telling the dealer what you want to bet. But be warned that the house edge on all the hard-way bets ranges from 9 percent to 11 percent. They don't call 'em "hard way" for nothing!

Out of Sequence: One-Roll Bets

A *one-roller* is a bet decided by the very next roll of the dice. There are two kinds of one-roll bets—bad and worse. Actually, that's not a lie, but they're really called: center, or proposition, bets (*except* the hard ways), and field bets.

A Proposition You *Should* Pass Up!

Although all the proposition bets (including the hard way bets) have high payoffs, the house edge on any of them is just too great to make them worthwhile wagers. The only logical reason for making one is to be able to throw a chip. Proposition bets are always *thrown*, or tossed, onto the table.

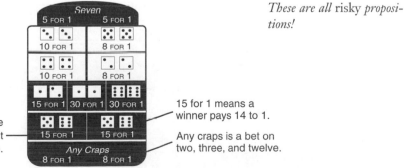

These are all risky *propositions!*

C and E bets go along the center edge when you want to bet craps and eleven.

15 for 1 means a winner pays 14 to 1.

Any craps is a bet on two, three, and twelve.

Playing the Field

At first glance, it looks like a wager in the large field box is a relatively smart bet because it covers the possibility of rolling seven out of eleven numbers (two, three, four, nine, ten, eleven, and twelve). But the four numbers that the bet doesn't cover (five, six, seven, and eight) happen to be the ones you're most likely to roll! If rolling a two or a twelve pays you double in the field, the house edge is 5.5 percent. If one of those numbers pays double and the other pays triple, the house edge on a field bet is 2.8 percent.

A Strategy for Learning

As we've said many times throughout this book, gambling is risky business, and if you play most casino games long enough, you will lose. Craps is no exception. But money can be won (and lost) very quickly in a fast craps game, so it's important for novices to start out slowly, get a feel for the game, enjoy the excitement, and learn! Each time you play, you gain more and more confidence and rely less and less on charts and table layout descriptions. For now, stick with the basics:

- Decide how much you're willing to risk on a session of craps. Then find a craps table that offers table limits to fit your bankroll.

- If you are in a friendly mood, be a right bettor. That means you should bet the pass and come, and place the six and eight.

- If you are feeling grouchy, be a wrong bettor. Bet the don't pass and the don't come.

- Always take or lay as much odds as allowed.

- Avoid all proposition, big 6 and big 8, and one-roll bets!

- If you lose your limit for the session, chalk it up to entertainment. Stand around, watch and learn for a while, or just leave and come back later. There will be many other opportunities for practice over the course of a long playing life. Craps takes time and patience to play with confidence.

The Least You Need to Know

- The same shooter rolls the dice until he or she sevens out.

- The best bets for right bettors are pass and come bets, with full odds on both.

- The best bets for wrong bettors are don't pass and don't come, with full odds on both.

- Center bets are good only for the house!

Chapter 13

Out of the Starting Gate

In This Chapter

- The different kinds of races in a daily program
- Reading the Official Program and *Daily Racing Form*
- Kinds of bets you can make
- How the track makes money on horse racing
- How *you* can make money on horse racing

A day at the track is as enjoyable as any afternoon at the beach. Sunshine, fresh air, relaxation, an occasional splash of stimulation, and a field of scantily clad thoroughbreds on which to gaze. Who could ask for more?

Stanford has three ways that an occasional race book customer can profit. We'll show you two out of three—which isn't bad for a day at the track! (The third way is to enter *handicapping tournaments*, which is too complex for this book. You can read about tournaments in Stanford's book *Betting Cheap Claimers.*)

Horse Racing: Then and Now

We know from the carvings on ancient artifacts that horse racing dates back thousands of years to a time when warriors raced their horse-drawn

A **jockey** is the rider of a thoroughbred horse in a race. A horse's **gait** refers to the style in which a horse has been bred and trained to move its legs while running. Standardbreds are required to move two legs in unison in either a trot or a pace while racing, whereas thoroughbreds are born and bred to gallop.

chariots in battle, much like today's *harness races*. Around 600 B.C., the saddle and stirrup were invented, allowing riders to mount their horses' backs, and *thoroughbred racing* was born.

Harness-race horses, called *standardbreds*, pull a driver and *sulky* (small, two-wheeled cart) around a track. Although they are descendants of the same three horses that have sired all of today's thoroughbreds, standardbreds are bred for their characteristics of *gait* and overall strength, whereas thoroughbreds are bred for speed and endurance. Because of these and other essential differences, we'll focus our attention on thoroughbreds and thoroughbred racing, which is the most popular form of horse racing today.

Off to the Races

Most thoroughbred racetracks offer nine races per day. All races have conditions that a horse must meet to be eligible for the race. For example, a race might be for 2-year-old females (*fillies*) that have won no more than one race. For that race, males (*colts* and *geldings*) need not apply, older horses (*mares* and *horses*) are out, and winners of more than one race are disqualified, too.

Gamb-lingo

A **filly** is a female 4 years old or younger. A **colt** is an uncastrated male horse aged 4 or less. A **gelding** was a colt before he was castrated, often to calm it for racing. A **mare** is a female 5 years old or older. In racing, the term *horse* refers to uncastrated males 5 years old or more.

The majority of each day's races are *claiming races*, which have the cheapest *purses*. A purse is the total prize money distributed to the owners of the winners of a race. As such, claiming races do not attract the best horses. A horse entered in a claiming race is called a *claimer*, which means the horse is for sale at the race for a set price. The claiming price puts a ceiling on the value of the horses in the race, which helps to ensure that the race is an even match.

Weight allowances are often given to certain categories of horses to make them more competitive. For example, a horse that hasn't won for a certain period of time might be allowed to carry less weight. A horse ridden by an apprentice *jockey* carries less weight, and a filly running against colts and geldings carries less weight than the males. (Fillies are allowed to run in races designated for colts and geldings, but males are not allowed to run in races designated for fillies.) The *weight* a horse carries includes the jockey and additional weights in the *saddlecloth* if the jockey is not heavy enough.

Maiden races are for horses (of either gender) that haven't won a race yet. Once a horse wins, it can no longer race in maiden races.

Stakes races attract the best horses by offering the largest purses and requiring owners to pay entrance and starting fees. Horses that run in stakes races are at the top of the thoroughbred hierarchy by virtue of their lineage and proven ability as consistent winners.

Gamb-lingo

The **purse** is the total prize money distributed to the top winners of a horse race. A **saddlecloth** is a piece of fabric between the horse and saddle in which weights can be placed.

The Kentucky Derby, Preakness, and Belmont Stakes are three of the most well-known stakes races. A horse that wins all three is hailed as a Triple Crown winner, which is the greatest honor in the horse racing world, and ensures that the horse will be remembered by horse racing historians forever.

Other common categories of races are *handicap* and *allowance*. In a *handicap* race, which also attracts a top field of horses, weights are allotted to each horse according to the rating that the racetrack handicapper assigns. Basically, weights are added to equalize the field. The handicapper's objective is for the race to end in a nine-way tie. Therefore, the strongest horse is given the greatest weight burden to carry, and the weakest horse carries considerably less.

In an *allowance* race, a horse must meet certain *conditions* to be allowed into the race, and weights are based on the number of races a horse has run or the amount of money won. A common allowance race condition is nonwinners of one, which means the horse can have at most one win on its record. If you buy a young, unraced thoroughbred, you race it in maiden races until it wins; then race it in nonwinners of one, nonwinners of two, and so on until your horse either proves exceptional and graduates to handicap and stakes races or proves average and is relegated to the ranks of claiming races.

The Inside Track

Once you're through the racetrack gates, hawkers try to sell you what appear to be racetrack memorabilia. What they're usually selling is the Official Program, which is the listing of the horses running in each race. They also sell the *Daily Racing Form*, a newspaper that contains valuable information about each horse and the racing conditions at the major tracks in your particular region of the country. (Different editions of the *Daily Racing Form* are printed for each part of the country.) The Official Program is worth the

Best Bet

Save yourself some money and avoid the racetrack tip sheets. Tip sheets are usually nothing more than one person's opinion about each race—and they're often wrong.

expense if you're there to do anything but catch a few rays. Both are essential if you want to handicap (or pick the likely winner) in each race.

Getting with the Program

Each racetrack offers its own Official Program, a guide to the day's events. Each race gets its own page in the guide. Even if all you want to do is bet on the jockey's colors or a horse's name, it's easier to do with a program in front of you. Otherwise, you'll be straining all day long to hear the announcer introduce each horse and jockey 15 minutes before *post time*.

As you can see in the sample program shown on the next page, the third race at Bay Meadows is the Jack Robinson Memorial race. This is a 6-*furlong* race, which in plain English means ¾ of a mile. (A furlong is ⅛ of a mile.)

Gamb-lingo

The time that a race starts is its **post time**. Horses line up at the starting gate a minute or two before post time.

A **furlong** is 220 yards; 8 furlongs equal 1 mile.

Gamb-lingo

When a horse has been **scratched**, it has been withdrawn from the race. Horses start a race abreast, and where a horse starts is its **post position**. Post positions are numbered consecutively, with number 1 being closest to the rail. An **entry** is two or more horses linked together for betting purposes. Typically, this means both horses have the same owner.

The program also shows that this is a claiming race for 4-year-olds and up, with a claiming price of $6,250. The fine print tells you the age and weight restrictions that apply to this race. Older horses are often required to carry additional weight because they are considered stronger, and in this race 5-year-olds and up carry an additional pound. Horses that haven't won at least two races since November 15 are given a 3-pound weight advantage, and those that haven't won any are allowed 5 pounds. The holder of the 6-furlong record on this track is Black Jack Road, a 6-year-old carrying 116 pounds.

Horses are listed by program number, which usually corresponds to their *post position*. Unless there is an *entry*, the number one horse is closest to the rail, and the other horses line up side by side in numeric order toward the outside of the rail. When you're at the track or a *satellite wagering race book* (an off-track establishment where you can bet on horse races), the program number is the number you'll use when you place your bet. In addition to the name and program number, you can find the vital statistics, including the horse's color, gender, year of birth, lineage, owners, trainer, jockey, and colors that the jockey is wearing.

A typical race program.

BAY MEADOWS

EXACTA / QUINELLA / PARLAY
PICK 3 (BM RACES 3-4-5) BM PICK 6 LEG B
APPROXIMATE POST 1:41

START →

	WIN	PLACE	SHOW

(6 Furlongs)

← FINISH

CLAIMING
PURSE $7,000

This oval shows the distance around the track and where to find the start and finish lines.

3

JACK ROBINSON MEMORIAL

FOR FOUR-YEAR-OLDS AND UPWARD. Four-year-olds 121 lbs., Older, 122 lbs.; Non-winners of two races since November 15 allowed 3 lbs.; a race since then, 5 lbs.; CLAIMING PRICE $6,250 (Maiden races, claiming, starter and classified handicap races for $5,000 or less not considered.)

Race conditions are listed here.

Track Record: 1:07.1, BLACK JACK ROAD (6) 116 lbs.; October 28, 1990

MAKE SELECTION BY PROGRAM NUMBER   PROBABLE ODDS

These are the "morning line" odds.

This is the track record for this distance.

OWNER	TRAINER	JOCKEY

TIM BELLASIS   OWNER   **15**

Cerise

1 BERIGHT BOY 🐎   L ***112**   CARLOS MADEIRA $6,250

Red. B. g.'90, Kundalini (Chi)-Jay J. May

The asterisk means there's a weight allowance. See the footnote below the last horse listed.

JIM R. ROBINSON   R. L. MARTIN
Asst. Tr. Bobby Martin   **6**

Red, White Stars on Blue Cross Sashes

2 GO GO LOUIE 🐎   L **117**   Chad Schvaneveldt $6,250

White. Ch. g.'91, No Points-Call Marie

Here's how much weight Go Go Louie will carry.

JOSE SILVA   OWNER
Asst. Tr. Jose L. Castro   **5/2**

White, White "E/S" In Green Clover on Back

3 BERING GIFTS   L **117**   VICTOR ESPINOZA $6,250

Blue. Ch. g.'88, Bering (GB)-Southern Fable

DENNIS CALHOUN, RON DONN   LEONARD SHOEMAKER
& MARIE YOUNG   Asst. Tr. Sergio Ledesma   **2**

White, Royal Blue Hoops and Bars

4 GRANBY   L **117**   RUSSELL BAZE $6,250

Yellow. Ch. g.'91, Groovy-For Safekeeping

MARK GLATT & DAVID REISING   RON GLATT
Asst. Tr. Mark Glatt   **7/2**

Red, Silver Clover on Back, Silver Sleeves

5 J. R. CIGAR   L **117**   CHRIS HUMMEL $6,250

Green. Ch. g.'90, Marshua's Dancer-Seine

VANGIE JACOBS   DONNA ELORDI   **9/2**

Dark Blue, Light Blue Diamonds

6 STREET VENDOR   L **117**   BRYAN CAMPBELL $6,250

Black B. g.'91, Lord Of The Apes-Crooked Halo

🐎 Registered California Bred - * 5 Lbs. Apprentice Allowance - L Treated with Lasix

These footnotes give you extra information.

The footnotes also show that every horse in this race is being treated with Lasix, which means they are all *bleeders*—horses who have a tendency to rupture blood vessels during strenuous workouts and races. Lasix is a medication that helps to control this common condition. A horse on Lasix for the first time often displays improved speed and endurance. You can find other relevant information about a particular

Gamb-lingo

It's difficult to compare horses by comparing their records because different races are run under different conditions. The **speed rating** helps; it relates a horse's speed to a standard. Historically, a speed rating of 100 meant the horse tied the track record.

Gamb-lingo

The **tote board** is a display of the totals bet on the various horses to win, place, and show, and the odds a bettor is likely to receive on win bets. It is generally updated at one-minute intervals before the start of the race.

horse's current condition by checking these notes and tracing the appropriate symbol back to the horse it relates to.

The carrying weight is listed in big bold numbers below the name of the owner. In this race, all but one of the horses are carrying 117 pounds because they're all 5 years old or older (122 lbs.) and haven't won a race since November 15 (-5 lbs.). If you look at the footnotes, you'll see that Beright Boy carries only 112 pounds because of an additional 5-pound weight allowance routinely given to apprentice jockeys.

The last item of major importance is the *morning line*, which shows the official track handicapper's predictions of the betting odds of each horse. The morning line odds in this race suggest that Beright Boy is a long shot at 15 to 1, and Granby is the favorite at 2 to 1. (When the odds are stated as a whole number, such as 15, you can assume the odds are "to 1," as in 15 to 1. When the odds are stated as a fraction, as in "5/2," they mean 5 to 2.)

Handicappers watch the *tote board* to see how the odds are changing on each horse right up until post time. The tote board reflects the actual bets being made.

*Form*ulating Your Own Opinions

We said earlier that if you wanted to properly handicap a race you should buy the *Daily Racing Form*. Although other racing papers are available, the *Daily Racing Form* gives you the best overall coverage of each horse's past performance, and each issue has a simple guide that shows you how to read the past performance charts. We aren't going to show you how to actually handicap a race, but we do suggest that if you want to become more than just a casual racetrack bettor, you should read some of the in-depth books that cover thoroughbred racing and handicapping exclusively.

The following figure shows a small sample of the information you'll find in the *Daily Racing Form*'s past performance charts.

This is the most recent
speed at which Granby ran.

Find the last race
Granby won.

BM PAGE 6	Sunday, January 7, 1996 DAILY RACING FORM

Granby won at this
speed rating.

Read across to see that it was a
6f race on Oct. 12, 1995. The
claiming price was $8,000.

Granby's past performance chart from the Daily Racing Form *says he should be able to win this one!*

How to Place a Bet

For those of you who want to jump right into the action without analyzing the odds, we'll show you how to lay your money down first. It may seem like an easy thing to do, but you'd be surprised how many people throw away winning tickets because they don't know what kind of bets they've made or when one of theirs has just won.

You can bet on a horse to win, place, or show. As the following table indicates, if you bet a horse to *win*, it must come in first. If you bet a horse to *place*, you'll win your bet if the horse comes in first *or* second. To win your bet whether the horse comes in first, second, *or* third, you must bet on the horse to *show*.

Basic Thoroughbred Race Bets

This Bet	Wins When Your Horse Comes in	Loses When Your Horse Comes in
Win	1st	2nd or worse
Place	1st *or* 2nd	3rd or worse
Show	1st, 2nd, *or* 3rd	4th or worse

When you're ready to make your bet, walk up to the wagering window and state how much money you are betting, the horse you're betting on (usually by program number rather than name), and the type of bet: to win, place, or show. "I'd like $2 on number 3 to win the third race," should do it. Don't walk away from the window until you make sure the ticket you received correctly reflects the bet you wanted. If the race starts before you notice that the bet you made is different from the bet you wanted, you're stuck with a bet you didn't want. Protect your tickets as though they were money because you must have the ticket to collect if you win; drop your ticket on the floor, and someone else could collect when your horse wins.

Gamb-lingo

A **win** bet is a bet that the horse will come in first. A **place** bet is a bet that the horse will come in first or second. A **show** bet is a bet that the horse will come in first, second, or third.

Best Bet

Sometimes a horse may be disqualified after the race, potentially changing the win, place, or show horse (or all three). Never toss out what you think is a losing ticket until the official race results have been posted.

The minimum bet is usually $2. Winning tickets are paid off according to the odds when the race goes off, not the odds that were posted when you placed your bet.

At the track, bets can be made right up to post time, at which instant further bets are locked out by computer. At a casino race book, no more betting is allowed after the first horse enters the gate. The final odds cannot possibly be displayed before post time, but are displayed almost immediately after post time unless there is some sort of computer malfunction.

Sometimes you are paid a little more than what you expected because the posted odds are rounded down. For example, the final odds might really be 2.2 to 1, but the tote would show 2 to 1. But don't worry; when you cash your ticket, you will be paid the correct amount.

A $2 bet on a horse that is shown as 2 to 1 on the final post will pay $6.00 to $6.80 if that horse wins. Think of 2 to 1 as meaning 3 for 1. The payoff is two times your original bet (2 × $2) *plus* the original bet ($2). If the payoff was $7.00, the odds would show as 5/2. Generally ticket prices are rounded down to the nearest 20 cents per $2 bet; this is called *breakage*. Some tracks round down to the nearest 10 cents, which of course is a better deal for the bettor.

It's more difficult to figure out what your payoff is on a place or show ticket because win, place, and show are separate pools. For example, when you make a place bet, your money becomes part of the place pool and affects potential place payoffs, but does not affect the win pool or potential win payoffs. Payoffs to place tickets are based on the place pool and the amounts of place bets made on the first two horses in the race. A place payoff can be greater than the win payoff, but it generally is smaller. Show payoffs are based on the show pool and the amounts bet on the top three horses to show. A show payoff can be larger than a place or win payoff, but it's generally smaller than both.

The easiest way to determine your payoff on place and show tickets is to wait until the final payouts are posted on the tote board at the end of the race. The final payoffs are posted something like what's shown in this next table.

Risky Business

Unlike sports betting where you're paid off based on the odds you accept when you place your bet, the odds on horses change right up until post time. You are paid according to the final odds, no matter when you place your bet.

	Horse	Win	Place	Show
1st	5	$5.80	$3.80	$3.20
2nd	6		$9.40	$4.20
3rd	4			$2.80

Not Exacta-ly a Science

Besides win, place, and show, you can make *exotic* bets. An *exacta* (sometimes called a *perfecta*) is a bet on the first two horses in a race. To win an exacta, you have to pick the winning horses in the correct order of finish. Often bettors pick two, three, or four horses they like and *box* them by buying an exacta box ticket that covers every possible exacta combination of those horses. For example, suppose you box three horses (A, B, and C), as shown in this next figure.

Gamb-lingo

An **exacta**, or **perfecta**, is a bet in which you select the first two horses in the correct order of finish. A **quinella** is a bet in which you select the first two horses in a race, and you win the bet if they finish in either order.

	1st Place:		
2nd Place:	A	B	C
A		BA	CA
B	AB		CB
C	AC	BC	

You have six ways to win: if A wins with B or C second, if B wins with A or C second, and if C wins with A or B second. The preceding chart shows the six exacta combinations you need to cover three horses. When you buy an exacta ticket to box three horses, it costs you the same amount of money (and has the same potential payoffs) as buying the six individual tickets. There is no advantage to boxing other than the convenience of buying multiple tickets at one time. You can also box two horses with two exacta combinations (also called an exacta *reverse*) or four horses with 12 possible exacta combinations.

Another way to play an exacta is to pick your favorite horse and *wheel* it with the most likely second-place finishers. If, for example, you're convinced horse A will win, but are not sure whether C, D, or F will finish in second place, you can buy an exacta ticket for each possibility: AC, AD, AF. A wheel costs the same and has the same potential payoffs as buying multiple single tickets.

In a *quinella* you select two horses. To win, your horses must be the first two finishers in a race, but you don't have to specify the order in which they will finish. A quinella is not the same as an exacta reverse if both bets are available because quinella bets go into a separate pool from exacta bets.

A *trifecta* bet is similar to an exacta, except you pick the first three finishers of a race, in the correct order of finish.

Multi-Race Wagers

To win a *daily-double* bet, you have to pick the winners of two consecutive races, which are usually the first two races of the day. (The Official Program tells you at the top of a race page whether daily-double wagering is offered.)

When a *triple* is offered, you must pick the winner of three consecutive races. This bet is sometimes called a "pick three."

A pick-six wager (when it is available) requires you to pick the winners of six consecutive races. If nobody picks six winners, the payoffs on pick-six tickets are split among bettors who picked the most winners. If nobody picks all six winners, some of the wagering pot may be carried over to the next day.

How the Track Makes Its Money

Before we get into showing you how you can make money betting horses, you need to understand how the track makes money. Here's an example that Stanford used in *Betting Cheap Claimers*:

"Suppose we flip a coin, heads you win and tails I win. Suppose we use a fair coin and completely random flip so that each of us has a 50 percent chance of winning. Suppose we bet $5 per flip. First flip is tails, and I win $5 from you. Next is heads, you win $5 from me. Then our friend PM wanders along and announces that he wants to play, too. Only PM doesn't like to lose—he wants to win $2 per flip without betting anything. Being nice guys, we allow PM to join our game. Next flip is heads, and I lose $5, of which you get $3 and PM gets $2. Next flip is tails, and you lose $5 of which I get $3, and PM gets $2.

"If we play this game long enough, you and I are both going to be losers and PM will have most of our money. It is difficult to imagine one of us being lucky enough to be ahead if we play more than a few games."

PM in this example is *pari-mutuel*. Flipping coins to either win $3 or lose $5, with the other $2 going to PM, is what happens when you bet in a pari-mutuel system, which is the wagering system that tracks use to make their money. In a pari-mutuel system, or pool, racetracks *take* a certain percentage of every dollar wagered before paying winning bets. The percentage is set by the state and often is higher for exotics than for straight bets. The money is used for the track's operating expenses, purses, and government tax. A track's *take* is usually 15 to 20 percent of all money wagered.

Gamb-lingo

In **pari-mutuel** betting, the odds are set by the bettors. The track takes a fixed percentage of wagers off the top and distributes the remainder to winning ticket holders. The **purse** is the total prize money distributed to the owners of first through fifth place horses in the race. The **take** is the amount of money deducted from the pari-mutuel pool for expenses, purses, and taxes.

Getting an Edge at the Races

As you might have guessed, you have to wager carefully (even judiciously) to keep your head above water when swimming in the pari-mutuel pool.

Basically, like the stock market, there are two ways to make money betting on horses: by using information not available to other bettors or by having a superior ability to evaluate public information.

The latter of the two, which is the most likely way any of us will gain useful information about a race, is called *handicapping*. Handicapping involves assigning a probability to a horse's chance of winning. The official track handicappers who set the morning line odds do a very good job of this themselves. From there, the betting public takes over, and their bets set the odds on each horse.

Instead of looking for the horse that's most likely to win, you should look for horses that are considerably more likely to win than the other bettors think. A horse whose actual probability of winning is high compared to the probability implied by the posted odds established by the bettors is called an *overlay*. A horse that has a smaller chance of winning than the betting crowd thinks is called an *underlay*, and you can profit by betting against them, too.

Gamb-lingo

Handicapping is using available information to assign a probability to a horse's chance of winning. An **overlay** is an event that has less money bet on its happening than can be justified by the probability of it happening. An **underlay** is an event that has more money bet on its happening than can be justified by the probability of it happening.

To summarize, there are two ways in which a race book (or racetrack) customer can find bets that give an edge. Instead of trying to pick the "winner" of a race, you should look for horses that fall into one of the following categories:

- ◆ Large overlay
- ◆ Large and foolish underlay

In the remaining sections of this chapter, we'll show you how to look for horses that fit either category.

Being Overlay Biased

Generally, the odds established by the bettors at a track are good estimates of how likely the horses are to win the race. Because the track take is so large, you need to find *big* mistakes being made by other bettors for your bets to be profitable. Because most handicapping systems require large investments of time and keeping up with daily racing information, an occasional race fan needs a more practical approach.

Gamb-lingo

If a horse is more likely to win when running on one part of the running surface than another, the surface is said to have a **bias**. The **rail** is the inside edge of the race track. With a **slow rail**, horses running well away from the rail have an edge over horses running close to it. With a **fast rail**, horses running close to the rail have the edge.

The best chance for an occasional horse bettor to find a large overlay is to look for *bias* in the track itself, which gives one horse an advantage over all the other horses in the race. A bias exists when a horse is more likely to win if it runs on one part of the track than on the other. A bias affects all horses, and when a running surface has a bias, how fast a horse runs depends on which route it takes. The two most common types of bias are a *fast rail* and a *slow rail*.

The condition of the rail (fast or slow) often depends on weather conditions. If a track is wet, the bias may change as it dries out, and as races are run. The same is true of a dry track that gets rained on. If the weather stays the same and the moisture content of the track stays the same, the bias should remain the same from one race to the next in the same day. If you notice a strong bias in the first race or two, watch each race to be sure the bias continues. You might want to check the track today and come back tomorrow to do all your wagering, or bet just the last few races.

A Fast Rail

When the rail is fast, inside horses have an edge over outside horses. Any track can have a fast rail on any given day. Some tracks always have fast rails. When more of the horses with an inside post position (that is, numbers 1 or 2) win, there may be a fast rail. If there is, the horses taking the early lead are more likely to be inside horses, instead of the horses that the racing newspaper(s) indicate have early speed. During the race, horses next to the rail will seem to run more strongly than horses away from the rail. A horse that takes the lead early and runs close to the rail usually stays ahead during the whole race.

A good rule of thumb to follow when you notice that the rail is fast is to bet the inside horse, or don't bet. The only exception is when the inside horse has no early speed and doesn't appear to be one of the better horses in the race, as indicated by a glance in your *Daily Racing Form*. If that's the case, don't bet the race when the rail is fast.

If the two best horses are in the two inside posts, you might consider combining them in an exacta or quinella.

A Slow Rail

A slow rail is the opposite of a fast rail. When the rail is slow, outside horses seem to run faster. Two indications of a slow rail are outside horses sprinting to the front, and the field bunching up during a race. The field bunches up because the lead jockey takes his or her horse to the rail where the distance around the track is shorter. The lead horse tires more quickly (because the rail is slow) and other horses bunch up behind and alongside, trying to pass. If the outside of the track is faster than the inside, catching up is easy even if the inside horse doesn't slow down.

Unless it is running far from the rail, the leader at the top of the stretch generally won't win the race. When the rail is slow, favorites seldom win. The outside third of the horses often win half or more of the races, and many races are won by long shots.

A good rule of thumb when the rail is slow is to bet the outside horse if the odds are 2 to 1 or more. Otherwise, don't bet.

Too Good to Be True?

When you bet against an underlay (the horse that has more money bet on it than it probably deserves), you are looking for the horse that everyone thinks is too good to be true (TGTB). With minimal analysis, you can easily determine whether it really is TGTB. If it is, don't bet. If it isn't TGTB, then you want to place a bet on all the horse's opponents, especially those who are likely to win at much higher odds.

It's easier to find TGTB horses to bet against in claiming races. The cheaper the claimer, the better. Here's an example of the kind of horse that Stanford considers too good to be true. All the horses entered in a particular claiming race were for sale for $5,000. One of the horses had a good performance record and had even won against horses for sale for $25,000 and more. By her record, she did not appear to belong in the same race with $5,000 claimers. But, if she were still capable of beating $25,000 horses, would her owner be willing to sell her for $5,000 today? It's highly unlikely. Yet the bettors at the track responded as if she were a $25,000 horse and would run away with the race. She went off at 3 to 5 and finished third.

Best Bet _____

You will only find a TGTB in approximately one race out of 100. If it's not bet down below even money (4 to 5 or less), it can't be TGTB.

Gamb-lingo _____

When excessive money is bet on one horse, that horse is said to be **bet down**. Betting a horse down reduces the amount bets on it will win if the horse wins.

The moral of the story is this: The TGTB horse certainly had a good enough chance to win, but the bettors were evaluating her as a $25,000 horse rather than the $5,000 horse she had become. There's hardly ever any reason for a cheap claimer to be bet down to 3 to 5 or 4 to 5. When you find one that is, it's usually TGTB! You should spread your bets among the other horses in the race in such a way that if TGTB loses, whichever horse wins will bring you a sizable profit.

Treasure Hunting (Finding TGTBs)

You're most likely to find TGTBs in races in which the purse size is greater than or approximately equal to the claiming price. Our earlier example of the third race at Bay Meadows is a likely candidate because the purse is $7,000 and the claiming price is $6,250.

After you check the Official Program to identify a race involving cheap claimers, watch the tote board to see if a horse is being *bet down* below even money (1 to 1; in other words, odds of 4 to 5 or less). If you find a likely candidate, use the *Daily Racing Form* to make sure the bettors are wrong in thinking this horse is much better than the rest of the field. Look up the following information:

- Claiming price and purse in the last few races

- Order of finish

- Speed

- Age

The value of a horse depends on how fast people think it can run, which is influenced by how fast it *does* run. Running fast and winning a race can raise the value of a horse, and losing can cause its value to drop. When a cheap claimer wins a race and then comes back at the same claiming price and purse, it can be TGTB. (It should have moved up to a higher claiming price after winning the race.) If it recently won by a wide margin against the same quality of horses it faces today, it's likely to get bet down for today's race, which also makes it TGTB. If a favorite horse is old, it's unlikely to be claimed at any price because it might not have too many races left in its legs. When bettors bet older horses down below even money, it may just be that the horse is superior to all its opponents, but nobody wants to buy it anyway, in which case it's *not* TGTB.

One word of caution before betting against a TGTB: *Don't* bet too early! Not only is there a chance that the TGTB won't be bet down far enough, there is a very real risk that the horse will be *scratched*. Of course, a horse would not be scratched just because it was bet down, but if a horse is being offered for sale at a bargain price because of a physical infirmity, the track vet might notice a limp and kick the horse out of the race. If that happens, it will greatly reduce the value of all your bets on the opponents.

The Least You Need to Know

- You can bet on horse races by being at the track (which is probably the most fun) or from a satellite wagering facility or casino race book.

- An occasional thoroughbred race fan can make money betting on horse races by looking for races in which either a large overlay or underlay exists.

- To find a large overlay (a horse that's more likely to win than the betting public believes), look for biases in the track. A slow rail favors horses with post positions far from the rail. A fast rail favors horses with post positions close to the rail.

- To find a large underlay (a horse that's less likely to win than the betting public believes), look at cheap claiming races in which the purse size is greater than or almost equal to the claiming price. When you find the horse that's too good to be true (TGTB), wait until only moments before post time and then bet on its opponents.

How About a Bet, Sport?

In This Chapter

- ◆ How casinos and sports books make money on wagering
- ◆ Basic principles every sports bettor should know
- ◆ How to read the sports big board
- ◆ Placing the most popular sports bets, and which bets to avoid

There's more sports betting in America than any other form of gambling. A friendly long-distance bet that keeps you in touch with Dad, a cutthroat rivalry with the neighbor next door, coworkers participating in a weekend office pool, diehard fans flying off to Nevada to bet their weekly picks (and everyone else's). Let's face it, sports fans: A friendly bet makes the game that much more exciting!

But if you're willing to wager, you should be betting to *win*! In this chapter, we'll show you how sports wagering works in Nevada, which is one of only three states in which placing a sports bet is legal. You'll learn how to read the betting line and the big board and see how casinos and sports books make their money on your bets. If you intend to get serious about sports wagering, we'll explain why winning takes a little more work than just knowing how to bet your favorite teams! Hang in there, sports fans—we've got a lot to cover.

Tuggin' the Line

Nevada has over 100 licensed sports books, and they're all kept busy year-round setting the *line* for a variety of wagering activities that include professional and collegiate sports, car racing, political elections, and other controversial events and topics of national interest (would you believe there's even a line on the likelihood of Elvis being found alive?). A line out of Las Vegas is usually what your local bookmaker bases his or her odds on and what the *USA Today* Sports section quotes on a daily basis.

Gamb-lingo _____

A sports-wagering facility that functions as a business on its own or as part of a casino is called a **sports book**. An athletic contest often pits two teams of unequal abilities. The **line** is how the sports book deals with this inequality so that wagers are placed equally on either team.

Although the term *sports book* sometimes encompasses a lot more than just sports wagering, we'll limit this chapter to the most popular *sports* bets made in Nevada: football, basketball, baseball, hockey, and boxing. After you learn how to read a betting line, you can understand the odds for and against you—and the expected payoff if you win—for any type of sports-book bet you make.

Bet You Didn't Know ...

Most Nevada sports books do not set their own lines. They buy lines from businesses whose function is to calculate (make) lines. It is more cost-effective for a small book to buy a line than hire its own in-house line-making expertise.

While we're on the subject, many of the "controversial" lines (like the odds of Elvis being found alive) are just publicity gimmicks. You can wager a nominal sum, but a big bet would be refused. Some Super Bowl bets fall into the same category. A book might offer a bet that looks too good to be true, but when you go to the casino to make that bet, you find you can make only a small wager. Offering the giveaway bet gets the casino publicity and brings in customers, but putting a cap on the wager size holds down the cost of the promotion.

How Casinos Make Money on Sports

To understand the betting line, you first have to understand a little bit about how casinos make money on sports bets. Casinos don't make their money by betting against the bettors, as they do in most other casino games. Rather, the goal of the sports book is to offer two equally attractive betting options so that an even amount of money is wagered on both teams. Then, like a stock broker, the casino charges a commission, or *vigorish*, on every bet made. (The commission is built into the odds you are paid on winning bets. We'll discuss the details of how that's done when we get down to wagering on individual sports.)

Because the house is also responsible for paying you off when you win (unlike a stock brokerage that buys only when a stock is for sale and sells when there is a buyer), if things don't work out evenly and more bets are placed on the winning team than the losing team, the house could wind up paying out a lot more money than it takes in.

Best Bet

Sports wagering is legal in only three states: Nevada, Delaware, and Oregon.

To minimize this risk, a sports book or *linemaker* creates a betting *line*, which is a method of handicapping that makes a bet on either team seem equally attractive. This is done by either penalizing a bet on the favored team or enhancing a bet on the opposing team. The betting line fluctuates right up until game time to attract more bets on the team that has been under-bet so far. By the start of the game, if the betting line has accomplished its intended job, the house can be assured of making money no matter which team wins or by how much.

Defining the Lines

There are two different types of betting lines in sports: the money line and the point-spread. The *money line*, also called simply the *line*, penalizes those who prefer to bet on the favorite by making them bet a lot to win a little. This is called *laying*, or giving odds, and it works like this: If you lay 8 to 5 odds that the Mets will win, you pay $8 to place the bet and get back $13 ($8 + $5) if you win. Of course, you could wager any other dollar amount at 8 to 5 odds, as long as your bet was within the sports book's betting limits.

If you bet on the Giants instead of the Mets in the same game, you're *taking odds* by betting $5 to win $7. (If you could bet $5 to win $8, there would be no edge for the casino—and the casino likes to have an edge.) You pay $5 to place the bet and get back $12 when you win. In this case, because the Mets are favored, you're enticed to bet on the Giants by the promise of winning more dollars than you bet. You're also assuming more risk by betting the underdog, but sometimes the potential profit is worth it.

In football and basketball, you generally see the betting information stated as a *point-spread*, also called the *spread*. The point-spread gives the

Gamb-lingo

The **money line** is the linemaker's estimate of the probability of a team winning, plus or minus a bit to give the casino a profit. A bettor **lays odds** when betting the favorite, and puts a big bet to win a small amount. A bettor **takes odds** when betting the underdog, and puts up a small bet to win a big amount.

underdog extra points for bets. So you don't just bet on the favorite; you bet on the favorite to win by more than the spread. A bet on the underdog wins if the underdog wins the game outright, and also if the favorite wins by less than the spread. For example, if the Knicks are favored by 11 points over the Clippers and you bet on the Clippers, the Clippers could lose by 10 points and you'd still win your bet. If the Knicks win by exactly 11 points, the game is a tie for betting purposes, and all who wagered at that spread will get their bets back. The Knicks have to win by 12 points or more—to "cover the spread"—for Knick bettors to get paid.

Gamb-lingo

The **point-spread** is the betting line that's quoted for football, basketball, and hockey where the favorite gives up points and the underdog takes points so that you can bet $11 to win $10 on either team. The outcome of a point-spread bet is determined by adding the spread to the underdog's final score (or subtracting the spread from the final score of the favorite).

Best Bet

The point-spread in a football game may fluctuate during the days leading up to the game. Pros bet early in the week because that's when the betting lines are weakest. As the lines move in response to the pros' bets, the lines become harder to beat because they more closely reflect the direction in which the money is moving, or being bet.

To bet on a point-spread game, whichever *side* you want to bet, you have to lay odds by paying 11 to win 10. You know what the points are when you make the bet. You read the line as being, say, "San Francisco –17," which means that San Francisco is favored and you give up 17 points. You can wager $11 to win $10 on either team at that line. After you make your bet, that spread is locked in for you even if the line subsequently changes. In the 1995 Super Bowl, for example, many bettors had San Francisco –17, although the final line was generally quoted as San Francisco –19.

That game was a classic example of how much excitement the point-spread can add to a game. One of the most thrilling highlights was whether the Chargers would score in the final seconds because the 49ers had a lead of 23. The 49ers had the game won, but a Charger touchdown would have cut the 49er lead to less than the spread. Those were intense moments for anyone who had a bet riding. As it turned out, the Chargers didn't score late, so the 49ers not only took the championship, they covered the spread. However, the game was a lot more exciting than anyone who didn't have a bet riding could have guessed.

Walking the Line (Basic Principles of Sports Betting)

Having a bet riding on your favorite team can make watching a sporting event more fun. (As if watching without betting isn't!) Just be sure you keep the amounts of your bets within the limits of what you're able to pay for the added excitement. Think of it as paying homage to your team by leaving little donations with the casino that takes your bet.

But, to win money on sports bets, you have to overcome the urge to bet only on your favorite team. You have to think in terms of making the bets that have value, even if that means betting against the home team—and sometimes that can be difficult to do. For example, Stanford personally thought a money-line bet on the San Francisco 49ers to win the 1995 Super Bowl was a value bet, and he was in Las Vegas a few days before the game and could have easily gotten the bet down. But he didn't, primarily because he lives in San Diego and had invited several other couples over for a Super Bowl party. He just didn't want to have money riding against the home team under those circumstances, even if it was a good bet.

If you're reading this section, we can assume you enjoy sports. You probably read your newspaper's sports section first, prefer *USA Today* over the *Wall Street Journal*, and may have been saving baseball cards since you were 6. In all those years, you've probably gathered more information about sports teams and individual players than you could fit in a book and may have forgotten more stuff about your game than most people will ever know. By applying self-discipline, logic, and time to your sports acumen, you can develop into a pretty good sports *handicapper* and turn a life-long interest into an occasional moneymaker. You already know how the casinos make their money; now it's time to find out how you can make yours!

> **Best Bet**
>
> If you like the favorite but aren't sure it can cover the points, a money-line bet is a reasonable alternative. You won't have to give up any points that way, but you have to bet more to win less compared to a point-spread bet.

First Down

The first point we want to stress is *don't* make a wager just to have some action. If all you want to do is make some bets to add some excitement to the games you watch on TV, that's one thing. But if you're wagering to make money, you must be selective about the games you bet on. To be a winner, you have to carefully weigh the pros and cons of the games that interest you and what you know about the teams and playing conditions, and then choose the select few bets that offer real winning potential because of the odds offered or the point-spread.

Second and 10

Which leads to point number two: Take the time to do your homework. You know how to read the sports section—you've been doing it for years. You can recite team and player statistics, and you know who's out for the season and who's just injured for a week. You know the strengths and weaknesses of your favorite teams, who the best rookies are, and what's expected of them. Before you get ready to make your picks, put it all together in your final analysis. Do what the pros do: Check the weather conditions where the game will be played, check the home-team advantage, and see who's been added to or removed from the injured list.

You've seen it happen time and again: Any one of these conditions can turn the tide against the assumed favorite. Do your homework and try to get an edge on the linemakers by finding their mistakes. Use all the up-to-the-minute information available in most local newspapers and on sports TV, which provides another great source of insight and information from ex-coaches, players, and sportscasters.

Third and One

Point number three: Crunch your own numbers! Don't leave the oddsmaking up to the pros. You can easily take the year-to-date averages posted in a good paper's sports section and see how and why the odds were figured the way they were and whether you agree with them. Use your analysis to draw your own conclusions and find the value in the wagers offered. Some odds will be right on the money and not worth giving or taking. You'll occasionally find some you don't agree with because of a change in the conditions or something you know about that the linemakers may have overlooked. Even if it's just a hunch, the anomaly is what you're looking for; when you find one, that's the game to focus in on.

And, most important, a word of caution that every recreational gambler should swear by: *Never wager more than you can afford to lose.* One problem with betting on sports is that if you want to bet several games, you might have to get all your bets down before you know the results of any of them. That's different from, say, blackjack, where you know the result of one hand before having to make a bet on the next hand.

Bet You Didn't Know ...

The Internet is a great place to get the latest statistics on all the leagues and teams. For example, the National Football League has its own website at www.nfl.com. The NFL site carries a professional history and stats for each player, stats for every game in the season, and gives you a play-by-play of a game while it's happening. The National Hockey League also has good coverage at www.nhl.com. Most league websites are also linked to team websites, too. If you'd like to check game schedules, go to the major sports networks. You can find ESPN at espn.go.com. For more information about the Internet and how to use it to find information, check out Chapter 27.

If you bet multiple games at the same time, you must be able to handle the risk of losing all your bets. Never count on winning *any* of them—no matter how certain you are of your predictions. For example, if you can't afford to lose more than $230, don't bet $110 each on four football games that will be played at the same time. You might think the worst that can happen is you'll lose three and win one, for a net loss of $230, but you must accept the possibility that you could go zero for four and lose the whole $440.

Also consider whether you will be augmenting your betting bankroll during the season. If not, don't risk so much money in one week that losing every game that week will knock you out of action for the entire season.

Now let's look at each sport individually.

> **Best Bet**
>
> When you're in Nevada, it pays to shop around to find the best value in sports betting. Sometimes all you have to do is walk across the street to find a sports book posting a different spread, better odds, or a different total.

Football

As predictable as the seasons, the start of Monday Night Football marks the passing of summer—and summer reruns. Few sports give their adoring fans as many long weekends as football, with college and professional games running from Thursday through Monday night during most weeks of the season.

Reading the Board

As you learned before, the most popular football wagers are based on the point-spread, in which the favorite team gives up points to the opposing team. When you bet a *side*, you're not actually wagering that your team will *win*, but on whether it will cover the spread. You can also wager on the *money line*, which is the outcome of the game without points, or on the *total*, which is whether the total number of points scored by both teams during the game will be *over* or *under* a given number. We'll explain each type of football wager as we show you how to read the line posted on the football big board in Nevada sports books. A typical line looks like this:

A	B	C			
Miami Dolphins	+140		OV	−110
San Francisco 49ers −3	−160	43	UN	−110

Betting the Spread

The point-spread line is listed first, in column A. In this example, San Francisco is favored by three points. That means if you bet on the 49ers, they need to win by *more* than three points to cover the spread for you to win your bet. A three-point win by San Francisco will result in a tie, and you'll get your money back, as will all other bettors who have the 49ers minus three or the Dolphins plus three. If San Francisco wins by only one or two points, Miami beats the spread and a bet on Miami wins.

You can always find a recent line quoted in the *USA Today* Sports section and in many local papers. A newspaper line, however, is only an approximation of the line you'll get in a casino, and it's invariably listed like this:

SAN FRANCISCO –3   Miami

(or)

SAN FRANCISCO   Miami +3

Best Bet

A casino takes a bet according to its own line, not the newspaper's. You can shop around to find the best casino line, too. If you like San Francisco at –3, you will like it even better when you find it at –2. Casino-to-casino differences of one point in a line are not uncommon.

It doesn't matter whether the points are shown as points that the favorite gives up (San Francisco –3) or as points that the underdog gets (Miami +3). But you'll always see the home team in capital letters, and the favorite team listed first. In this case, San Francisco happens to be both.

How the House Makes Its Bread on the Spread

Whenever you place a point-spread bet, you lay 11 to win 10. That means if you want to win $100, you have to wager $110, no matter which team you're betting on. If you win, you're paid $210 (your $110 wager plus the $100 you just won). If you'd rather bet an even amount of money, such as $50, the sports book will accommodate you by rounding down the payoff. That means that a $50 bet will win $45, instead of the 10 to 11 payoff of $45.45.

Risky Business

If you'd rather bet round numbers, sports books round down the winnings. For example, instead of betting $11 to win $10, you can bet $10 to win $9. If the payoff was completely consistent with $11 wins $10, however, you'd receive $9.09. Rounding down costs you only pennies, but it does cost you.

The difference between an even-money bet of 10 to 10 and the 11 to 10 bet you're required to make is the house's vigorish, which amounts to a 4.54 percent commission on every point-spread bet you make. To see how the vigorish can add up and negatively affect your expected-win rate, let's see what would happen if you placed ten point-spread bets and won five:

Five wins @ $100 per win	=	$500
Five losses @ $110 per loss	=	−$550
		−$50

As you can see, even though you won half your bets, you still lost $50. To break even against the house edge, you have to win at least 52.38 percent of any point-spread bets you make, whether they're on football or basketball.

A Money Line in Football?

If you want to bet on the actual outcome of a game instead of a point-spread, you can place a *money-line* bet on a football game. Column B on the following big board example represents the money-line odds, expressed in betting units of $100. The pluses and minuses indicate that a $100 wager on the Dolphins will earn you $140. To bet on the 49ers, however, you have to wager $160 to win $100, because they're the favorite and you're laying odds. (That does not mean you have to wager $160; you can wager whatever sum you want, and the amount you win will be calculated on the basis of 100 to 160.)

A	B	C		
Miami Dolphins	+140		OV	−110
San Francisco 49ers −3	−160	43	UN	−110

The house edge on money-line bets is comparable to the house edge on bets with a spread.

The Football Totals

The number shown in column C of the following example is used if you want to bet on the total number of points that will be scored by both teams during the game; it has nothing to do with who wins or loses.

A	B	C		
Miami Dolphins	+140		OV	−110
San Francisco 49ers −3	−160	43	UN	−110

In this example, the *total* is 43. If you think more than 43 points will be scored in the game (by both teams, collectively) you can wager 11 to 10 on the *over* (OV). If, on the other hand, you don't think the total score will reach 43, wager 11 to 10 on the *under* (UN).

Don't bet the over just because you have a game between two powerhouse offensive teams capable of putting a lot of points on the board. The linemakers also know that offensive powerhouses score a lot of points, so they put up a big number for the total.

Gamb-lingo

You can wager on the combined total of points scored by both teams during a game. Winning an **over** bet requires that more points be scored than the linemaker's total, and winning an **under** bet requires that fewer total points are scored. Scores that fall right on the total are ties, and bets are returned.

You don't win a bet on the over just because two teams score more points than average; you win betting the over when the two teams score more points than the total posted on the board. Same with the under. If you think two powerhouse defensive teams probably won't let each other score, the linemakers think that, too, and they put up a small number for the total.

Successfully betting the over or under takes just as much handicapping skill as betting a side via a point-spread or money-line bet. Like a point-spread bet, your payoff on an over or an under is figured on the basis of 11 to win 10.

Football Come-Ons (Parlays and Teasers)

Parlays are sports bets in which you select multiple teams, and all your selections have to win for you to win your bet. The *teaser* is one popular form of a parlay. The menu of options the casino allows you to link on a parlay is printed on a *parlay card*.

You can also bet a parlay without a parlay card. For example, you can bet a two-team parlay and receive 13 to 5 in most sports books. You select two teams (sides or totals) and give your $5 to the person behind the counter. In turn, they give you a piece of paper to hang onto like money, because that piece of paper is your only proof of having made the wager. If both teams win, that piece of paper is worth $18. If either or both teams lose, that piece of paper is useful only to prove to a tax auditor that you had some gambling losses during the year. If one team ties, your bet plays as a straight $5 on the other team. So if one team ties and the other *wins*, that piece of paper is worth $11.50. If *both* teams tie, that piece of paper is worth the $5 you paid for it.

If you elect to bet a parlay card, the results of at least three games are tied together. You are not given extra points on any team in a parlay and should always check the card for the details. Some cards specify that ties lose, and others specify that ties win. Other parlay cards have no ties because all the spreads end in 1/2.

Here's an example of how a parlay card works: Suppose you want to bet on three games. You want to lay $10 to win $9 that team A will win. (That's not quite as good as laying 11 to 10, but we're keeping the math simple.) If that bet wins, you want to take the whole payoff and wager at 11 to 10 that team B will win. If that bet also wins, you want to take the whole payoff and wager at 11 to 10 that team C wins.

If all three of your teams win, your original $10 has grown into almost $70. If any of your teams lose, your original $10 is now the sports book's $10. This is exactly what a parlay does. A three-team parlay returns about $70 (depending on which sports book you are patronizing) for a $10 wager if all three teams win.

Gamb-lingo

A sports bet that ties multiple games together in one bet, with the outcome determined by winning all games, is a **parlay**. A **teaser** is a type of parlay that offers more generous spreads, but pays off at lower odds.

Of course, the true odds of having all three winners are 7 to 1, so if there were no house edge, your $10 would turn into $80. The house edge on a three-team parlay is 10/80, or 12.5 percent. To someone who picks more than 52.38 percent winners, a parlay is as good an investment as a straight bet; to someone who is betting just for fun and likely to average 50 percent winners, however, a parlay is worse in terms of giving the casino a higher percentage.

Bet You Didn't Know ...

Parlay cards can be good bets if you can parlay together bets that are likely to win. Of course, it still doesn't *always* work out, but that's what makes it exciting! Here's an example from Stanford:

"For the 1996 Super Bowl, the Santa Fe sports book in Las Vegas offered 6.5:1 on a parlay of which team would score the first field goal, the shortest field goal, and the longest field goal. Since the first field goal could also have been the shortest, longest, or *only* field goal, that looked like a good bet to me. I bet it both ways: *both* Dallas and Pittsburgh to have the first, shortest, and longest field goals. The Pittsburgh parlay lost when Dallas kicked the first field goal. Dallas had first, shortest, *and* longest until the fourth quarter, when Pittsburgh, behind 20-7, kicked a long field goal that caused the Dallas parlay to lose."

In a teaser, you select three or more different teams, and each team has to beat a special spread for you to win your bet. Teaser bets are special because sports books give you additional points over the regular point-spreads. For example, if Air Force is favored by 9 over Wyoming, a teaser card might let you select Air Force –3 or Wyoming +15.

Because teaser cards give you more attractive spreads, they pay off at lower odds than other parlays. Some teaser cards specify that ties lose, and others specify that ties win, and others have no ties because all the spreads end in 1/2. One sports book might offer several different teaser cards; each teaser card has all the applicable details printed on it.

The advantage to a parlay is that if you win, you get a huge payoff for a small bet. The downside is that to get paid, you have to win all the games you select, instead of just one or two out of three.

A Little Football Handicapping

Linemakers use the points-for (PF) and points-against (PA) for each team (along with other information) to set the totals. Here's how you can use the PF and PA to decide whether you think it's worth betting over or under a total. Most of the football statistics you need are listed in *USA Today* or a good local paper under the NFL standings.

Here's what you might learn about tomorrow's Pittsburgh vs. Green Bay game, at Pittsburgh:

	Wins	Losses	PF	PA
Pittsburgh	11	4	388	303
Green Bay	10	5	380	295

From this information, you can calculate the average PF to date by dividing each team's PF by the total number of games played. Then do the same for the PA. Add the PF and PA averages to get the average total points per game.

	Avg. PF	Avg. PA	Total Points/Game
Pittsburgh	25.86	20.2	46.06
Green Bay	25.33	19.6	44.93

As you can see, these teams match up pretty well. The actual line on this game was quoted as GB –3 1/2 42. That means Green Bay was favored by 3 1/2 points and the total was 42. With both teams averaging more than 44 total points per game, you might be tempted to bet the over. The outcome of the game was close to the line-maker's prediction, with Green Bay winning 24 to 19, for a total of 43 points scored.

Of course, you need a lot more information than we've given you to win more than 52.4 percent of your games, but it's a start. (Besides, doing the research is half the fun, right?) When you're analyzing all the latest information you have available, remember that the linemakers have already factored in most of what you have discovered.

For example, they'll usually add two to three points for the home-team advantage. Although it's not obvious in the point-spread for this game, without Pittsburgh's home-team advantage, Green Bay might have been favored by six points. Injuries are another critical factor that linemakers and professional handicappers figure in, and you can, too. You'll find injury lists published in *USA Today* and other papers with good sports sections. They're usually arranged by team, and they list the current status of all injured players. Key player injuries can swing the point-spread one to five points, depending on the position they play, their value to the team, and the quality of their replacements.

Best Bet

Newspapers typically print much more about their home teams than about teams from other cities. For inside information, get the appropriate hometown newspapers from your local library or special book/newspaper stores.

Some teams are very deep in personnel in some positions and very weak in others (meaning that one team might rely on a particular quarterback or defensive lineman, but could replace anyone else who gets injured). It helps to know the strengths and weaknesses of the teams you bet on, so you can anticipate how they will be exploited during the game.

Hoop Dreams

Basketball can be the sports fan's great escape from the harsh realities of a long, cold, lonely winter. With NBA and NCAA games played daily, basketball can be a virtual oasis, with an occasional double- and triple-header thrown in to satisfy even the most voracious sports fan's appetite for action.

The NBA currently has 29 teams scattered across the United States and Canada. These teams are divided into two conferences, each with two divisions of seven or eight teams that each play an 82-game season. It's important to realize just how vast the NBA playing field is so that you can imagine the scheduling nightmare each team and each player faces in terms of travel, work, and preparation—not to mention the heavy toll that running on those hardwood floors must take on their knees! We'll get back to how all this can affect your basketball betting strategy, but first we'll show you how to read the hoops line and what kinds of bets you can make.

Basketball bets are based on the point-spread, as in football. When you bet the favorite you give points, and when you bet the underdog you take points. You bet 11 to win 10, and it really doesn't matter who wins the game, as long as you make your point-spread. Basketball odds are often posted to indicate who has the home-team advantage and who is favored. Here's how a typical basketball game is posted on the big board:

A	B
Knicks	O/U
BULLS +3	208

The Knicks being listed first in column A indicates that they're the favorite. The Bulls are in capital letters, so they are the home team. The line is Bulls plus three, so three points will be added to their final score to decide bets on the teams. That means the Knicks have to win by more than three points for a bet on them to pay off. The Bulls can lose by three and the bet would still be considered a tie. They could lose by two points and a bet on them would still win.

The total on this game is 208 points, shown in column B. That means if you bet the over, you win if the teams score more than 208 points. If you bet the under, you win if the teams score fewer than 208 points. If the teams score a combined total of exactly 208 points, over and under bets are refunded.

A teaser bet is usually offered in addition to the point-spread and total. As in football, a teaser is a bet in which additional points are given or taken, and all teams selected have to win for you to win the bet.

Handicapping Hoops

With such a rigorous schedule, the home team has an advantage that is always re-flected in the point-spread. Those guys are glad to be home for a while, and the fans are usually glad the boys are back in town! Because road trips are tedious and can last for a week or two at a time, it's a good idea to look for teams that tend to travel well. Notice which teams win more of their away games than they lose, and, like the pros, use that knowledge to judge a team's overall strength. Teams that can win on the road have more seasoned players and can weather the hardships better, or perhaps they're more committed to a winning season. If you notice winning and losing streaks, you may not want to buck the trend. An ordinarily good team that's been losing at home is less likely to start winning at the beginning of a road trip. The opposite is probably true, too. If they've been winning at home, they're likely to keep it up on the road.

Again, as in football, check the stats often and keep records of the teams you're interested in if you want to bet basketball to win. Know who's on the injured list and who's coming off, what the latest game results have been with and without injured players, and how many points have been scored for (PF) and against (PA) so far. Use all the information you can gather from newspapers, television, and books to make informed betting decisions.

Baseball's Field of Dreams

Baseball may be America's favorite pastime, but it's slipping in recent years in terms of the amount of money wagered in Nevada's sports books. Nevertheless, it has always enjoyed its share of popularity as a betting option. Baseball odds are quoted in terms of a money line, and bettors must decide who will win the game, period. A typical baseball quote is posted on the sports book board like this:

A	B
METS - Padres	6 1/2 – 7 1/2

The favorite team is always listed first in column A, and the underdog is underneath or alongside it. The home team is almost always capitalized. In column B, the money line is expressed in terms of how much you will win with a $5 bet on the underdog and how much you need to lay on the favorite to win $5, in that order. In this example, if you prefer to bet on the Padres and take the odds, you need to wager $5 to win $6.50. A bet on the favorite (the Mets) will cost you $7.50 to win $5.

In the following example, the money line is quoted differently:

Cubs - REDS   +130 –150

In this game, in which the Cubs are favored over the Reds in Cincinnati, you see the odds expressed as how much money you need to lay or give to win $100. In this case, you can bet $150 on the Cubs to win $100 (or any other multiple of 1.5 to 1), or you can bet $100 on the underdog Reds to win $130.

Where's the Vig?

If you're wondering how the house makes its money in baseball, it's in the difference between what a bettor on the favorite has to lay to win $100, and what a bettor on the underdog gets paid if the underdog wins. (Usually it amounts to $20, but it can be more.) In the latter baseball example above, if one person bets $150 on the Cubs and someone else bets $100 on the Reds, one bet will pay the other if the Cubs win, and the casino will make $20 if the Reds win. Of course, the casino would rather have $110 or so wagered on the Reds so it will profit no matter which team wins the game.

In the first baseball example above, the numbers are similar. If one person bets $150 on the Mets while someone else bets $100 on the Padres, the casino will either break even or make $20.

Making Your Baseball Picks

The single most important factor in picking a winning baseball team is the pitcher. A good pitcher can make it very difficult for even the best team to score against him. If you're a baseball fan, you probably won't have to do that much brushing up on your statistics to find the best pitchers (but you'll have to do a lot of homework to keep up with the linemakers!).

Study pitchers' earned run averages (ERA) and win-loss records. You want to find those who don't give up too many runs, so their ERAs should be low and their win-loss percentages high. See how the pitcher you're thinking about betting on has been doing lately. Is he in a slump? Was he robbed of a win last week and ready to fight for one this week? If your favorite pitcher isn't doing well lately, find out why before betting on him again. Check the stats to see how he's done against individual teams, and then consider the changes that have been made since then.

Check the team stats, too. All major newspapers carry good baseball coverage, and there's always *USA Today*. Focus on the team's winning percentage, record for the past 10 games, and the number of games won or lost in succession. Know as much as you can about the teams you're betting on.

Because the linemakers usually know more about each team than you do, good handicapping can't guarantee you a win. What it can do is help you be

> **Risky Business**
>
> In baseball, when you bet on favorites you have to bet a lot to win a little, so you have to win a larger percentage of your bets to break even. The higher the odds, the higher percentage of wins you need to break even. The same is true when you bet the money line in football.

an informed bettor, and increase your likelihood of finding opportunities that the linemaker or betting public might have missed. These are the two most likely ways you can win by handicapping baseball (or any sport):

♦ When you get opportunities to bet on new information before it's reflected in the linemaker's odds—go for it!

♦ Bet any information you know to be important but you think is overlooked or being misvalued by other bettors.

Hockey

The hockey line reflects a point-spread, like basketball and football, which is based on the number of goals scored. A typical hockey line looks like this:

BOSTON BRUINS   1.5   Chicago Blackhawks

In this example, the Bruins are not only the home team, as you can tell by the capital letters, they're also favored to win this game by 1.5 goals. You know the Bruins are favored because they are listed first on the board. Again, as in football and basketball, you would wager $11 to win $10 on either team, and the Bruins have to win by at least two goals for a bet on them to win. If the Blackhawks lose by only one goal, they are considered the winners because they were given the points. If the Blackhawks lose by two goals or more, a bet on them loses. A game with half a point in the point-spread can't end in a tie because it's not possible to score a half-point goal.

Boxing

Boxing prizefights are so few and far between that they can almost be considered special events, although there are many avid fans who follow the sport closely and bet heavily when they get the chance. Betting on prizefights relies on the money line, and like baseball, quotes are based on $5 wagers. But the vig charged on boxing wagers is usually about twice as steep as baseball bets, so fans have to be extra careful of the odds they give or take when placing a boxing bet. Here's a typical boxing line:

Ali 9   Frazier 7

In this hypothetical fight, Ali is favored and you must bet $9 to win $5 if you bet Ali. To bet Frazier, the underdog, you bet $5 to win $7.

Unless you follow boxing routinely—and most people don't—it's very difficult to handicap or determine whether the money line represents favorable odds. In most cases, the casual sports fan bets boxing matches with his or her heart, based on the reputations of the titleholder and the opponent. Most prizefights are well-hyped, so there's usually enough information and opinion available to help you make a decision if you're determined to wager. But if you don't follow prizefighting seriously, you should avoid putting down any serious money.

Best Bet

SharpSportsBetting.com is a website for sports bettors that is owned and operated by Stanford. According to Stanford: "It is a place to share picks and compare analyses. Most of the pages of SharpSportsBetting.com are message boards. Some of those pages can be accessed by anyone who visits SharpSportsBetting.com, and other pages require a password for entry. The password-protected pages are hosted by people who spend a lot of time studying their sports, and who bet big on their own picks. The hosts interact with each other, and with visitors to the site. When a number of sharp individuals bring their own individual skills and viewpoints to a discussion, the result of the discussion often is a more complete understanding of a situation than what any one member of the group had initially."

The Least You Need to Know

- There are point-spread bets in football, basketball, and hockey, and money-line bets in football, baseball, and boxing.

- You pay a vig for the privilege of making a sports bet in a sports book.

- You're betting into a line rather than simply making an even-money bet that a team will win. This line generally recognizes all available information about the game.

Part 4

The ROYALS (A Lot of Ways to Play Poker)

At this very moment, thousands of people all over the world are picking up their poker hands and praying for a Royal Flush. Only one in approximately 650,000 will have it. By the time you finish reading this section, one of those lucky winners could be you! In Part 4, you'll learn how to play five different casino games that are all based on basic five card draw poker.

In Chapter 15, you'll get your first taste of poker as we introduce you to Seven Card Stud and Texas Hold 'em. In Chapter 16, we'll show you how to match your knowledge of poker and Stanford's winning strategy against a machine as you learn to play video poker. In Chapters 17 and 18, we'll cover Let It Ride and Multiple Play Video Poker, two of the hottest new poker games that are played on the main floor (not in a poker room) of most casinos. And in Chapter 19, we'll explain Pai Gow Poker—American poker and Chinese Pai Gow combined.

Bluffing Your Way to the Top—Poker

In This Chapter

- What makes poker such a popular card game?
- What's the object of the game?
- How to play seven-card stud
- How hold 'em differs from seven-card stud

I remember the Great Poker Game in the Blizzard of '77 as if it were yesterday. It was snowing fiercely in the Garden State and folks had been leaving work early, but I had to stay 'til 7:00 p.m. A commute that normally took 35 minutes took almost 4 hours.

When I finally got home, dad and his poker buddies (who had traveled just as far as I had), were engrossed in a game, oblivious to a storm I had thought would surely take my life. While I and millions of other commuters struggled home seeking the comfort of our loved ones and shelter from the storm, these guys couldn't wait to get together for their weekly session! In this chapter, Stanford and I show you what it's all about. Of course, to get as good as my dad, you're gonna have to learn a whole lot more—and practice, practice, practice!

Is Poker Bluffing Its Way to the Top?

Poker is a very popular game. Almost every major casino in the country has a poker room, and even states that have only limited legalized gambling have poker rooms. Kids in college dormitories play poker. Friends and neighbors play poker. Retired people play poker. Professionals play poker. People enter poker tournaments. Swarms of people play video poker. Wyatt Earp played poker. Wild Bill Hickok *died* playing poker. Nowadays, women are giving men a run for their money in what used to be considered a "man's game." Poker is, and always has been, a *very* popular game.

Gamb-lingo

A poker player **bluffs** by betting and raising to give the impression that a hand is better than it really is. A player **raises** by matching the previous bet and then betting more, to increase the stake for remaining players

Poker combines the traditional elements of skill and luck with the extra gratification that comes from "psyching out" your opponent. As in the game of life, a good poker player can turn a bad hand into a winner by *bluffing* his or her way to the top.

What It Takes to Be a Winner

Unlike other casino card games, poker is a game in which players bet and play against each other, not against the house. The objective of poker is to win the *pot*, the money that accumulates as players who remain in the game keep *raising* their bets. There are two ways to win: by holding the highest hand in the game, or by making your opponents *think* you've got the highest hand—in which case everyone else *folds*, leaving you to win the pot!

Gamb-lingo

The chips that accumulate in a poker hand as each player bets and raises are called the **pot**, and they go to the winner of the hand. A player **folds** by throwing in his or her cards. A player who has folded makes no more bets on that hand and cannot win the pot.

Poker has many variations. In some games, you're dealt a five-card hand; in others, it's seven. In stud poker (5- or 7-card), some cards are dealt face-up and some face-down. In hold 'em, each player is dealt two cards face-down, and then five community cards are dealt face-up. Draw poker is a closed game, meaning all cards are dealt face-down. In a game called lowball, players compete for the lowest rather than the highest hand. In each of these games (except lowball), although the rules of play and strategy differ, the hierarchy of winning hands remains the same. That's where we'll start.

The Hierarchy of Winning Hands

Most poker games are played with a standard 52-card deck. The highest ranking card is the ace (A), followed by the king (K), queen (Q), jack (J), 10, 9, 8, 7, 6, 5, 4, 3, and 2. The ace can also be used as a 1 in lowball or when it is needed to complete a 5-high straight: A, 2, 3, 4, 5. Five cards of the same suit compose a flush, but other than that, suits have no ranking.

Unlike blackjack or baccarat, cards in a hand are not given a point value and totaled to determine the winner. Rather, each five-card hand is ranked according to a hierarchy, with the order descending from a once- or twice-in-a-lifetime royal flush to a very ordinary pair, or less. The following table explains the hierarchy of poker hands.

The Hierarchy of Poker Hands

Royal Flush	A ♥ K ♥ Q ♥ J ♥ 10 ♥	A, K, Q, J, and 10 all of the same suit.
Straight Flush	A ♣ K ♣ Q ♣ J ♣ 10 ♣	Five cards in any sequence, all of the same suit (such as Q, J, 10, 9, 8 of clubs).
Four of a Kind	Q ♥ Q ♣ Q ♦ Q ♠ 3 ♦	Four cards of the same rank, one in each suit, plus an additional card that doesn't matter.
Full House	K ♣ K ♦ K ♥ 2 ♦ 2 ♥	Three cards of one rank, plus another two cards of another rank.
Flush	Q ♠ 10 ♠ 9 ♠ 6 ♠ 4 ♠	Any five cards of the same suit, in any order.
Straight	10 ♦ 9 ♠ 8 ♣ 7 ♥ 6 ♥	Any five cards in sequence.
Three of a Kind	J ♣ J ♠ J ♦ 7 ♣ 2 ♦	Three cards of the same rank, plus two additional cards.
Two Pair	K ♣ K ♥ 7 ♠ 7 ♣ A ♦	Two cards of one rank and two cards of another rank, plus one additional card.
One Pair	8 ♥ 8 ♦ A ♣ 10 ♥ 3 ♠	Two cards of the same rank and three additional cards.
No Pair	A ♠ J ♣ 9 ♦ 7 ♠ 2 ♥	All five cards of different ranks and not all of one suit.

In the Event of a Tie

If a hand comes down to a *showdown* between two or more players, the player with the highest-ranking hand wins. If two or more players have the same hand (such as both hands having two pair), the winner is decided by looking at the individual cards.

In full house against full house, the three-of-a-kind cards from the two hands are compared with each other; high rank determines the winner. If two full houses have the same threes of a kind (which can happen if community cards are used), then the rank of the pair cards are compared.

Gamb-lingo

In most poker games, **high poker** is played. In high poker, high hands win and high cards (ace, king, queen, and jack) are ranked higher than low cards. The ace is the highest ranking card, and the two (deuce) is the lowest. In **low poker**, also called **lowball**, low hands win and the ace is the lowest card because it counts as 1. The best hand you can get in low poker is A-2-3-4-5.

If two or more players have flushes, the highest card that is part of the flush determines the winner. If the highest cards are another tie, then the next-highest card determines the winner. Two flushes are equal and split the pot only if every card matches rank for rank.

With straights, the high end of the straight determines the ranking, not the highest card; for example, a 6-high straight (6-5-4-3-2) beats a 5-high straight (5-4-3-2-A). Two straights that are equal card for card are tied and split the pot.

Two three-of-a-kind hands are compared by looking at the rank of the threes of a kind. Only if both hands have the same three of a kind would you compare the higher singletons, and then the fifth cards.

Two hands with two pair are ranked by looking at the rank of the higher pair in each hand. If both hands have identical high pairs, then compare the second pair in each hand. If the second pairs also are equal, then the winner is decided by the fifth card in each hand.

Two hands with one pair are ranked by looking at the rank of the pair. If both pairs are equal, then compare the highest singleton in one hand with the highest singleton in the other. If those highest singletons also match, then compare second-highest singletons. If those cards also match, then compare fifth cards.

Two hands that have nothing in the way of pairs or flushes or straights are compared card for card, starting with the highest card in each hand and going down through five cards.

A sixth card is never used to rank poker hands. In a poker game where each player gets to select a five-card hand from among more than five cards, the pot is split if the two five-card hands are equal, even though the sixth card of one hand might be of higher rank than the sixth card of another hand.

Playing the Game

Poker played in a casino or card room differs only slightly from the poker friends play around the kitchen table. The most noticeable difference is that in a casino or card room you have a dealer, who in addition to dealing each round of cards also exchanges your cash for chips when you buy in. The poker-room dealer also makes sure that all bets are for the correct amount and that everyone has the right number of cards. The dealer also calls the *game* and lets you know whose turn it is to bet first on each round. Unfortunately, the dealer won't fix the gang a sandwich between hands, but can probably tell you where the best place to get one is.

Another major difference is that many poker rooms won't allow you to play cash on the table (like you can when the action heats up in the kitchen). Because of this chips-only rule, it's important that you keep an adequate supply of chips available. If you have a good hand and run out of chips, you'll be allowed to play out your hand, but you'll be excluded from betting in the remaining rounds. The other players will continue to bet in a *side pot*, which excludes you. If you win that hand, you'll win the original pot, but the side pot would go to the highest-ranking hand that had contributed chips to it. After the showdown is over, you can buy more chips.

Most poker games start with a shuffle and cut of the deck, and then the players *ante*, which means that before the dealer deals a card, players put up some money (usually a percentage of the minimum bet). The antes "sweeten" the pot before the first round of betting and ensure that if no one makes a bet, the player with the best hand will win at least something.

Best Bet

When you want to enter a poker game, instead of walking up to a game that's in progress, ask the poker-room manager if a seat is available at a game you want to play in. If all the games are full, the manager will add your name to a waiting list.

Gamb-lingo

Poker players **ante** when they place a small bet into the pot before a new hand starts. A **blind bet** is a bet that selected players are required by the rules to make.

In hold 'em, selected players are required to make a *blind bet* before the cards are dealt. The first two players to act are the ones singled out to make blind bets. As with the antes, blind bets serve to raise the stakes and get some early action going. After everyone antes, the dealer deals one or five cards face-down to each player, depending on the game, and maybe a few cards face-up, again depending on the game, and the players peek at their cards to decide whether to bet. Most versions of poker contain additional rounds of dealing cards and betting.

Betting Business

Strict rules govern betting order, which also varies with the type of poker game. In some games, the player to the left of the *designated dealer* bets first, which is called *opening*. In other games, the player whose first up card is high or low opens. The betting order is important because the player who bets first has the disadvantage of giving other players information about his or her hand before getting information about any other player's hand. The player who bets last has the advantage of seeing how everyone else bets before deciding whether to play his or her hand.

There are different numbers of betting rounds in different poker games. For example, in seven-card stud there are five betting rounds; in hold 'em there are only four rounds.

Gamb-lingo

The player who bets first is said to **open**. In some games, including hold 'em, the player to the left of the dealer opens. When there is a resident dealer (a casino employee who deals every hand), a different player is the **designated dealer** for each hand. The player to the designated dealer's left opens the betting.

During each round, betting moves clockwise around the table and players can either check, call, raise, or fold. When you *check*, that means that you want to stay in, but don't want to bet. When you check, you forfeit the right to raise in the current round of betting unless "check and raise" is allowed in your game. After someone makes the first bet, all other players can only *call*, *raise*, or *fold*. When you call, you match the most recent bet by saying "Call" and placing the appropriate stack of chips in front of you. It's very important in a card room or casino that you don't throw your chips into the pot as they do on TV; instead, let the dealer count and place them into the pot for you.

If somebody else has already bet, you can *raise* the amount of the bet when it's your turn by matching the previous bet, and then saying "Raise" and placing the amount of chips by which you would like to increase the bet in front of you. After the bet has been raised, all other players remaining in the pot must call with the higher amount of chips, or fold. In many poker games, the bet can be raised only three times in the same betting round.

When you don't think your hand is good enough to win and don't feel like bluffing, get out of the game by folding instead of calling on your next turn. Depending on the game, there might be several rounds of betting, with a card or cards dealt between rounds.

Let's summarize the betting options we've covered so far:

1. The player who bets first can check or open unless required to bet blind, in which case the person must bet.

2. As the opportunity to bet moves around the table, if nobody ahead of you has opened you can check or you can open, but you cannot raise. When you *check* during a round of betting, you can later decide to call a bet, but unless the rules of the game permit, you cannot check and raise.

3. After the first bet is made, the other players can call, raise, or fold, but they cannot check.

4. You *call* by matching the amount of the previous player's bet. If the previous player has called and raised, you call that bet by wagering the full amount of the call plus the raise.

5. When you raise, you really call and raise by matching the previous bet *and* adding in the raise amount.

Gamb-lingo

A player can **check** to stay in the game, but not bet. You can check only when no one has made a bet in the current round. When a player matches a previous bet or raise, he or she **calls** the bet. Sometimes this is referred to as **seeing** a bet.

Best Bet

It's important player etiquette to always let the dealer and other players know what you are doing before you actually do it. For example, if you want to call and raise, say, "Call X dollars and raise X dollars."

6. After a raise, even players who have already bet in the round must match the raise or fold, or they can re-raise. Some poker games limit the number of raises to three per round of betting.

7. When you do not want to spend additional money to match another player's raise, you *fold*.

Risky Business

It's important to set the appropriate betting limits for your bankroll. You don't want to be making decisions on the basis of how much money you have to bet instead of on how strong your cards are. Better to be able to play at a level that affords you the opportunity to play your hands correctly.

When two or more players remain in the game at the end of the last round of betting, each of the players show their cards in the *showdown*. It doesn't matter whose cards are shown first. *Cards speak.* That means the hand with the highest poker value wins the pot, regardless of whether the owner of the hand realizes how good or bad the hand is. So if you get to the showdown, always show your hand instead of just throwing it away because there is a chance you have a winner without realizing it. The remaining player whose hand ranks the highest wins the pot. If only one player remains in the game, that player automatically wins the pot. If you folded, you can't win the pot.

The Game Has Its Limitations

When you play in a poker room or casino, you'll find the name of the game posted somewhere above or alongside the poker table, along with the betting limits. Most games have a two-tiered betting limit, like $1–$4, $2–$4, or $5–$10. Usually the second figure is double the first, but occasionally you'll find games with a larger spread. In a *structured*, or *fixed-limit* game, the first dollar amount is what you can bet or raise in the early rounds, and the second amount is what you can bet or raise in later rounds. In a *spread limit* game, any bet between the two limits is allowed at any time.

Raking It In

As you learned earlier, players don't bet against the house in poker; they bet against each other. You're probably wondering, then, how the casino or card room can afford to provide the dealers, card room staff, playing tables, lighting, and even food and beverage service?

Gamb-lingo

The **rake** is the money that the casino or card room charges for each hand of poker. It is usually a percentage or flat fee that is taken from the pot after each round of betting.

The answer is in the *rake*, which is a percentage of each pot that the house takes for itself. The rake percentage varies from 2 to 10 percent, depending on the card room or casino where you play. In some casinos, the rake can't exceed a maximum dollar amount no matter how large the pot gets; in other casinos, the rake is a flat fee instead of a percentage. In hold 'em, you might hear the rake referred to as the *big blind*. No matter how you slice it, the rake is *their* take.

Getting Started

Seven-card stud and hold 'em are two of the best poker games to start out with because (1) Seven-card stud is similar to the basic poker you might already play at home and is easy to learn, and (2) They are the most popular poker games played in card rooms today. We'll walk you through a typical game of seven-card stud and provide some basic strategy pointers along the way. Then we'll point out the major differences between seven-card stud and hold 'em.

Although it won't make you a winner right off the bat, our coverage will give you an idea of what to expect when you first sit down in a poker room. After you get over that hurdle, you'll quickly learn through experience and watching other people play their hands. As you've probably noticed, poker has a rich and colorful language all its own. After you play a while and get used to the lingo, you'll more fully appreciate and understand the valuable information offered in many of the in-depth poker books available. Books by the leading poker experts, such as Doyle Brunson, Mike Caro, David Sklansky, and Mason Malmuth, are recommended to help you get a greater understanding of the variety of poker games and strategies.

Playing Seven-Card Stud

In seven-card stud, each player receives three cards before the first round of betting, and then four additional cards, each of which is followed by another round of betting.

A winning hand is decided by the best five-card hand out of the seven cards dealt, or by whatever hand the last remaining player holds.

Gamb-lingo

In seven-card stud, the **bring-in** is a mandatory bet made by the player with the lowest up card in the first round of betting.

Players start the game by anteing before the deal. In this $2–$4 game, each of the eight players puts in 50 cents. The dealer deals each player two down cards and one up card, and the first round of betting begins with the player who has the lowest up card *bringing it in*.

As you can see in the following example, there is a tie for low card between players D and F. The dealer determines the first bettor by the suits of their 4s. Although suits don't ordinarily have a ranking, when used to decide a tie for the bring-in, the suits are ranked in alphabetical order: clubs, diamonds, hearts, and spades. You can't tell from this example, but player D bets first because he holds the 4 of spades, which is the lowest ranked suit.

Players' cards in the first round of betting. (# indicates a card dealt face-down.)

Player	Up Card
A	#-#-9
B	#-#-Q
C	#-#-8
D	#-#-4
E	#-#-A
F	#-#-4
G	#-#-Q

The *bring-in* means that the first bettor (player D) is forced to start the game rolling by opening with a $1 bet. The bring-in is lower than the minimum betting limits ($2 in this $2–$4 game) only until someone at the table raises to the minimum bet level. The second player to bet (to the left of the first bettor) has three options: fold, call the bring-in, or raise to the minimum bet level. After the bet has been raised to the minimum bet, it usually stays at that level for bets and raises for the remainder of the first betting round, which is called *third street*, and for the second betting round, called *fourth street*. If one of the players has a pair showing on fourth street, the betting limit can be raised to the maximum bet.

As you might have guessed, player E was the second bettor; with an A showing, he raised by placing $1 and $2 in front of him. Players F, C, and D folded, and players G, A, and B called by matching player E's $3 bet. No one raised again, and the remaining players were dealt another card:

Players' cards in the second round. (# indicates a card dealt face-down.)

Player	Up Cards
A	#-#-9-7
B	#-#-Q-4
E	#-#-A-2
G	#-#-Q-9

On fourth street and later rounds, the player with the highest hand showing bets first. In this case, it's player E with an ace. (If there's a tie from here on out, the player to the left of the designated dealer bets first.) Because none of the players has a pair showing, the betting limit remains at $2 for this round. (If anyone showed a pair, the betting limit would be $4.) Player E bets $2, and player G raises by placing $4 on the table. Because player G has raised, the betting goes around the table again, stopping when all remaining players have bet the same amount in this round. Player A calls player G's $4 bet, and player B folds. Player E raises by betting $6. Players G and A both call without further raising, and the next card is dealt to the remaining players:

Player	Up Cards
A	#-#-9-7-K
E	#-#-A-2-A
G	#-#-Q-9-4

Players' cards in the third round. (# indicates a card dealt face-down.)

We're now on *fifth street*, and the betting limit is $4. Player E still has the highest hand showing with a pair of aces, and he bets $4. Player G raises $4, placing a total of $8 in the pot. Player A no longer thinks his hand is worth the cost of continued bets, so he folds. Player E re-raises another by putting another $8 into the pot. Player G calls by placing another $4 in the pot. The next card is dealt:

Player	Up Cards
E	#-#-A-2-A-10
G	#-#-Q-9-4-6

Players' cards in the fourth round. (# indicates a card dealt face-down.)

On *sixth street*, player E bets $4 and player G raises $4. Player E calls. So on this round of betting, each player has placed $8 in the pot.

The last card is dealt face-down:

Player	Up Card
E	#-#-#-A-2-A-10
G	#-#-#-Q-9-4-6

Players' cards in the fifth round. (# indicates a card dealt face-down.)

In the final round of betting (*seventh street*), player E bets $4, player G raises $4, and player E calls. The *showdown* reveals that player G wins with a Q-high straight, against player E's three aces.

Gamb-lingo _____

The first round of betting in seven-card stud is called **third street** because players have three cards. The second round is called **fourth street** with four cards, the third round is **fifth street** with five cards, the fourth round is called **sixth street** with six cards, and the fifth round is **seventh street** with seven cards. Phew!

Gamb-lingo _____

After the last betting round, the players that haven't folded show their cards in the **showdown** to determine the winner.

Some Basic Strategy for Stud

Poker is a game of chance as well as skill and psychology. The skill comes in knowing how to play each hand and making the right playing decisions. The more you know about the makeup of a deck and the rules of the game, the more likely you are to make good playing decisions.

For example, if you hold three cards of a flush, you know that in a 52-card deck there are only 10 other cards of the same suit that can help you make your flush. When cards are dealt face-up, it's easy to see how many other cards of that suit have already been dealt. When a card you need gets dealt to someone else, you won't be getting it. Any other information you can pick up from the way other players play their hands, the cards discarded in a folded hand, and so on, can also be used to your advantage.

It's hard to bluff successfully if bluffing makes your hands shake. As you gain more experience, you'll be better equipped to handle the psychological aspects of the game, but don't overlook them as you're learning. They're often what separates winners from losers and pros from amateurs.

Playing Hold 'Em

There are a few fundamental differences between seven-card stud and hold 'em. The most significant difference is that each player is dealt just two personal cards, and the remaining five cards in each player's hand are dealt as community cards and shared by all the players. The advantage of this format over seven-card stud is there can be more players; you can't play seven-card stud with more than seven players without risking running out of cards.

The first round of betting comes after each player has received two face-down cards. Then three community cards are dealt face-up, followed by a second round of betting. Then a fourth community card is dealt face-up, followed by a third round of betting. Then the fifth and final community card is dealt face-up, followed by the fourth and final round of betting. All players bet on their own two cards plus the community card(s). The winning hand is decided by the best five cards in a player's seven-card hand, which includes five community cards. If the showdown results in a tie, the pot is split among the remaining players. The sixth and seventh cards are not used to break ties. If the community cards for the best hand are left for everybody left at the showdown, then those players split the pot.

There are four rounds of betting in hold 'em. Betting can be either fixed or spread limits, as in seven-card stud. Instead of deciding which player bets first by high or low card for each round of play, the player to the left of the designated dealer bets first throughout the hand. The designated dealer is indicated by a round *button* that is moved clockwise around the table after each hand.

Gamb-lingo

A small **button** marker is moved from player to player after each hand of poker to designate the dealer position. The community cards that are dealt face-up in the center of the table are referred to as the **board**.

Before the first two cards are dealt to each player, the first two players to the left of the designated dealer put up a *blind* bet, which is equivalent to an ante in seven-card stud. The first player puts up the small blind, and the second player on the left puts up the big blind. The big blind is generally equal to the first-round bet, and the small blind is generally half as big.

After the first two cards are dealt face down to each player, the player to the left of the big blind starts the betting action by either calling the big blind, raising, or folding. Each succeeding player calls, raises, or folds. The player who put up the small blind must either fold or put in additional money so that his or her contribution is the same as that of the other players, and the small blind also has the option of raising. The player who put up the big blind also has the option of raising, even if all the other players have merely folded or called.

Gamb-lingo

The three cards dealt face-up in the center of the table are called the **flop**. In hold 'em, **fourth street** is the fourth card on board and the third round of betting. **Fifth street** is the fifth card on board and the final round of betting.

After everyone has finished betting on the first round, the *flop*—which consists of three face-up community cards—is dealt. Then comes the second round of betting. Each player bets the two cards she or he was dealt originally plus the three community cards. The player to the left of the designated dealer starts the betting in this round and the remaining rounds. If this player folds, the player to his or her left bets first in remaining rounds.

After this round of betting, a fourth community card is placed face-up in the center of the table. Then comes a round of betting referred to as *fourth street*. A fifth community card is then placed face-up in the center of the table, followed by a round of betting called *fifth street*.

The showdown comes after all rounds of betting are complete. Of the remaining players, the one with the best poker hand wins the pot. Because five out of seven cards are shared by all players, it's not unusual for more than one player to tie with the best hand at the showdown. When a hand ends in a tie, the pot is split between the players with the tied hands.

The Least You Need to Know

- The player who bets first is usually at a disadvantage, and the player betting last has the advantage of seeing how everyone else has played their hands.

- Never *throw* your chips or cards into the pot. Place them in front of you and tell the table what you're doing: calling, raising, or folding. The dealer will count your chips and move them into the pot, or scoop up your cards.

- Always wait until it's your turn to bet. Betting moves clockwise around the table, starting with the first bettor.

- You call by matching the amount of the previous player's bet.

- When you raise, you really call and raise by matching the previous bet *and* adding in the raise amount.

- If you run out of chips in the middle of a hand, you can stay in the hand, but you're precluded from winning whatever accumulates in the pot after you run out of money. Always have enough chips to play out your hand and win a big pot!

- Seven-card stud has five rounds of betting, with four cards dealt face down and three cards dealt face-up. In hold 'em, there are four betting rounds and two cards dealt face down to each player; the remaining cards are dealt face-up, as community cards.

Chapter 16

For Those Who Just Can't Bluff—Video Poker

In This Chapter

◆ What it's like to be obsessed with a machine

◆ How video poker machines work and why they're so popular

◆ Being a discriminating player and choosing your video poker machine carefully

◆ What strategies work best for the machines you're most likely to find

You might say I'm a "reformed" video poker junkie. My fascination started back in the '80s when I noticed blackjack dealers returning from their breaks all pumped up. I checked around and learned that they weren't sipping a new blend of coffee; they just couldn't wait to get back to video poker.

One day, while visiting my favorite casino, I noticed these new machines strategically installed at the casino bar. I also found out that if you purchased a roll of quarters from the bartender to play a machine, your drink(s) were free. So, while innocently sipping a free cup of coffee, I found out what a powerful grasp this seemingly innocuous game could have on an otherwise rational being. As I sat there playing, I grew less and less interested in what was going on at the blackjack tables and more and more committed to the royal flush and all the free drinks a few rolls of quarters could buy. I knew nothing about getting an edge at video poker; I just knew the game required some thinking, was fun and fast, and took my adrenaline to new levels! I didn't care what was happening to my bankroll (or my heart rate)—I was hooked!

Well, maybe I exaggerate—but I do like video poker, and I'm not alone. In this chapter, we'll explore America's attraction to this compelling game and share many of the secrets of winning that Stanford reveals in his book *Professional Video Poker*. You'll also find out what made me kick my habit and why I'm now very selective about the machines I play.

The Second Wave

While the oil embargo held us hostage in the '70s, Las Vegas fell on difficult times. Gas prices were high, the country entered a recession, many casinos changed hands, and fewer players came to Vegas. Maybe it's just coincidence, but at the same time, slot machines finally entered the information age, and a new wave of computer-controlled machines and video games was invented. Video blackjack was the first, but it was video poker that put Vegas back on the road to recovery. As word of the game spread, more and more casinos installed poker machines in just about every nook and cranny they could find. Soon everyone was playing video poker … and all was well again in Vegas.

What's the Attraction?

Video poker ingeniously combines the most intriguing aspects of luck, skill, psychology, and modern technology to give you hours of entertainment, stimulation, and, yes, isolation. In an age when you spend the majority of each working day proving your value to people who hold your future in the palms of their hands, the idea of parking yourself in front of a machine that has no expectations about your ability, behavior, the color of your skin, your mother's maiden name, whether you take cream with your coffee, or what time you showed up, has a certain appeal. In an Orwellian sense, it's a place where you can be alone without being lonely, take your brain out for a walk and make some meaningful decisions *all by yourself!*

The point is that the machine makes you focus and think. Unlike slots, video poker requires you to do more than just pull a handle to win, and people like that. Some of us do some of our best thinking alone in front of a machine. The rest … well, maybe they just like poker.

Five-Card Draw Some More

The majority of video poker games are based on five-card draw poker. In five-card draw, players are dealt five cards and can throw away any of them to try to improve their hands. New cards are dealt to replace the discarded ones, and the final five cards decide your fate. When playing the most popular video form of five-card draw, known as Jacks or Better, you win if your final hand has at least a pair of jacks or better (get it?). Jacks or Better was the original video poker game. Although there are now many more types, including Joker's Wild, Deuces Wild, Bonus Poker, and even Double Bonus Poker, we'll focus on Jacks or Better because it has the widest appeal and is the easiest to learn.

Instead of beating your opponent's hand or bluffing, as you do to win a "live" poker hand, in most of the video versions you win whenever you hold any of the five-card winning combinations listed in the hierarchy of winning hands (see the following table). In Jacks or Better, for example, you aren't paid for a pair of 10s or a pair of 2s, but you are paid for any hand higher than a pair of 10s, including a pair of jacks, queens, kings, or aces, and any two pairs of anything, right up the line to the most regal of hands, the royal flush. Video poker games often differ in terms of what the lowest-paying winning hand is and what it might pay, but you can find out by reading the *payout table* posted on the machine or the video screen. You can even press a Help button (on some of the multi-game video machines) to learn the rules of each particular game.

Best Bet

Video poker machines are so popular that many slot clubs comp video poker players as well. If you're an avid player, you can probably earn comp credits and collect your freebies while playing your favorite game.

Gamb-lingo

A **payout table** is somewhere on the front of every video poker machine or on the screen itself. It tells you what you win, which varies depending on the hand you win with and how many coins you bet.

The Hierarchy of Poker Hands (for Jacks or Better Video Poker)

Royal Flush	A, K, Q, J, and 10 all of the same suit.
Straight Flush	Five cards in sequence, and all of the same suit (such as Q, J, 10, 9, 8 of clubs).
Four of a Kind	Four cards of the same rank.
Full House	Three of a kind, plus a pair.

continues

The Hierarchy of Poker Hands (for Jacks or Better Video Poker) (continued)

Flush	Five cards of the same suit.
Straight	Five cards in sequence (ace can be high or low).
Three of a Kind	Three cards of the same rank.
Two Pair	Two cards of one rank and two cards of another rank.
Jacks or Better	A pair of jacks, queens, kings, or aces.

What Makes It Tick?

All video poker machines (and video gambling games in general) work on the same principles discussed in Chapters 5 and 6. (For a more detailed account, we suggest you review those chapters because many of the same "control yourself, this is a money-eating machine" principles apply here, as well.) Basically, a computer chip controls the video poker machine.

A computer program contains all five-card combinations that can be dealt from a 52-card deck, along with the odds of actually hitting each combination. It also contains the payoff schedule for each winning combination. Whether you win, and the amount you win, depends on how you play each hand.

When You've Played One, You've Played 'Em All

A typical video poker machine is about the same size as a regular slot machine and comes in a tabletop configuration or the standard desktop unit. Some of the newer models are wrapped in multi-game packages in which you're also likely to find a number of the latest video poker, blackjack, keno, and even slot games. You can find nickel, quarter, dollar, and even $5 video poker machines, and no matter which machine you play, it's basically the same. After you insert your money, either as a bill in the cash slot or as coins in the coin drop, you select the game you want, which in this case is Jacks or Better. If you inserted cash and are working off credits, press the **BET 1 CREDIT** or **MAX CREDITS** button to place your bet. (**MAX CREDITS** automatically wagers the maximum number of coins/credits the game allows.)

Best Bet

When you insert a bill into a cash/credit machine, make sure you get the proper amount of credits. Sometimes these machines mess up. Don't worry if there's a mistake. A slot mechanic or technician will spot it easily, retrieve the bill, and fix the machine. Just ask a change person to locate someone who is authorized to fix the machine.

After you make your bet, press the **DEAL** button. Once all five cards are dealt, some machines automatically tell you which cards to hold. If you want to get rid of a card that the computer suggests you hold (and you probably will once you get the hang of it), press the **HOLD** button under that card.

If your machine doesn't make a selection for you, consider yourself lucky and make your own selection. On most machines, you press the **HOLD** button under the cards you want to keep or tap the cards you want to keep on a multi-game touch screen. After you make your decision (and don't worry, we'll give you plenty of advice about that later), the word **Held** or **Hold** appears above the cards you want to keep, indicating that they will not be discarded with the rest of the trash you're throwing away.

Best Bet _____

Once in a while, you'll be dealt a five-card winning hand. Before you do *anything else*, press the **STAND** button to automatically hold all cards, or press the **HOLD** button under each card. Then, press **DEAL** again (as though you were drawing cards), and the win will register.

Now press the **DEAL** button again to get your replacement cards. If your replacement cards are good, you may hear bells and whistles, or maybe just see a small flash on the screen that tells you you're a winner and how much you've won. If you're working off credits, they will be added to the credit count. If you're into coins clanking, I hope it's a long and loud payoff! You can usually turn the coin-clanking off by switching to credit play, if your machine is so equipped. Just press the **CREDIT** button until it lights up. When you're ready to quit, press **CASH OUT** or **COLLECT** before the credits are gone.

If you didn't win, you'll probably see **Game Over** displayed on the screen, and, refusing to be beaten by some stupid machine, you'll do what many people are prone to ....

Bet You Didn't Know ...

People used to believe that video poker machines dealt five replacement cards at the same time they dealt your original five cards. When you discarded a card, the replacement was waiting behind it to be called into play. With the variety of machines on the market today, this is no longer always the case.

It really makes no difference which way your particular machine works. It's just that sometimes, as you sit there playing and realize that the first two replacement cards would have given you a royal had you discarded different cards, you can't help but wonder how these things work and whether the machine is really playing *you!*

Press the appropriate **BET** button (or drop in more coins) and do it again. Repeat this procedure approximately 40,000 times and you're likely to wind up with a royal (royal flush). Of course, there *are* no guarantees, and if you're not playing to win, a royal might not even get you ahead. We'll show you why next!

The *Big* Secret

It's hard for someone who's played as much video poker as I have to believe that professionals actually earn a living doing it. But they do, and although it may take a heavy bankroll to get the same results, there's a lot that recreational players can do to get an edge. According to Stanford, there are only two ways to win at video poker:

♦ Pick your machines *very* carefully.

♦ Use the basic strategy that we'll show you soon, and play max coins.

Make no mistake about it. You can get lucky sometimes, and you can enjoy yourself every time, but unless you play the right machines—the right way—you won't get even or win in the long run!

A Machine Worthy of Your Time and $$$

As we mentioned earlier, the payout table tells you how much you win for each winning hand, and it's usually posted at the top of older machines or on the video screen of the newer models. What we *didn't* tell you is that although you may be playing the same game (say, Jacks or Better) on different machines, the payout schedules could differ.

For instance, in some varieties of Jacks or Better, a one-coin full house pays you nine coins and a flush pays six coins. In other versions, the same one-coin full house pays only eight or six coins, and the flush might pay only six or five. The amount of money a machine pays off for each winning hand is how the casino controls the machine's *payout percentage*, which is the proportion of your money you can expect the machine to pay you back in the long run. (The rest feeds the house!)

The average payback for video poker is between 90 and 100+ percent, with proper play. Unfortunately,

Best Bet

Some nonprogressive poker machines pay out as much as you'll need to break even, and you can do well playing them in lieu of a high progressive. (For example, some 9/6 machines pay $5,000 for a one-coin royal flush.) The problem is that you probably won't find these machines in too many places—and when you do, you'll probably have to stand in line!

you won't even come close to those figures if you don't hit the royal flush because it, too, is calculated into the machine's overall payout percentage.

The only way you can expect to win at video poker is to hit the royal flush. To hit the royal, you have to be willing to play until you get it. You know from Chapters 5 and 6 on slots that there's really no way to predict when you will get a royal (which is the equivalent of a slot machine jackpot). However, you know from the poker chapter (Chapter 15) that a player can expect a royal flush approximately once in 40,000 hands. So, if you want to win, you have to be able to keep playing by feeding the machine from your pocket or by collecting more money from the intermediate hands that you *do* win. The following table will help you compare the most common video poker payout schedules.

Bet You Didn't Know ...

Many newer video poker machines have a Hi-Lo double-or-nothing feature that entices you to double your money after winning a hand. All you have to do is figure out whether a card selected from the deck will be a high card (9 or higher) or a low card (2 through 7). If you guess correctly, you double your winnings. If you guess wrong, you lose your winnings. After winning a Hi-Lo side bet, many machines ask if you want to do it again—as many as four more times. Now that's gambling! (If you don't want to play Hi-Lo, press the **TAKE SCORE** button after each win.)

As you can see, the payouts for all Jacks or Better machines (and most other video poker games, too) are the same *except* for the payout on a flush, full house, and royal flush. To spend less of your own money pursuing the royal, you have to play *only* the highest-paying machines you can find and avoid the lower-paying ones. The best machines, which are, of course, hard to find, are those that pay nine coins for a full house and six for a flush (appropriately referred to as a *9/6 machine*). The next best machines are the *8/5 machines*, especially if they offer a high *progressive jackpot*. (We'll get into the difference a progressive jackpot makes in a minute.) Avoid *6/5 machines* (which are more prevalent in Atlantic City and some Indian reservations than in Nevada casinos), unless the progressive jackpot more than makes up for the weaker payouts.

Gamb-lingo

A **flat-top** is a video machine (or slot machine) whose jackpot is always a fixed amount. A **progressive** is a machine whose jackpot keeps increasing each time a coin is played. When the jackpot finally hits, the jackpot goes back down to the starting number.

Video Poker Machine One-Coin Payouts

Hand	Payoff, by Type of Video Poker Machine			
	9/6–1,000	8/5–1,000	8/5–250	6/5–250
Royal Flush	1,000 coins	1,000 coins	250 coins	250 coins
Straight Flush	50	50	50	50
Four of a Kind	25	25	25	25
Full House	9	8	8	6
Flush	6	5	5	5
Straight	4	4	4	4
Three of a Kind	3	3	3	3
Two Pair	2	2	2	2
Pair, Jacks or Better	1	1	1	1
Payback percent:	100.07%	97.81%	96.06%	93.76%
Average losses between Royals				
1 quarter/hand	$244	$440	$440	$620
1 dollar/hand	$976	$1,760	$1,760	$2,480

How Big a Jackpot Do You Need?

The preceding chart also shows you that most *flat-top* video-poker payouts for a royal aren't big enough to pay you back the coins you're likely to play while waiting for the royal. (That's why *I* could never get ahead, even though I had my fair share of royals.) For example, a one-coin royal flush that pays only 250 quarters gets you $62.50. *However*, it can cost you $440 or more to hit the royal! (The casino averages $377.50 profit on your one-coin royal.) The most likely way to find a video poker machine worth playing is to find a 9/6, 8/5, or even 6/5 machine with a *large*, *progressive* jackpot.

Gamb-lingo

The **break-even point** is the point at which if you play forever, and play correctly, the coins you feed in will approximately equal the payoffs you'll receive.

A progressive jackpot can never get too big. In fact, most video poker progressives (and slots, too) start out too low and aren't worth playing until they've been fed long enough to get BIG. On the average, if you're playing an 8/5 progressive quarter machine (or even a flat-top), the *break-even point* is $2,200 because you must play five coins at a time to be eligible for the progressive jackpot. That means you have to be able to win at least $2,200 on a royal to get back in payoff what you expect to lose between royals.

After the progressive jackpot on a quarter video machine exceeds $2,200, you're actually playing at a slight advantage—if you use Stanford's video poker strategy, which we describe next. But you *must* load the machine up (play max coins, usually $1.25 per hand on a quarter machine) to win the progressive jackpot. If you don't play max coins, you won't be eligible for the higher jackpot and you won't have an edge at all. In short, a one-, two-, three-, or four-coin royal won't return the money you missed by not getting the progressive jackpot.

Bet You Didn't Know ...

Years ago, the Lady Luck casino in Las Vegas offered a large progressive jackpot that would be won by any player who played eight quarters and received a blackjack hand of ace, 2, 3, 4, and 5 of the same suit. When the jackpot on these machines reached $33,000, Stanford informed his newsletter readers that the jackpot was worth pursuing.

Many months passed, and the jackpot continued to grow. Stanford was in town when the jackpot passed $40,000 and decided to give the machines another try. Before finishing his second roll of quarters, he hit the ace, 2, 3, 4, and 5 of hearts and won $40,370! Unfortunately for the rest of us, he hasn't seen a progressive blackjack machine of this type since.

An 8/5 dollar machine requires you to play $5 per hand to win the progressive jackpot. On these machines you need a jackpot of at least $8,800 to break even. Any amount higher than that will give you an advantage as long as you continue to play max coins and proper strategy.

If you play a 6/5 machine, you need a large progressive jackpot to compensate for the lower payouts you'll be getting as you wait for the royal. You'll need a quarter jackpot of $3,100 and above, and on a dollar, you'll need at least $12,400 for the royal.

8/5 Machine Strategy

The professionals don't mess with machines that pay anything less than what we prescribed in the preceding section. If you just want to have fun and are willing to let the chips fall where they may, play any machine, but do yourself a favor and use Stanford's video poker strategies to make your playing decisions. They're the most profitable way to play each hand based on the type of machine and the level of the jackpot. (We include strategies for the 8/5 and 6/5 machines because they are the ones you're most likely to find.)

You can use the strategy in the following table with any 8/5 machine and the one in the following table for any 6/5 machine.

Strategy for 8/5 Video Poker Machines

# Cards To Hold	Best Cards Dealt	What Do I Do?
5	SF	Keep pat straight flush except draw to four cards of RF only for jackpots larger than $2,900.
4	RF	Draw one card.
5	flush	Keep flush unless four cards of RF (then draw one card).
3	three of a kind	Draw two cards.
5	straight	Keep.
4	ss Q-J-10-9	Draw one card.
3	RF	Draw two cards.
4	two pair	Draw one card.
4	SF	Draw one card.
2	high pair	Keep and draw three to full house.
4	flush	Draw one card.
4	K-Q-J-10	Draw one card.
2	low pair	Draw three cards.
4	Q-J-10-9	Draw one card.
4	J-10-9-8	Draw one card.
3	ss Q-J-9	Draw two cards.
2	ss HC-HC	Draw three cards. If choice of two suits, drop suit with an ace.
4	consec–no HC	Draw one card.
3	ss J-10-9	Draw two cards.
3	SF–1 gap, 1 HC	Draw two cards.
3	SF consec–no deuce	Draw two cards.
2	ss HC-10	Draw three cards.
4	ace-high straight	Draw one card.
3	K-Q-J	Draw two cards.

# Cards To Hold	Best Cards Dealt	What Do I Do?
2	HC-HC	Draw three cards. If ace-HC-HC, discard ace.
1	HC	Draw four cards.
3	SF	Draw two cards.

Key:
HC = high card (A, K, Q, or J only)
RF = royal flush
SF = straight flush
ss = same suit
consec = consecutive

6/5 Machine Strategy

Whenever you get the opportunity to play an 8/5 or 9/6 machine instead of a 6/5 machine, take it! Just in case your options are limited to 6/5 machines, however, and you still want to play, we've included the following table. Remember, play for the biggest progressive jackpots and load 'em up!

Strategy for 6/5 Video Poker Machines

# Cards To Hold	Best Cards Dealt	What Do I Do?
5	SF	Keep pat straight flush except draw to four cards of RF only for jackpots larger than $2,900.
4	RF	Draw one card.
5	flush	Keep flush unless four cards of RF (then draw one card).
3	three of a kind	Draw two cards.
5	straight	Keep.
4	ss Q-J-10-9	Draw one card.
3	RF	Draw two cards.
4	two pair	Draw one card.
4	SF	Draw one card.
2	high pair	Draw three cards.
4	flush	Draw one card.
4	K-Q-J-10	Draw one card.

continues

Strategy for 6/5 Video Poker Machines (continued)

# Cards To Hold	Best Cards Dealt	What Do I Do?
4	Q-J-10-9	Draw one card.
2	low pair	Draw three cards.
4	J-10-9-8	Draw one card.
2	ss HC-HC	Draw three cards. If choice of two suits, drop suit with an ace.
4	consec–no HC	Draw one card.
3	ss J-10-9	Draw two cards.
3	SF–1 gap 1 HC	Draw two cards.
3	SF consec–no deuce	Draw two cards.
2	ss HC-10	Draw three cards.
4	ace-high straight	Draw one card.
3	K-Q-J	Draw two cards.
2	HC-HC	Draw three cards. If ace-HC-HC, discard ace.
1	HC	Draw four cards.
3	SF	Draw two cards.

Key:
HC = high card (A, K, Q, or J only)
RF = royal flush
SF = straight flush
ss = same suit
consec = consecutive

Strategy for 8/5 and 6/5 Machines

Use the strategy in the preceding table for 8/5 machines and the strategy in the table above for 6/5 machines. First look at your hand and figure out what you have. Then, take the best potential hand and find it on the chart. For example, if you have three same-suit cards to a potential straight flush (SF) *and* a pair of high cards (such as 4-5-6-J-J where the 4-5-6 are all the same suit), first look for the three-card SF on the chart, and then look for the high pair. Notice that the high pair is listed higher, so it outranks the possible SF. That means you should hold the high pair and draw three cards because it has a higher average expected win than holding the three-card possible SF.

Best Bet

You can use almost any video poker game program to practice basic strategy on your home computer.

If you can't find anything from your hand on the chart, draw five cards. For example, with 3-4-6-7-8 of assorted suits, your best play is to draw five cards.

The chart takes a bit of getting used to, and that's why you should carry it with you when you play. (Stanford keeps a pocket-size one in his wallet at all times.) To make it easier for you to carry around, we've included a handy copy on the tear-out card in the front of the book (without the *What Do I Do?* column, which you'll need only when you practice at home). Copy it, cut it out, carry it with you.

Best Bet

Many casinos hold regular video poker tournaments. For those who enjoy playing (beginners included!), it's a good opportunity to practice the basic strategy, have a good time, and win some big tournament bucks. Entry fees are usually lower than you might spend playing max coins for an hour.

More Insider Information

Some "basic truths" about video poker strategy aren't included on the card because they're taken for granted. Here they are:

When it says *draw* on the strategy tables, it means hold the cards described in that row, and discard the other cards so that you can be dealt (*draw*) new cards. The new cards will combine with the held cards to make a winning hand—you hope.

Never draw to an inside straight, unless it's an ace-high straight. An inside straight is a sequence of cards missing a link in the middle. One example of an inside straight is 8-7-5-4. Another example is 5-4-3-A. Draw to an *outside* or *two-way* straight, such as 5-4-3-2, which is twice as likely to be successful.

Gamb-lingo

A potential straight that can be completed only one way is called an **inside straight**. A single high card (A, K, Q, J) that has the potential to turn into a winning pair is called a **kicker**.

Don't draw to three of a straight except for K-Q-J. (Don't hold three high cards of assorted ranks and suits unless the three cards are K-Q-J.) When you hold K-Q-J, you have two possible straights: ace-high and king-high. If you draw to A-K-Q, A-K-J, or A-Q-J, you can make only one possible straight. The difference is enough to justify discarding the ace, if you have one, whenever you start with three high cards of assorted ranks and suits.

Never **hold a kicker with any pair or with three of a kind.** A *kicker* is a single high card (not including the 10) that has the potential to turn into a winning pair. Of course, you should hold the pair and draw three new cards, or hold the three of a kind and draw two new cards. Hold just one card, a high card, when that's the best you can do with your hand.

Don't draw to three of a flush, unless it is a potential straight flush.

Variations on the Video Poker Theme

There are so many Video Poker variations available that it would probably be almost impossible (*and* very redundant) to cover them all in this book. Before you start playing a video poker game that's new to you take a few minutes to learn about the game. Look at the machine's pay table and read the Help screens if they are available. You'll find there are many subtle and not so subtle variations. In Jacks or Better, for example, you need a pair of Jacks or better to win. But in Joker Poker, you need a pair of Kings or better. In Deuces Wild, a pair doesn't win at all.

Playing Joker Poker

There's only one Joker in a 52 deck of cards and one potential Joker in each hand of Joker Poker video. When you get a Joker, don't throw it away! That single card can turn a weak hand into a winner. Unlike Jacks or Better, you need a pair of Kings or better to win. One King with a Joker qualifies as a winning pair. The following table shows you the payouts for the typical Joker Poker video machine.

One-Coin Payouts for 7/5 Joker Poker Machine

Hand	Payout
Royal Flush	800
Five of a Kind (Four with Joker)	200
Wild Royal Flush (with Joker)	100
Straight Flush	50
Four of a Kind	20
Full House	7
Flush	5
Straight	3
Three of a Kind	2
Two Pair	1
Kings or Better	1

The most important points to remember in this game are that the Joker is wild and you only get paid for a pair of Kings or Aces. (Jacks and Queens don't count here.) Here's a simple strategy:

◆ Always keep the Joker.

◆ Always keep a Royal Flush.

◆ Draw to four cards of anything except an inside straight (i.e. 3♣ ,4♣, 6♦, 7♠). Which means, draw to a Straight, Flush, Royal Flush or 5 of a Kind.

◆ Throw away a single Jack or Queen, but keep a single King or Ace.

Playing Deuces Wild

Deuces Wild is a video poker change of pace. In fact, I sometimes marvel at how little this game actually resembles traditional Video Poker. Don't bother looking for a 9/6, 8/5 or even 6/5 Deuces Wild machine. These pay tables don't match the traditional Video Poker pay tables simply because the deuces (twos) are wild, which means that whenever you are dealt a two in any suit it serves to fill in for whatever card you need to have a winning hand. If you are dealt a Ten ♥, Jack ♥, Queen ♥, Two ♦, Two ♣, you have a Royal Flush with Deuces. It doesn't pay as much as a real Royal Flush (no Deuces), but it does pay well. The following table shows you the payouts for a typical Deuces Wild machine.

One-Coin Payouts for Deuces Wild Machine

Hand	Payout
Royal Flush	800
4 Deuces (plus any card)	200
Wild Royal Flush (no Deuces)	25
Five of a Kind	15
Straight Flush	9
Four of a Kind	5
Full House	3
Flush	2
Straight	2
Three of a Kind	1

Once you get used to the fact that pairs don't pay in Deuces Wild, you'll find yourself throwing away more hands than you keep and starting with five new cards on the second deal. This simple strategy will save you some money:

- Hold 5 of a kind no matter how many deuces make up the hand.

- Don't touch a Royal Flush! Let the machine do its Royal gyration and wait patiently to get paid.

- Hold all of your deuces.

- Don't hold two pairs. Hold one pair and hope for a deuce or better on the draw.

- Don't hold single Jacks, Queens, Kings or Aces. Discard and hope for a better hand with deuces.

- Draw to an inside straight (i.e. 3♣ ,4♣, 6♦, 7♠). Because deuces are wild, you're more likely to get an inside straight.

The Least You Need to Know

- The only way to beat a video poker machine is to hit a high-paying Royal Flush.

- When playing a machine with a large progressive jackpot, always play MAX coins.

- *Never* hold a kicker (a single high card that has the potential to turn into a pair) unless you are drawing four cards.

- Don't draw to an inside straight unless it's an ace-high straight or you're playing Deuces Wild.

- If you don't find any cards worth holding from your hand on the chart, draw five cards.

- In Deuces Wild, you'll probably be throwing away more hands than you keep.

Chapter 17

Letting It Ride!

In This Chapter

- ◆ How to spot a Let It Ride table
- ◆ A basic strategy to keep you in the game
- ◆ Knowing when to "let it ride"
- ◆ Knowing if and when to put up the extra "bonus" dollar

What first attracted me to Let It Ride wasn't the throngs of carefree players, nor the victory song that blasted from the stereo speakers letting everyone within earshot know when someone won. For me, it was the sight of an empty table and a "no time to waste" shuffle machine standing idly by.

I sat down expecting to play a few fast hands of blackjack and found that I had stumbled upon a very different game indeed. Of course, the dealer coached me through a few hands before I marched off to breakfast—knowing full well that I'd be calling Stanford for his expert advice.

Since then, I've used the strategy that Stanford gave me and have been quite successful. We'll share that strategy with you in this chapter. For those of you who have been playing Let It Ride for years, we'll also explain the most recent changes in the bonus dollar game.

Born and Raised in Las Vegas

Let It Ride is a table game that was introduced by ShuffleMaster, Inc., in 1993. Shuffle-Master is a company that makes those contraptions that automatically shuffle a deck of cards while the dealer deals from another deck. I happen to like these machines—

Best Bet

Although the Let It Ride table accommodates seven players, it is more comfortable with only four or five. With fewer than four players, however, you lose some of the camaraderie and carnival atmosphere that quickly develops when the cards get hot!

they're quick, honest, and keep the game moving without *shuffle-interruptus*. Some people don't like them, for the same reasons. Whatever your feelings, I suspect we'll be seeing more and more ShuffleMaster machines sitting on card tables in the future. Let It Ride was probably born out of ShuffleMaster's desire to promote more fast-action, single-deck games, and they've certainly accomplished their mission with Let It Ride!

Let It Ride is based on five-card stud poker and is played with as many as seven players on a standard blackjack table, as shown next.

Each player is dealt three cards, and the remaining two cards are community cards that every player uses to complete his or her hand. The object of the game is to make a pair of 10s or better from the combination of your three cards and the two community cards. The poker hands are rated and paid according to the following table.

With the exception of the lowest winning hand, you'll see this chart is the same as the one in the poker and video poker chapters. In poker, any hand can be a winner, and in video poker, you usually need a pair of jacks or better to win. In Let It Ride, you're a winner with a pair of 10s or better. The excitement comes from knowing whether you have a good hand and whether to let your bet ride.

The Hierarchy of Poker Hands (for Let It Ride)

Royal Flush	A, K, Q, J, and 10 of the same suit.
Straight Flush	Five cards in sequence and all of the same suit (such as Q, J, 10, 9, 8 of clubs).
Four of a Kind	Four cards of the same rank.
Full House	Three of a kind, plus a pair.
Flush	Five cards of the same suit.
Straight	Five cards in sequence (ace can be high or low).
Three of a Kind	Three cards of the same rank.
Two Pair	Two cards of one rank and two cards of another rank.
10's or Better	A pair of 10s, jacks, queens, kings, or aces.

Playing Let It Ride

Unlike blackjack or poker, where your objective is to either beat the dealer or your opponent, Let It Ride has more camaraderie than competition because each player has an equal opportunity to win the hand based on the merits of the cards dealt to him or her.

To start the game, each player places equal bets in each of three betting circles before the cards are dealt. Although a $5 minimum requires each player to bet $15 per hand initially, you'll see that as the game progresses you have the option of reducing the amount down to only one betting unit per hand (which amounts to $5 at a $5 minimum table).

The use of the ShuffleMaster machine and the dealing of the Let It Ride cards is quite a ritual in itself. After players place their bets, the machine slides the newly shuffled cards down to the dealing tray, three cards at a time. The dealer places the first three-card stack face down in front of the first player's betting circles, the next stack in front of the second player's betting circles, and so on until each player has three face-down cards. The last three-card stack is dealt face down to the dealer. One of the dealer's three cards is placed in the discard tray, leaving two cards face down in front of the dealer; those cards will be the community cards.

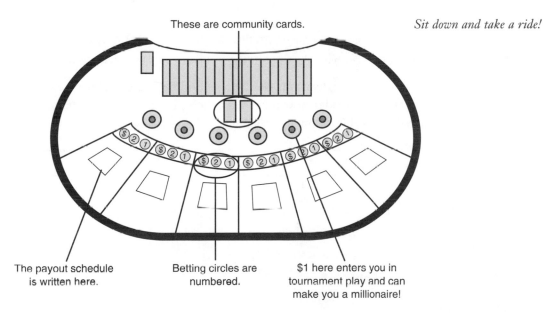

These are community cards.

Sit down and take a ride!

The payout schedule is written here.

Betting circles are numbered.

$1 here enters you in tournament play and can make you a millionaire!

When all 52 cards have been accounted for, the dealer picks up each player's stack of cards in turn, placing it on the player side of the betting circles; that's the all-clear signal for you to pick up your cards and smile. Now you look at your three cards and decide whether to pull back one of your bets. The dealer asks each player in turn whether he or she would like to take back the first bet or let it ride. When it's your turn to tell the dealer what you want to do (we'll give you advice later in the section "Riding Your Way to the Top"), do one of the following:

Best Bet

The ShuffleMaster people have introduced a video game version of their Let It Ride table game. The video game has become almost as popular as the table game, and the strategy you learn in this chapter will serve you well playing against the machine version.

◆ If you want to take back the first bet, indicate this by scratching the surface of the table toward you with your cards (like taking a hit in blackjack). The dealer will push this bet back to you. Do *not* try to remove the bet yourself! (The cameras will be watching you, and they *don't* like you touching or reaching over a bet once you have cards.)

◆ If you want to let your first bet ride, place your three cards face down under your first bet or in front of the betting circles.

After all the first betting decisions have been made, the dealer turns up the first community card. With four out of five cards revealed, you now have the opportunity to take back your second bet or "let it ride!" You *are* allowed to take back your second bet even if you let your first bet ride. Tell the dealer what you want to do, and then place your three cards face down under your chips in the third betting spot (which is labeled "$"). At this point, you have no further opportunities to take back a bet.

After all players have made their decisions on their second bets, the dealer reveals the second community card. The dealer now turns over each player's cards and pays all winning hands according to the following schedule:

Let It Ride Payout Schedule	
Royal Flush	1,000 to 1
Straight Flush	200 to 1
Four of a Kind	50 to 1
Full House	11 to 1
Flush	8 to 1
Straight	5 to 1
Three of a Kind	3 to 1
Two Pair	2 to 1
Pair of 10s or better	1 to 1

A player with a winning hand is paid for all bets riding in the betting circles. A full house with two bets riding, for example, is paid 11 to 1 on both bets. If a player had $10 riding on each of two betting circles, for example, the payoff would be $220 for the full house and the player would still have the original $20, too.

You can see that when luck is on your side, it's not too difficult to amass a small fortune quickly. To limit their losses, however, many casinos have imposed a $25,000 table limit on each Let It Ride game. That means if you let $15 ride on each of three betting circles and you catch a royal flush, you're paid only the $25,000 table limit, instead of the $45,000 you should be entitled to. (Of course, royal flushes are rare in a five-card game with no opportunity to draw—just one in 649,740.) To avoid unpleasant surprises, always ask about the maximum table limits before deciding how to place your bets.

In the unlucky event that you don't have a winning hand (a pair of 10s or higher), the dealer collects all the bets riding on your losing hand.

Best Bet _____

To make sure you get paid all that's coming to you if you're dealt a royal flush, divide the game's maximum payout by $3,000, and don't bet any more than this amount in each of your three betting circles. For a $25,000 maximum, this means holding your bets at $8-$8-$8 or less.

Riding Your Way to the Top

As we mentioned before, the strategy in this game involves knowing when to let your bets ride. You start out by placing bets in each of the three betting circles, and then you make two betting decisions:

◆ After seeing your first three cards, you must decide whether to let bet #1 ride (or not).

◆ After seeing the fourth card, you must decide whether to let bet #2 ride (or not).

You already saw how you can earn money quickly if you get good hands. But really good hands (like a flush or better) don't come very often, and there's no bluffing in this game. With that in mind, Stanley Ko, in his book _Mastering the_

Risky Business _____

Many people believe they can take their second bet back only if they took their first bet back. This is _wrong!_ If your hand isn't as good as it should be by the time the fourth card is revealed, take your second bet back regardless of what you did with the first bet. Your first and third bets _can_ remain in play while your second bet is removed.

Game of Let It Ride, has worked out a basic strategy to determine when to let your first bet ride and when to let your second bet ride. Here it is:

When to Let It Ride!

With Three Cards Known (Bet #1 Decision)	With Four Cards Known (Bet #2 Decision)
A paying hand already (a pair of 10s or better).	A paying hand already (a pair of 10s or better).
Three consecutive cards of the same suit (a possible open-ended straight) of 3-4-5 or higher. (Don't let the first bet ride with A-2-3 suited or 2-3-4 suited.)	A possible flush.
Three almost consecutive cards of the same suit with one hole and at least one high card (for example, 7-8-10 suited) smaller than *7-8-9-10* or with J-Q-K-A.	Four consecutive cards headed by 10, J, Q, or K. Don't let the second bet ride with a four-card straight unless you also have a possible flush. A, K, Q, J, and 10 of all the same suit.
Three almost consecutive cards of the same suit with two holes and at least two high cards (for example, 7-10-J).	

Times Have Changed: What an Extra Buck *Used* to Buy

It used to be that if you wagered an extra "bonus" buck on your Let It Ride hand and were lucky enough to win one of the top 100 hands played since the last tournament (about every 3 or 4 months) you'd be invited by the Let It Ride folks to participate in the next tournament. The Let It Ride tournament offered quite an incentive for players to wager the extra buck because each Grand Prize winner became an instant millionaire.

Unfortunately, times have changed, and the Let It Ride folks no longer sponsor the tournament—so your extra dollar won't pave your way to riches. To make up for the loss of incentive, however, the bonus payouts have been increased in the new game, which is now called Let It Ride Bonus, rather than Let It Ride: The Tournament.

The Good News Is ...

If you'd like to win bonus payouts, all you need to do is bet another dollar ($1) coin or chip in the extra *red* betting circle in front of you. The additional dollar will earn you extra money for winning hands—on the spot! You used to need a straight or better to be eligible for bonus payouts, but now you get paid for two pair or better. Although bonus payouts vary from casino to casino, and even table to table within a casino, a typical bonus payout schedule looks like this:

Let It Ride Bonus Payout Schedule	
Royal Flush	$20,000
Straight Flush	$2,000
Four of a Kind	$100
Full House	$75
Flush	$50
Straight	$25
Three of a Kind	$9
Two Pair	$6

The Fine Print

According to Stanley Ko, the casino's take (the house edge) in Let It Ride is about 3.5 percent of one bet, or 35 cents if you bet $10-$10-$10. The bonus payout that you get with the extra dollar returns approximately 45 cents of every dollar wagered, on average, depending on the bonus payout schedule. The bonus bet was never a good one to make, but now, without the possibility of winning the million-dollar tournament, it's worse than ever.

Let It Ride isn't a game in which you're likely to find yourself seated next to a professional, but it is a game you might want to play for a chance at a big score and a relatively small investment. If you're there to have fun, check it out!

Best Bet _____

When your hand looks bleak and you think you're going to lose, all is not entirely lost. Although you should always bet your hand according to the strategy in this chapter, it's possible that the dealer will turn up a high pair for the community cards, and then everybody wins!

Bet You Didn't Know ...

I've played Let It Ride many times to test the strategy we've presented here and have found it to be a fast-paced and enjoyable game. It keeps my interest without taxing my brain too much, and it offers an exciting alternative to mindless slot play, low-budget blackjack, and hard-driving video poker.

On two occasions, after losing almost my entire session bankroll, I miraculously brought myself back and left with more than I started with. In both cases I hit a flush, and in one session I got a straight. The large payouts definitely make the game worth playing—and worth sticking around for when luck seems to have taken a temporary siesta.

Unlike blackjack, you don't need to bet big to win big, or even to get your money back. Although I didn't put my extra dollar up because it's not good strategy, I might in the future, because in a few short hours I gave up about $150 worth of bonus payouts.

The Least You Need to Know

- Let It Ride is based on poker, but you don't play against the dealer or your opponents. Your goal is the same as everyone else's at the table: to get dealt a good poker hand.

- You are initially dealt three of your own cards, and you share two community cards that are turned up one at a time as the game progresses.

- You must start out with identical bets in each of three betting circles, but you can take two of the bets back.

- You can remove the first bet after seeing your first three cards.

- You can remove the second bet after seeing the fourth card, which is the first community card. You're allowed to take your second bet back even if you let your first bet ride.

- An extra $1 bet entitles you to receive an extra bonus payout in addition to the regular payout when you're dealt a two pair or better.

What Will They Think of Next? (Multiple Play Video Poker!)

In This Chapter

◆ How to multiply your video poker fun

◆ How to figure out how much you're betting when you play multi-play

◆ How to play different multi-play video poker games

One evening while wandering through a local casino on the way to dinner, I noticed a fellow gamer playing a new kind of video poker machine. It caught my eye because there were three, count them T-H-R-E-E, bright red Royal Flushes displayed on the screen, along with a $6,000 payout. What a beautiful sight! The machine was a fifty-cent Three Play Video Poker machine, and I was interested. In this chapter, I'll tell you what I found out about these new fangled machines, and what you need to know to play them.

What is Multiple Play Video Poker?

Multiple Play Video Poker machines enable you to play most of the old video poker games that you've come to know and love. But instead of playing just one game at a time, you play three, five, ten, fifty, or one hundred games (depending upon the machine) at the same time. Does it sound like overkill to you? Maybe. But I think it's genius! Genius because Action Gaming, the inventor of multiple play video poker, has found a simple way for you to spend more money playing a game they know you love, faster. The premise being that the more hands you play, the more you'll win. While that may or may not be true, it is an exciting and exhilarating concept.

Best Bet

When you play the Triple Double Bonus Triple Play machines both the Royal Flush and four Aces with a kicker (2,3,or 4) pay 4,000 credits. The Double Bonus Triple Play machines only pay 2,000 credits for four Aces with a kicker. So, if you like the Bonus games, look at the pay tables and try to find the ones that offer higher payouts.

Best Bet

Most multiple-play game payouts are based on the payouts of a Jacks or Better game but you should always look at a machine's payout table before deciding to play. Look for multi-play machines with full-house to flush payout ratios of 10/7, 9/6, or 8/5.

How Multi-Play Video Poker Games Work

In Multiple Play Video Poker you play three or more poker hands at the same time. Like regular Video Poker, each hand is played from one 52-card deck, draw cards are dealt from the same deck and the deck is shuffled at the end of each hand. A different deck is used for each of the multiple hands played in a multi-play game.

Playing Triple-Play

Triple-Play Video Poker is a good place to start learning about multi-play Video Poker because you only have to play three hands simultaneously rather than five, ten, fifty or more. Here's what a Triple Play machine looks like:

Unlike single play video poker where a maximum bet is 5 credits to play one hand, the maximum bet in Triple Play is 5 credits for each hand played, or 15 credits total. With that in mind, when you sit down at a Triple Play machine select the denomination of coin you want to play by touching the denomination circle on the screen.

Some machines offer a choice of \$.05, \$.10 and \$.25 games, other machines offer \$.25, \$.50 and \$1.00 games. High roller Triple Play machines offer \$1.00, \$2.00 and \$5.00 games.

Now, select the game you want to play. Most Triple Play machines provide a variety of at least six different Triple Play games. It may be a good idea when you're starting out to avoid the Bonus games and stick with plain Triple Play. Don't forget to check the payout tables on the game before you start playing so you know what to expect.

Gamb-lingo

In Video Poker a **kicker** is a low card, usually an Ace, 2, 3, or 4, that turns a winning hand into a higher paying hand in special bonus games.

After you've made your bet, press the Deal button and fifteen cards will be dealt: the top two rows of five cards will be face down and the bottom five cards will be dealt face up, like this:

⊠	⊠	⊠	⊠	⊠
⊠	⊠	⊠	⊠	⊠
A♠	3♦	Q♥	A♥	4♣

The machine will automatically suggest which cards to hold based on Jacks or Better rules, unless otherwise noted on the payout table. Our machine in this example has suggested we hold the pair of Aces and we see nothing wrong with that.

If you don't agree with the machine's suggestion you can change the Hold cards by tapping each card held on the bottom row of the screen, or pressing the corresponding Hold button on the front of the machine. This will release the Hold. To select a different Hold, just touch the screen or press the Hold button corresponding to the cards you want to keep. When you hold a card in the first row of cards, it automatically holds the same card in the other two rows.

After deciding which cards to hold, press the Draw button and a new set of draw cards will be dealt to each of the three hands. Since each of the hands is dealt from a different deck, you probably won't draw the same cards on all three rows. Although when it happens, it can be quite profitable!

A♠	J♣	6♣	A♥	3♣
A♠	A♦	3♦	A♥	A♣
A♠	A♦	Q♥	A♥	A♣

As you can see, we've just drawn a winner—four Aces on two rows and a pair of Aces on the third row. That's 255 credits (125 + 125 + 5)! Had we been playing a Bonus game rather than the standard Triple Play game, the kicker (3♦) in one of our four-of-a-kind hands would have paid a substantial bonus payout.

What to Bet

To get the maximum payout from a Multi-Play machine you have to load it up, which means betting five coins for each hand you play. On a fifty cent Triple Play machine, that comes to $2.50 per hand, or $7.50 for all three hands.

Bet You Didn't Know ...

There are many Multi-Play Video Poker games that offer extra payouts for special hands. For example, in Double Double Bonus Poker you are paid 1,000 credits and in Triple Double Bonus Poker 2,000 credits for four 2s with a "kicker". You're paid 2,000 credits in Double Double and 4,000 credits in Triple Double for four Aces with a "kicker" (that's what a Royal pays!) Always check your machine's payout schedule so that you know what the bonus hands are. When I'm playing a Triple Double machine, I throw away the second pair when I have two pairs and one of them is Aces. The two pair would pay 5 credits and a Full House would pay 45. But it's worth it to hold the Aces and go for the four of a kind for 4,000 credits. (High payouts are what we're looking for, and you can't beat 4,000 credits in this game—unless of course you're dealt four Aces for 12,000 credits. It pays to read the payout table and adjust your play accordingly.

If you play less than maximum coins on a multi-play machine the first five coins bet will apply only to the first hand dealt. The next five coins bet will apply to the second hand and the last five coins apply to the third hand. Playing 12 coins on a Three-Play machine will afford you the maximum payouts for the bottom and middle hands, but only a 2-coin payout for the top hand. If you don't load up the machine, hope that when you hit a Royal it's on the bottom line so that you win the full payout.

 Risky Business _____

When recklessly playing out the last few coins in a multi-play game rather than cashing out, I've hit the Royal Flush (more than once!). And though it's always nice to hit a Royal, 1,200 credits isn't nearly as rewarding as the 4,000 credits I would have received had I still been playing max bet. Please think of me the next time you're tempted to press the Deal button with only a few credits left in the machine and cash out instead!

Endless Variety

Most of the popular multi-play games listed below are based on regular Jacks or Better draw poker and are available on Triple, Five, Ten, Fifty, or One Hundred Play machines.

Multi-play machines are usually multi-denominational, which means they give you a choice of the denomination you'd like to play. You'll find Fifty Play and One Hundred Play machines that offer one cent, two cent, five cent and twenty five cent games and all varieties of Triple, Five, and Ten Play machines offering five cent all the way up to $5 games.

Beware before you sit down at a Multi-Play machine that it will cost a lot more than the denomination you chose to play a hand. To calculate how much, multiply the denomination by 5 for the cost of playing maximum bet on one hand. Then, multiply that result by the number of hands you are going to play.

To put it in perspective, betting two cents a game on a Fifty Play machine will cost you $5.00 per game to play maximum bet.

> The wager on one hand = $.02 × 5 = $.10
>
> The number of hands wagered = 50
>
> The cost of the maximum wager in two cent fifty play game = $5.00 (the wager multiplied by the number of hands)

Playing the same Fifty Play game on a one-dollar machine would cost a whopping $250 per hand:

> The wager on one hand = $1.00 × 5 = $5.00
>
> The number of hands wagered = 50
>
> The Cost of the Maximum wager in one dollar fifty play game = $250.00 (the wager multiplied by the number of hands)

For obvious reasons, most Fifty and One Hundred Play machines are of a lower denomination, like .01, .02, and .05.

These are the most popular Multi-Play video games available today:

- Multi-Play
- Bonus Play
- Bonus Deluxe Multiple Play
- Double Bonus
- Super Aces Bonus
- Double Double Bonus

- Triple Double Bonus
- Super Double Bonus Triple Pay
- Spin Poker
- Matrix Poker
- Fast Action Poker

- Chase the Royal
- Double Pay Poker
- Flex Play Poker
- Millionaire Triple Play

Bet You Didn't Know ...

Although the rules and strategy for playing Multi-Play Video Poker are the same as single play Jacks or Better, your break-even point for each hand differs. For example, in single play Jacks or Better one pair of Jacks or better returns your five-coin bet. Anything higher than that makes you a winner. In Triple Play you need three pairs of Jacks or Better (one pair in *each* of the three hands) to get your 15 credit bet back, or at least one 15 point 3-of-a-kind. In Fifty Play, because each max bet costs you 250 credits, you need a combination of winning hands that equal at least 250 credits, or one Straight Flush that pays 250 credits. In One Hundred Play you would need to accumulate 500 credits on a hand in order to win, so if all you got was one Straight Flush (which is unlikely out of 100 hands), you'd lose! Because you are wagering 500 credits when you play One Hundred Play, you need to hit a Royal Flush (4,000 credits) on 33.3 hands in order to get the same return that one Royal Flush on a Triple Play machine would pay.

Royal Chasers

Those of us who play Video Poker are in it for one thing—a Royal Flush! The folks at Action Gaming knew that when they brought out the "Chase the Royal" game, which is another Multi-Play Video Poker Game. The beauty of Chase the Royal is that it lets you go after Royals all day long. Here's how it works:

First, find a Chase the Royal machine that you like. They currently come in Triple, Five, and Ten Play varieties, but who knows, they'll probably introduce Fifty and One Hundred Play versions soon, too. When you place your maximum bet you play your hand according to regular Jacks or Better rules. But, if you've been dealt either a pair of Jacks, Queens, or Kings a special bonus screen appears giving you two choices:

- You can keep your original hand and be guaranteed to be paid five credits on the pair, or whatever hand you win on the draw, or
- You can choose to Chase the Royal!

If you should decide to Chase the Royal (and why wouldn't you if you're playing this game?) your original cards are discarded and you're dealt three new cards from a single-suit deck that only contains the Ten, Jack, Queen, King, Ace. That's a guaranteed Royal, right?

Wrong! The remaining two cards are drawn from a fresh 52 card deck for each hand played. (Heck, this is *gambling*, not heaven!).

Best Bet

There are many books available to help you become a serious Video Poker player. One that we recommend is *Video Poker—Optimum Play* by Dan Paymar.

After you've gotten over the initial shock of not getting your automatic Royal, you'll find that if you catch a Straight or Flush the payout is at least double what the payout would have been if you had drawn those cards without Chasing the Royal. And, there's always the possibility that you will catch the Royal, which pays out the usual 4,000 credits per hand. Because this game is totally Royal-centric, Action Gaming assures us that the game pays out four times more Royal Flushes than a standard Video Poker machine.

Double Pay, Olay!

There's nothing wrong with getting paid, is there? That's what Double Pay Multi-Play is all about. First you get paid for any winning hands you draw on the initial deal. For example, if you're dealt a pair of Queens, you are paid for the pair even before the draw cards are dealt. Then, you get paid again for whatever winning combination you wind up with on the final draw.

And, Double Pay *also* gives you the option of playing a Double or Nothing bonus round after winning hands. When you elect to play the bonus round the screen changes and you play high card against the imaginary dealer. One card is dealt face up to the dealer, and four cards are dealt face down to you. You have to choose one of the face down cards and hope it beats the dealer's. If it doesn't, you loose what you just won on your winning hand. If it does, you win double the amount of your previous winning hand, and the chance to play Double or Nothing again!

Spinning the Poker

Spin Poker is a cross between a Triple-Play Video Poker game and a multi-line video slot machine. Instead of betting 5 credits for each hand played as you would in Triple Play, you bet lines for each hand as you would in multi-line slots.

There are three poker hands played in Spin Poker and nine lines to play, so each Poker hand gets three lines. You don't have to activate all nine lines but if you don't you won't get the maximum payout. (It's very important to read the payout tables on this game!)

When you press the Deal button, the first hand is dealt on the center line and the other two hands are dealt above and below it. Whatever cards you hold in the first hand are also held in the other hands. The fun starts when you press the Draw button for your final cards. Pressing the Draw button sets the rows of discard cards spinning like a slot machine. You don't know what your final hand is until they stop!

The rules and strategy for Spin Poker are the same as regular Triple Play Video Poker. It's the anticipation of the final draw that will have you sitting on the edge of your seat!

Matrix Poker

You may have seen the movie *The Matrix*, and you may have once been a product of "matrix" management. Now there's Matrix Poker, another multi-play Video Poker marvel that thinks it's a slot machine.

The easiest way to imagine this game is to think of it as a modified Ten Play game that lets you win on horizontal rows of cards (like a regular Five Play game) and vertical rows, too (which are the other five plays that make it like a Ten Play game).

Like a multi-line video slot machine, you decide how many lines you want to play. You can play from 1 to 10 lines at a cost of 5 credits per line. So, like a Ten Play machine, the maximum bet costs 50 credits. When you press Deal, five cards are dealt in the bottom hand, row #1. The cards you decide to hold will also be held in the other ten hands. But because we've now got poker hands running up and down and left and right across the screen, the hold cards are scattered all over the place!

Fortunately, when you press the Draw button the machine automatically calculates your winning hands. You'll probably need a few minutes to figure out which hands won, and why, but at least it will make more sense than the multi-line slot machine wins. Good luck with your Matrix play!

What the Future Holds

It's hard to imagine that they haven't already thought of everything as far as Video Poker is concerned. But, as technology evolves and our appetite for Royals shows no sign of letting up, you can be sure there will always be better games!

Perhaps we'll be enticed with fully reclining leather seats and a remote control game pad to hold in our hand so we don't wear out our fingers and wrists pressing the buttons. Perhaps they'll provide magnifying lenses that will enable us to see 500 hands played at a time, or 1,000, or more! Perhaps they'll open up a casino that will let me pay $50 dollars to play all of the latest and greatest video poker games I want to play all night long! I can dream can't I?

The Least You Need To Know

- Multiple-play video poker costs more money to play than standard video poker, but you can win more money, too.

- Always check your denomination of play, look at the pay table schedule and figure out how much it will cost you to play maximum bet before you put your money in.

- There are currently five basic multiple-play machines; Triple Play, Five Play, Ten Play, Fifty Play, and One Hundred Play. There are many different versions of video poker you can play on each, such as variations of Jacks or Better, Deuces Wild, etc.

- Play most multiple-play video poker machines according to Jacks or Better strategy. However, if there are extra bonuses paid for specific combinations, such as four Aces, vary your play accordingly by going after the bonus combinations.

Chapter

19

How Now Pai Gow?

In This Chapter

- ◆ How do you say "pai gow" and how do you play the game?
- ◆ How to know who wins
- ◆ The best strategy to use when starting out

Pai gow poker is growing in popularity as more and more people learn to play. Although the game has been around for years, people are starting to see it played in casinos and card rooms everywhere—and they seem to like what they see! The game attracts a sociable crowd who enjoy interacting with other players at their table. Everyone's success depends on the outcome of the banker's hand so there's a natural "us against them" spirit. And, unlike blackjack, there's never any reason to debate whether you would have won if only the guy on the end played the way you do!

In his book *Optimal Strategy for Pai Gow Poker*, Stanford explains how to win. We'll share some of his secrets with you in this chapter.

What *Is* Pai Gow Poker?

Pai gow (which rhymes with *pie now*) poker is a card game played with 53 cards: a standard 52-card deck plus one joker. It's rumored that this ingenious game is a combination of American poker and the Chinese domino game of pai gow invented by the Chinese laborers who built our railroads in the late 1800s.

In pai gow poker, players wager against a *banker*. The players and banker are each dealt seven cards, which they skillfully separate, or *set*, into two hands of five and two cards. The object of the game is to beat the banker's five-card hand with your five-card hand and also beat the banker's two-card hand with your two-card hand.

Gamb-lingo

A card game **banker** is a player who books the action of the other bettors at the table. For the banker in pai gow poker to win money, the banker's five-card hand must beat or copy the player's five-card hand, and the banker's two-card hand must beat or copy the player's two-card hand.

When pai gow poker is played in card rooms, players take turns banking the game with their own money. When played in a casino, the house is usually the bank and the dealer is the banker, although players can bank a game, if they want.

Like other poker games played in casinos and card rooms, the house makes its money in one of two ways: by taking 5 percent out of each winning pai gow poker bet, or by taking a flat fee from each bet.

It Takes Two Hands to Win

To win, your five-card hand must have a higher poker ranking than the banker's five-card hand, *and* your two-card hand must also have a higher poker ranking than the banker's two-card hand.

If your two-card hand and the banker's two-card hand have equal poker value, they are said to be *copies*. Your five-card hand can also be a copy of the banker's five-card hand if they have equal poker value, but it's less likely. The banker wins copies (which gives the banker an advantage). If your five-card hand has equal or lower ranking than the banker's five-card hand, and your two-card hand has equal or lower ranking than the banker's two-card hand, you lose.

Gamb-lingo

A **copy** is when a player and the banker have the same two-card hand or the same five-card hand. Copies go to the banker, giving him or her a natural advantage over the player.

If your two-card hand beats the banker's two-card hand but the banker's five-card hand beats your five-card hand, you have a *tie* and no money changes hands. If your five-card hand beats the banker's five-card hand but the banker's two-card hand beats your two-card hand, you also have a tie, and no money changes hands.

How to Play the Game

Pai gow poker is played with one to six players and a banker. The players and banker are usually seated around a special pai gow poker table, shown here.

The minimum and maximum betting limits for players for each pai gow hand are posted at the pai gow table. The amount of money the banker risks is limited to what the banker places on the table; the banker is not required to dig into a wallet or purse for additional money after the cards have been dealt. The banker may be expected to place enough money on the table to cover all the players' bets, or the banker might be allowed to risk less. After all 53 cards are well shuffled, the dealer deals seven stacks of seven cards each. The banker then rolls dice from a teacup to determine which player gets the first stack of cards. All bets must be placed before the banker rolls the dice.

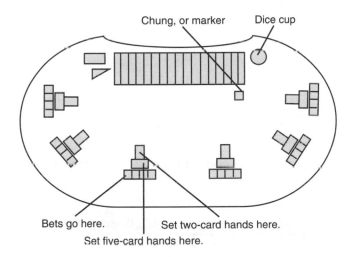

Chung, or marker   Dice cup

A pai gow poker table setting.

Bets go here.   Set two-card hands here.

Set five-card hands here.

After the players get their cards, they *set* the cards into two separate hands of five and two cards. (The banker's cards remain face down.) The two-card hand is called the *low hand*, and the five-card hand is called the *high hand*. Each five-card hand is ranked according to the pai gow poker hierarchy shown in the following table. This hierarchy varies from the standard poker hierarchy in that five aces (four aces and the joker) beats a royal flush. (We'll tell you more later about how the joker can be used.) Also, some house rules say that the A-2-3-4-5 is the second-highest straight instead of the lowest straight.

The two-card hand is either a pair or no pair. The highest two-card hand is a pair of aces. Hands are ranked according to the standard poker ranking of ace (A), king (K), queen (Q), jack (J), 10, 9, 8, 7, 6, 5, 4, 3, 2. Each suit (spades, clubs, hearts, and diamonds) is of equal rank.

In setting the hands, players take care not to show their cards to the banker. They must be sure that the five-card hand has a higher poker ranking than the two-card hand. If the two-card hand turns out to be higher, the hand is *foul* and is an automatic loser. An example of a foul hand is a K-K for the two-card hand and an A-Q-7-6-5 of assorted suits for the five-card hand. Because there is no pair or better in the five-card hand, the two-card hand in this example is ranked higher. Had the pair of kings been played as part of the five-card hand, the hand would not have been foul.

The Hierarchy of Pai Gow Poker Hands

Five Aces	Four aces plus the joker.
Royal Flush	A, K, Q, J, and 10 all of the same suit.
Straight Flush	Five cards in a row, all of the same suit (such as Q, J, 10, 9, 8 of clubs). Ace can be high or low.
Four of a Kind	Four cards of the same rank, plus an additional card that doesn't matter.
Full House	Three cards of one rank plus another two cards of a different rank.
Flush	Any five cards of the same suit, in any order.
Straight	Any five cards in a row. Ace can be high or low.
Three of a Kind	Three cards of the same rank, plus two additional cards.
Two Pair	Two cards of one rank and two cards of another rank, plus an additional card.
One Pair	Two cards of the same rank and three additional cards.
No Pair	All five cards of different ranks and not all of one suit.

Risky Business

A pai gow poker player skillfully **sets** seven cards into two separate hands of two and five cards. A pai gow poker hand is **foul** when the hands have the wrong number of cards or the two-card low hand has higher poker value than the five-card high hand. A foul hand is a losing hand.

The banker cards are kept face down until all player hands are set. Each player hand plays against the banker only, not against other players. After every player has set his or her hands, the dealer turns up the banker's cards. The banker's cards are then arranged into a two-card hand and a five-card hand, with the five-card hand having a higher poker value. The banker, not the dealer, decides how to set the banker's hands.

Next, the banker hands are compared to each player's hands, one player at a time, starting with the player who received cards first and going clockwise around the table. If a player wins (player's five-card hand beats banker's five-card hand, and player's two-card hand beats banker's two-card hand), the dealer uses the banker's money to pay the player even money. If the player's hand loses (banker's five-card hand beats or copies the player's five-card hand, and banker's two-card hand beats or copies the player's two-card hand), the dealer awards the player's bet to the banker. In a casino or card room in which the 5 percent commission is taken from each winning hand, the dealer takes the commission from each winning player hand and from the aggregate win of the banker, if any.

Best Bet

Flushes and straights are easy to overlook. So, when picking up your seven-card hand, look for a straight and look for a flush before looking for cards of the same rank.

The Joker

The *joker* serves as a *wild card* in straights, flushes, and straight flushes. You can also use it as an ace. In some casinos or card rooms, the joker can be used to fill in any hand.

Get Ready, Get "Set"

To win, you need to set your high and low hands properly. With the exception of two-pair hands, most hands can be set with minimum thought, according to the ranking of cards and hands and the basic pai gow poker strategy guidelines shown in the following table.

Setting a two-pair hand is sometimes a more difficult decision to make, but it's a very important one because the hand occurs so frequently, and because how you set your hand can make a big difference in the outcome. Whether the lower of the two pair should be played as the two-card hand depends primarily on the highest *singleton*; the higher the singleton, the more likely both pairs should be played as part of the five-card hand. A high singleton can sometimes be enough to turn a two-card hand into a winner. The general advice included on the

Gamb-lingo

A **joker** is often referred to as a **wild card** because it can be used as an ace or to fill a straight, flush, or straight flush.

Gamb-lingo

A card that is the only one of its rank is called a **singleton**.

chart is to keep the two pair in the five-card hand if one of the singletons is an ace. If none of the singletons are high cards, consider playing the lower pair in the two-card hand.

(See Stanford's book *Optimal Strategy for Pai Gow Poker* for precise advice on playing every possible hand.)

Basic Pai Gow Poker Strategy

If You Hold	Play Your Hand This Way
No Pairs No Straight No Flush	**Two-card hand:** Use your second and third highest cards. **Five-card hand:** Use your highest card.
A Pair No Straight No Flush	**Two-card hand:** Use your two highest singletons. **Five-card hand:** Use the pair.
Two Pair	If you have a singleton ace, use the ace in the two-card hand and keep the pairs together in the five-card hand. If you do not have a singleton ace, split the pairs as follows: **Two-card hand:** Use the lower pair. **Five-card hand:** Use the higher pair.
Three Pair	**Two-card hand:** Use the highest pair. **Five-card hand:** Use the second and third highest pairs.
Straight *and* Two Pair	Play as two pair, ignoring the straight.
Five-card Straight	**Two-card hand:** Use the two cards not in the straight. **Five-card hand:** Play it straight.
Six-card Straight	**Two-card hand:** Use the two highest cards that you can, subject to keeping a straight. **Five-card hand:** Use the remaining straight.
Flush *and* Two Pair	Play as two pair, ignoring the flush.

If You Hold	Play Your Hand This Way
Other Flush	**Two-card hand:** Play the highest cards in this hand, but don't break up the flush.
	Five-card hand: Play as a flush.
Full House	**Two-card hand:** Use the pair.
	Five-card hand: Use the three of a kind.

Why It Pays to Be a Banker

Because the banker wins all copies, the best way for a player to get an edge in pai gow poker is to be the banker. In casinos, the house (or dealer) banks first. Then the banker position moves from player to player around the table, changing after every hand or every other hand. If the first player doesn't want to bank, the next player is given the opportunity. A marker, or *chung*, is set in front of the banker's betting area. If no one wants to bank, the house continues to bank until a player asks to bank again or a new player/banker enters the game. When a player rather than the house dealer is the banker, the dealer places a bet and plays a hand as a player.

In casinos, to be a banker you must be willing to cover the bets of all players at the table from your own bankroll. If you can't cover all bets, you can't be the banker, which is probably why most people don't want to bank. This is not always the case in card rooms, where people can often split the banker position with others who are willing to bank only part of the amounts being wagered.

Generally, you can bank for only one or two hands before relinquishing the bank to someone else. If you want to get an edge, you should bank as much as possible and play as small as you can get away with when it's your turn to be a player. To break even when the house takes a commission of 5 percent of all winning bets, you need to bank 6 to 14 times as many dollars as you bet when you are a player. The exact break-even point depends on how skillful you are at setting hands compared to your opponents. An example of a break-even situation is when you are given the opportunity to be banker every other hand, the minimum bet is $10, and your opponents are betting a total in the range of $60 to $140. If your opponents are betting more than that, you will have a slight edge as the banker.

The Least You Need to Know

◆ In pai gow poker, the joker is generally used for aces, straights, and flushes, but in some casinos, it is completely wild. Always ask before you start playing.

◆ Five aces is the highest hand, followed by the royal flush and the rest of the basic hierarchy for poker.

◆ To win, you have to beat both of the banker's hands with both of your hands. Bankers win copies. Winning one hand and losing the other is a tie, and no money changes hands.

◆ The basic strategy for setting a pai gow hand is easy. Always check your hand for straights and flushes first, and then set your hand according to the strategy rules.

◆ Your best opportunity to win in pai gow poker is to be the banker. To be the banker, you should be willing to risk enough money to cover 6 to 14 times the table's minimum bet.

Chapter 20

Caribbean Stud–The Tropical Storm That's Sweeping the Country!

In This Chapter

◆ What's so hot about Caribbean Stud?

◆ How does a dealer get "qualified"?

◆ The best strategy to use when starting out

Caribbean Stud is a relatively new game on the American casino scene. So new, in fact, that when the first *The Complete Idiot's Guide to Gambling Like a Pro* was released, I hadn't played it yet. Now that I've tried it and liked what I've seen, we've decided to help you avoid some of the mistakes I made. In this chapter, we'll explain the rules of the game and some of the basic strategy that Stanford says works better than the one I was playing.

A Hot New Game

Transplanted from the shores of the Caribbean islands to America's favorite casinos, Caribbean Stud has been sweeping the country like a tropical storm. It's like Let It Ride in many ways. You play this game in the main casino, not a poker room; you bet against the dealer instead of the other players at your table; and there are bonus pay-outs for winning hands. But that's where the similarity ends. If you try to apply the Let It Ride strategy to this game, you're bound to lose!

Unlike Let It Ride, you can't take your bet back in Caribbean Stud. Instead, like seven-card stud, you can increase your bet when you think you have a winning hand. If you do have a winning hand, however, you're eligible for a "bonus payout" only when the dealer's hand is good enough to qualify (we'll explain this later).

Sound complicated? It is, kind of. But the huge progressive jackpot makes it all seem worthwhile. If you happen to hold a royal flush (the odds are about one in 650,000) and you've put your extra dollar up to play the progressive, you can win anywhere from $5,000 to whatever the progressive meter above the table flashes when the hand is played. Depending on where you play and how many Caribbean Stud tables are linked in the progressive pool, that can amount to hundreds of thousands of dollars!

The Geography

Caribbean Stud, based on five-card stud poker, is played with as many as six or seven players, depending on the size and layout of the table. As you can see, in front of each player there is a betting circle, an *ante box*, and a place to make an extra wager on the progressive jackpot.

Gamb-lingo

In Caribbean Stud, players must **ante** to start the game. The amount they wager in the **ante box** must match or exceed the table minimum.

The first of three marked betting spots in front of each player on a Caribbean Stud table is called the betting circle. You do not have to bet in the betting circle, but when you do, it must be double the amount of money in the *ante*.

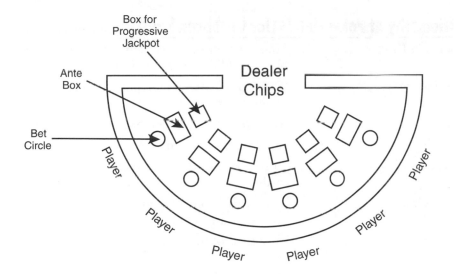

How to Play

The game starts when players place their opening wagers in the ante box (in the middle) in front of their seats. The ante amount to get the game started is usually $5, although during off-hours you may be able to find a game with a lower minimum. While anteing up, you should decide whether you want to get in on the progressive jackpot. If you do, place one dollar (some casinos charge more) in the progressive jackpot slot.

After everyone has anted up, the dealer locks the progressive wagers and starts the game.

Out of a standard 52-card deck, each player is dealt five cards face down. The dealer also gets five cards, but one card is face-up. After looking at their cards, players decide whether to stay in the game. Players judge the quality of their hands based on the hierarchy of Caribbean Stud hands shown in the following table and the dealer's up card. An ace-king combination is the lowest ranking hand that counts as anything in Caribbean Stud. The rest of the rankings are the same as in regular poker.

The Hierarchy of Poker Hands (for Caribbean Stud)

Royal Flush	A, K, Q, J, and 10 all of the same suit.
Straight Flush	Five cards in any sequence, all of the same suit (such as Q, J, 10, 9, 8 of clubs).

continues

The Hierarchy of Poker Hands (for Caribbean Stud)   (continued)

Four of a Kind	Four cards of the same rank, one in each suit, plus an additional card that doesn't matter.
Full House	Three cards of one rank plus another two cards of another rank.
Flush	Any five cards of the same suit, in any order.
Straight	Any five cards in sequence.
Three of a Kind	Three cards of the same rank, plus two additional cards.
Two Pair	Two cards of one rank and two cards of another rank, plus an additional card.
One Pair	Two cards of the same rank and three additional cards.
Ace-King Hand	One ace and one king of any suit.

If a player has a hand he or she thinks is strong enough to beat the dealer's hand, the player *calls* by placing double the ante bet in the betting circle. The additional bet pays according to a bonus payout schedule that's based on the hierarchy of winning hands. Players who don't have any of the winning Caribbean Stud hands should *fold* by placing their cards face down in front of them. When a player folds, he or she loses his or her ante bet and is out of that hand.

Best Bet

Wait for all the cards to be dealt before picking up your cards. Then wait for the dealer to tell everyone it's okay to pick up their hands.

After the betting round is over, the dealer turns all of his or her cards face up.

Is Your Dealer Qualified?

The quality of the dealer's hand determines whether players holding stronger hands will earn bonus payouts. The dealer needs to hold at least an ace of any suit and a king of any suit, or a higher ranking hand, for the round to qualify for bonus payouts.

If the dealer's hand is *qualified* (holds an ace and a king, or higher):

◆ The player either wins or loses both the ante bet and call bet, depending on the strength of his or her hand. The player's hand must beat the dealer's hand, according to the hierarchy of winning hands, for the player to be paid.

◆ If the player's hand beats the dealer's hand, the player is paid even money for his or her ante bet; for the call bet, he or she is paid according to the rank of his or her hand and the bonus payout schedule posted on the table (see the following section).

◆ If the dealer's hand wins, the player loses both his or her ante bet and call bet.

Gamb-lingo

When a Caribbean Stud player places an additional bet after seeing his or her cards, he or she **calls** the previous bet.

When a player does not have a strong hand, he or she can **fold** by turning his or her cards in.

If the dealer's hand is *not qualified*:

◆ Every player who stayed in the game wins his or her ante bet. The bet pays even money, or 1 to 1. Players who folded in the betting round forfeited their ante and are not paid.

◆ All call bets are returned to the players.

The Bonus Payout Schedule

If the dealer holds a qualified hand but your hand is better, your call bet is paid according to the Caribbean Stud bonus payout schedule.

Hand	Payout
Royal Flush	100 to 1
Straight Flush	50 to 1
Four of a Kind	20 to 1
Full House	7 to 1
Flush	5 to 1
Straight	4 to 1
Three of a Kind	3 to 1
Two Pair	2 to 1
One Pair	1 to 1

Here's how it works: If you made a $5 ante bet and were dealt a flush, you would call by placing double the ante bet, or $10, in the betting circle. When your hand beat the dealer's qualified pair of eights, you would be paid $55: $5 even money on the ante bet plus $50 on the call bet, which pays 5 to 1 for a flush. If the dealer didn't have a pair, or even an ace and a king of any suit, his or her hand wouldn't be qualified and you would have won only $5 for your ante bet. Quite a disappointment!

Like Let It Ride, Caribbean Stud tables often limit the amount the casino pays on the bonus payout. You should adjust your betting strategy accordingly. Divide the maximum table limit by 100 and don't wager more than that amount on your call bets. Your ante bet will be one half of that amount. So, if the maximum payout for the table is $5,000, the most you should wager is $50 to call (5,000 ÷ 100) and $25 to ante (50 × ½).

Not Really Better Than Nothing!

Imagine how frustrating it would be to not get paid when you're dealt a straight or a flush, or worse yet—the big one! Well, that's exactly what happens in Caribbean Stud when the dealer's hand doesn't qualify. You don't receive bonus payouts no matter how good your hand is when the dealer's hand doesn't pass the A-K minimum test.

However, if you'd put your dollar up to play the progressive jackpot at the beginning of the hand, your flush would get paid out of the progressive pool. The progressive jackpot pool pays additional sums for those who have wagered their extra dollar and are dealt a flush or better. It doesn't matter whether your hand beat the dealer's hand or whether the dealer's hand even qualified. If you wager your dollar on the progressive payout and receive a flush or better, you will be paid out of the progressive jackpot pool. Although it varies from casino to casino, the typical progressive jackpot pay schedule looks like this:

Best Bet

When you wager your extra dollar for the progressive bet, always make sure the dealer pays you for a flush or better even if his or her hand beat yours.

Hand	Payout
Royal Flush	100% of jackpot
Straight Flush	10% of jackpot
Four of a Kind	$100
Full House	$75
Flush	$50

Risky Business _____

In the unlikely event that you get a straight flush or royal flush at the same time as someone else at your table, you'll have to split the 10 percent or 100 percent progressive payout. That's because the progressive pool is an aggregate total, which means that's the most the casino will pay off on a single deal.

The Only Reason to Bet the Progressive

The extra dollar you bet on the progressive jackpot is not a very good bet to make. It can't really ease your pain, as I suggested earlier, because the extra dollar per hand adds up when you play long enough to hit the Big One. So, it increases the amount of money you need to win to break even.

Most people who make the extra wager on the progressive jackpot do so because it's fun and it gives them a shot at winning tens or even hundreds of thousands of dollars—kind of like the lottery!

If you do bet the extra $1, keep in mind that the progressive payoff will be the same (either a fixed dollar amount or a percentage of the jackpot) whether you bet $15 or $150 on a hand. Don't bother increasing your bet so that you can get a bigger progressive payoff.

At times like this, it's good to bet the extra dollar!

(Photo courtesy of Brian Spector)

Some Sound Advice

There's no doubt Caribbean Stud is fun, but it's still a negative-expectation game, which means that in the long run, you're more likely to lose than win.

That said, here's some simple basic strategy that can help you stay at the table and enjoy the game a little longer:

♦ Look for Caribbean Stud tables where the jackpot has reached $200,000 or more.

♦ Play in casinos where the progressive payout schedule pays more for a flush, full house, and four of a kind.

♦ Make the call bet whenever you hold a pair or higher in your hand.

♦ If your best cards are an ace-king combination, place the call bet if you also hold a jack or a queen. Otherwise, you should probably fold, especially if the dealer's up card is an ace or a king.

The Least You Need to Know

♦ Caribbean Stud is based on poker, but you play at a special table in the main casino and you bet against the dealer's hand instead of other players.

♦ The object of Caribbean Stud is to have a higher ranking poker hand than the dealer's hand.

♦ The dealer must have at least an ace and a king or any other ranking poker hand to qualify. If the dealer's hand doesn't qualify, players win their ante bets but their call bets are returned to them, no matter what hand they hold. If the dealer's hand qualifies, players have to beat the dealer's hand to win even money on the ante bet and to be paid according to the bonus payout schedule on the call bet.

♦ The progressive jackpot pays *big* money, but it's not really a good bet!

Chapter 21

Two Fast and Easy Poker Games—3 Card Poker and WAR

In This Chapter

- ◆ How to play poker with only three cards
- ◆ Betting against the dealer vs. betting on yourself
- ◆ What means WAR in a casino

Are you a video poker player looking for an easy-to-learn table game to play while your favorite poker machines are occupied? If that sounds like you, you'll probably enjoy either of these fast-paced poker variations: Three Card Poker and War. There are no complicated rules and strategies to learn so you're almost an expert already!

Three Card Poker

Although Three Card Poker is played with fewer cards than most poker games (three vs. five), it gives you more playing options. There are three ways to bet:

- ◆ Bet that your hand will beat the dealer's hand, and raise your bet if your cards are good—just like in a real poker game.

◆ Bet that your hand will contain at least a pair or better.

◆ Bet that your hand will contain a pair or better *and* beat the dealer's hand.

In Three Card Poker, each three-card hand is rated based on the standard poker ranking: Ace, King, Queen, Jack, ten, and so on. If player and dealer both have a pair, straight, or flush, the high card hand wins. The following table shows you how three card poker hands are ranked.

The Hierarchy of Three Card Poker Hands

Royal Flush	Sorry! Since you only get three cards, you can't get a Royal Flush in this game.
Straight Flush	Three consecutive cards of the same rank.
Flush	Three cards of the same suit.
Straight	Three cards in sequence.
Three of a Kind	Three cards of the same rank.
Pair	Two cards of the same rank.

Table Layout

There are three betting circles in front of each player's seat on a Three Card Poker table. The one closest to you is labeled "Play", the middle one is labeled "Ante", and the top one is labeled "Pair Plus."

What makes Three Card Poker most exciting is that the rules allow you to play two different poker games at once. In the first game, which we'll call "Beat the Dealer", you bet that your hand will beat the dealer's hand. You place your bets in the Ante and Play betting circles, as we'll explain in greater detail soon. In the other game, you don't bet against the dealer. Rather, you bet on the strength of your own hand hoping that it will contain at least a pair or better. This game is called "Pair Plus" for obvious reasons, and you play this game by placing a wager in the Pair Plus betting circle. You do not have to play Beat the Dealer when you play Pair Plus, but you can play both. Since Pair Plus is easier, let's see how to play it first.

Playing Pair Plus

When you play Pair Plus, you're betting on the strength of your own hand. All you need to win is to be dealt one pair (i.e. 2 twos, 2 tens, 2 Kings, 2 Aces, etc.). In most casinos, the Pair Plus bet pays off as follows:

If You Have A	You Get Paid
Straight Flush	40 to 1
Three of a Kind	30 to 1
Straight	6 to 1
Flush	4 to 1
Pair	1 to 1
High Card	1 to 1

Playing "Beat the Dealer"

When you play Beat the Dealer, you have to place a bet in the Ante circle. Then, you and the dealer are both dealt three cards facedown. Before the dealer shows his or her cards, you have the opportunity to look at your cards and raise your bet if you think you have a chance of winning. If you decide to raise your bet, place another bet equal to your Ante bet in the Play circle. If you don't have a good hand, fold by placing your cards face down toward the dealer. The dealer will pick up your cards and your Ante bet.

After all players have looked at their cards and decided to raise or fold, the dealer turns over his cards. Like Caribbean Stud, the dealer's hand must qualify in order to continue play. To qualify in Three Card Poker, the dealer's hand must hold a high card of Queen or better (i.e. a King or an Ace), or it must contain a Pair, Flush, Straight, Straight Flush or Three of a Kind.

If the dealer's hand does not qualify, he or she will fold, return each Play bet and pay 1:1 for each Ante bet. Unfortunately, if you folded before the dealer folds, you're not paid at all.

Gamb-lingo

Players must wager in the **Ante circle** or **Pair Plus** betting circle in order to start the game. The amount they wager in either circle must match the table minimum, or more. If a player wants to continue betting against the dealer after looking at his or her cards, he or she must place an additional bet equal to the Ante wager in the **Play** circle. When a player or dealer does not have a strong hand, he or she can **fold**, or turn his or her cards in and stop betting.

Best Bet

Stanley Ko has also calculated the optimal play for Three Card Poker. According to Stanley, only make Play bets when all three of your cards are no lower than this combination: Queen-Six-Four.

If the dealer's hand qualifies, the players' hands are opened and compared to the dealer's hand. If the dealer's hand ranks higher, you lose both your Ante and Play bets. If your hand is better, you'll be paid 1:1 for the Ante bet and 1:1 for the Play bet.

In addition, if your hand contains a Straight, Three of a Kind, or Straight Flush you're paid a bonus on your Ante bet no matter whether the dealer's hand beats your hand. The extra bonus is paid as follows:

If You Have A	You Get Paid
Straight Flush	5 to 1
Three of a Kind	4 to 1
Straight	1 to 1

Risky Business

When you're playing against the dealer in Three Card Poker, the house edge rises to 7.7 percent if you always make the Play bet regardless of your hand.

Three Card Poker Strategy

In Three Card Poker, placing both bets in the Beat the Dealer game gives the house a higher advantage (3.4 percent) than if you only made a Pair Plus bet (2.3 percent). So, Beat the Dealer is a little riskier.

In Pair Plus, there's no basic strategy; place your bet and hope for the best!

In Beat the Dealer, just follow the same rules the dealer uses to qualify his or her hand. Fold if your hand does not contain any of the winning ranks or at least a Queen, King, or Ace high card. Only place the Play bet if you have a qualifying hand.

War: What Is It Good For?

You might remember playing War, the card game, when you were a kid. It was easy to learn, easy to play and easy for your brother to cheat you out of your allowance if you didn't keep your eyes on the deck!

Well, casinos have revived this simple, action-packed card game and players seem to enjoy stepping back in time.

War isn't really a poker game at all, but it uses the Poker ranking of cards. Cards are ranked from high to low regardless of suit, with Ace high, and two low.

To start playing, just place your bet in the betting circle in front of you. The dealer will deal each player one card, face up. Then he or she will deal him- or herself a card face up. The following scenarios can occur:

◆ If the dealer's card is higher than yours, you lose your bet.

◆ If your card is higher than the dealer's, you win and are paid even money for your bet (1 to 1).

◆ If your card and the dealer card are the same rank (i.e. two Kings, or two twos, etc.) you are tied and must decide your next move.

When you and the dealer are tied, you can either walk away from the battlefield by surrendering your hand, or you can stand up and fight!

When you surrender, you forfeit one half of your bet.

When you decide to fight, you go to War with the dealer, which means that you both play one more hand to see who wins.

To signal that you want to go to war, place another bet equal to your original bet on top of your card. (Note: the dealer doesn't have to double his or her original bet to go to war, but you do. This is where the house gets its advantage in the game of War.)

Next, the dealer will deal both of you a second card. These are the possible scenarios:

◆ If your card is higher, you win 2:1 on the second bet.

◆ If your card is lower, you lose both bets.

◆ If you tie again, you win 3:1 on the second bet and the game is over.

There *is* one more bet that you can make in War that's a bit like playing against my brother. At the start of each game, you can bet that your card and the dealer's card will tie. The tie bet is placed in the Tie betting circle and usually requires a $1 minimum. If you and the dealer tie on that hand, you'll be paid 10 to 1. But, the house edge on tie bets is a whopping 16 percent. It doesn't pay to make the Tie bet unless you've got a really strong hunch!

Risky Business

If you go to war and win, you win one bet. But if you go to war and lose you lose two bets. What a deal?

The Least You Need To Know

♦ Three Card Poker and War are both easy games to learn, but you won't come out ahead if they're the only games you play. Both games favor the house!

♦ In Three Card Poker you can play two different games: Beat the Dealer (Ante and Play bets), and Pair Plus. You can either play both games at the same time, or just one. Each game requires its own bet.

♦ War is just like the game you played as a kid. You play against the dealer and whoever has the higher card wins. When you tie, you go to War!

♦ You can place a side bet in War that will pay you 10 to 1 if you and the dealer tie. But, probability tells us that you're not going to tie too often so this bet gives the house a 16 percent advantage. Avoid the tie bet unless you have a big bankroll and a lot of really good hunches!

Part 5

Nothing But Numbers

Some people are into numerology and have their own lucky numbers that they play all the time. Other people like to let strangers pick their numbers for them. No matter which strategy you use, if you're a "numbers" person, you'll be glad to know we've devoted Part 5 to the games of chance that involve nothing more than picking and playing numbers. The object of all the number games is to have as many of your numbers come up as it takes to win in a random drawing.

The features that distinguish one numbers game from another are how many numbers you get to pick from and whether you do the picking or someone else does it for you. We'll help you sort out all of the differences and show you how to play each of these games: lottery, bingo, keno, video keno.

Chapter 22

The Ancient Art of Keno

In This Chapter

- ◆ Where to find the keno game in a crowded casino
- ◆ The object of the game
- ◆ How to place a simple bet
- ◆ Your best bets
- ◆ "Ways" to increase your keno potential

Keno is a numbers game similar to lottery that came to us from China. The game played in ancient China involved selecting 10 out of 120 Chinese characters. Those 120 Chinese characters were unusual in that they told a story, and no character was used more than once. Can you imagine writing a 120-word essay without ever using the same word twice? We won't go into the history of how keno came to America, but it has evolved considerably. Today it is a popular casino game in which players bet on the outcome of 20 numbers randomly selected from a pool of 80.

In this chapter, we'll explain how live, big-board keno is played and how to mark a keno ticket to place a bet. You'll also see some pretty awesome odds and find out why most keno players believe that the high payouts are "occasionally" worth the risk! We'll even show you ways to place your keno bets that will make you look like a pro the first time out. Keep your crayons handy; we're ready to start.

Fries with Your Ticket, Ma'am?

When an establishment offers "live" keno (as opposed to video keno, which is covered in Chapter 25), you'll find *keno boards* like the one shown in the next figure conspicuously placed throughout the casino, *keno lounge*, and restaurants.

Although the keno lounge is where the game actually takes place, you'll find more keno players eating dinner or enjoying a cocktail at the bar while they play. The game comes to them; they don't have to go to the game. *Keno runners* circulate throughout the casino to enter players in the next game. It's simple: You fill out a blank keno ticket, which you can find on almost any table in any restaurant, and then hand the ticket and your money to a keno runner.

Gamb-lingo

The **keno lounge** is the area in a casino where keno is played. Keno numbers are **called**, or drawn, for each game. The **keno board** is a large electronic board posted in many places throughout a casino to display the winning numbers. A **keno runner** takes your bet from anywhere in the casino to the keno lounge counter and also delivers payment for winning tickets. The **ticket** is the paper you use to mark the numbers you select and the amount you bet on a game.

The runner takes your money and ticket to the *keno counter*, where a *keno writer* accepts your bet and issues an official keno ticket indicating which numbers you have selected and how much you have bet. The runner brings the official ticket back to you at your table. As long as the runner gets your ticket to the writer before the game starts, you have a bet, regardless of when the ticket actually gets back to you.

There are at least 5 minutes between games, and each game takes about 30 seconds to *call*. Most keno lounges run between 200 and 240 keno games per day. When you win, the keno runner will cash your ticket for you (hoping for a small piece of the prize as a tip!), or you can go to the keno lounge yourself to collect your winnings *before* the next game starts.

Although a good deal slower than most casino games, keno offers you the possibility of winning a substantial reward for relatively little investment. The odds (which we'll discuss later) are horrendous, but where else can you sit down, pass the day quietly, enjoy free drinks, and still be part of the action?

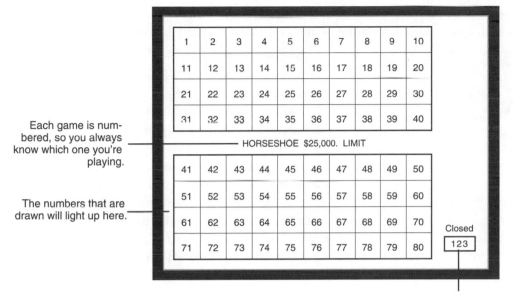

Each game is numbered, so you always know which one you're playing.

The numbers that are drawn will light up here.

HORSESHOE $25,000. LIMIT

Closed

When the sign says "Closed," wait for the next game. This one is ready to start!

I'll have a hamburger, iced tea, 4, 6, 7, 22, 54, and 72, please.

Lounging Around

If you're interested in seeing how a keno game is run, sit in the keno lounge. To play, use the crayon markers provided to fill out a keno ticket, and then step up to the keno counter to place your bets. The counter person/ticket writer takes the bet and enters your numbers into a computer terminal. The computer issues an official ticket with the game number, date, ticket code, writer code, your choices, and the amount of the bet.

Immediately check the computer-generated ticket against your original crayon-marked copy for any discrepancies between the two sets of numbers. (If you give your bet to a keno runner, he or she returns the computer ticket before the game starts. You've still got to check the numbers.) If you find an error, make sure you get the computer-generated ticket corrected before the game starts. Otherwise, you are paid according to the numbers on the official ticket instead of on the numbers you wanted. Once the game is ready to start, no more bets are taken, and no tickets are changed.

The keno numbers (1 to 80) are printed on 80 individual ping-pong balls. For each game, 20 balls are drawn from either a wire birdcage that spins, or a round air bubble that keeps the balls up in the air until all 20 are captured in two separate "goosenecks." As each ball is picked, its winning number is electronically highlighted on the casino's keno boards.

Risky Business

Unless you're playing a multi-game ticket, you will forfeit your winnings if you don't collect them *before* the start of the very next game. *Always* check your game tickets as soon as the numbers are drawn and then collect your winnings *immediately!*

After all 20 numbers are selected, check your tickets to see if you won. Winning depends on how many numbers you selected and how many of those numbers actually came in. The payouts vary with each betting option, so if you're unsure, have a keno ticket writer or runner check your ticket before the start of the next game. Remember, with the exception of a multi-game ticket, all winning keno tickets must be turned in at the keno counter in the lounge or to a keno runner *before* the start of the next game (more on the multi-game tickets later).

Reading the Menu

When you sit down in a keno lounge or even a casino restaurant, you'll find blank keno tickets, crayons, and instruction booklets everywhere. If you decide to bet your two favorite numbers, you're not getting the most bang for your keno buck. But who can blame you? Most in-house instructions do little more than explain the most basic bets and what the house pays if you win them. Once you understand the game better, you'll see that there are actually many other ways to bet—and many ways to increase both your odds and your payoffs.

Gamb-lingo

Straight keno is the basic keno game, played by marking individual numbers or *spots* on a keno ticket. A **spot** can be any number (from 1 to 80) that a player selects on a keno ticket. The term is derived from the phrase "X marks the spot," as in treasure hunting. It also refers to the amount of numbers marked on a ticket. A 6-spot ticket, for example, has six marked numbers.

Novice keno players generally start out placing basic, or *straight*, keno bets. More complicated strategies involve *way tickets* and *combinations*, which we'll cover later.

Getting It Straight

Placing a straight keno bet involves deciding how many numbers you want to bet and marking your ticket to indicate your choices. To decide how many numbers to bet, consider the following:

The maximum number of *spots* (or numbers) that can be marked on a straight bet ticket. Most casinos allow a maximum of 15 numbers, but some may cover bets on a maximum of only 10 numbers. Some casinos offer special keno tickets that allow you to bet 20 numbers at a higher minimum bet. Ask your keno runner or ticket writer for specifics.

The betting limits. (Usually a 70-cent or $1.00 minimum.) With 70-cent minimum, you can make bets in increments of 70 cents: $0.70, $1.40, $2.10, $2.80, $70, and so on.

Your potential payout (what a winning bet will pay).

Your chances of winning.

Your minimum bet and payoff for winning tickets differ from casino to casino, but you can get this information from the casino's keno instruction booklet or at the keno lounge. In most casinos, if you play only one number and it is drawn, you triple your money (if you paid $1 to play the single number, you get back $3 when you win).

By the same token, if you play ten numbers for the same dollar, your potential payout is terrific, but you have to *catch* at least five numbers. That means five or more of the ten numbers have to be drawn before you win anything. The more numbers you catch, the more money you win. For example, a $1 bet on ten spots usually wins $25,000 when you catch all ten numbers. If five of the ten numbers come in, you get back your dollar and they call it winning. If you catch six out of ten numbers, you receive $20, of which $1 is your original dollar; seven out of ten numbers pays $140; eight out of ten pays $1,000; and catching nine out of ten numbers pays you $4,000.

Gamb-lingo

When you **catch** a keno number, that means a number you've marked on your keno ticket has been drawn.

Gamb-lingo

The **house edge** is the percentage of each bet you make (win or lose) that the house takes in. It's like payment for letting you play, an entertainment tax.

The **ticket** is the paper you use to mark the numbers you select and the amount you bet on a game.

Taking a Chance

Keno is a popular pastime because it offers the possibility of winning spectacular payouts on relatively small wagers. As we just mentioned, in some casinos, a $1 bet on ten numbers can generate a $25,000 return when all ten numbers are drawn. However, there are more than 1.6 *trillion* ways to select ten different numbers from a pool of 80, and your odds of picking 10 of the 20 that are drawn are approximately one in 8.9 million. The more numbers you try to pick, the harder it is to hit them all.

For that reason, the most popular keno bets are often the 6-, 7-, and 8-spot tickets because the payout for selecting six numbers on any of these tickets is still high compared to a $1 bet, and (as you can see in the following table) your odds of hitting eight out of eight are considerably better than your odds of hitting ten out of ten.

Take a Look at Your Keno Odds

Your Chances of Hitting	Are 1 in	$1 Bet Pays (Typically)
10 out of 10	8,911,711	$25,000
9 out of 10	163,381	$4,000
8 out of 10	7,384	$1,000
7 out of 10	621	$140
6 out of 10	87	$20
8 out of 8	230,114	$25,000
7 out of 8	6,232	$1,480
6 out of 8	423	$90
7 out of 7	40,979	$8,100
6 out of 7	1,366	$400
6 out of 6	7,752	$1,480
5 out of 6	323	$90

Bet You Didn't Know ...

When the house edge is 30 percent, on the average you receive 70 percent back. So what you spend compared to what you get is 1.00 ÷ .70 = 1.43. Therefore, a 30 percent house edge means you spend 43 percent more than you receive in payoffs.

Something else you should know about keno: If you were to cover all the possible ways to pick ten out of ten numbers by placing an equal bet on every combination of ten numbers you could make, you would spend 40 percent more (or thereabouts) than you would get for all the winning numbers and combinations. That's the *house edge* on a 10-spot ticket. The house edge in keno varies from casino to casino, depending on the payout schedule. Usually, the house keeps 25 percent *or more* of all possible wins (30 percent is common), no matter how many numbers you choose.

"On Your Mark ..."

After you pick your numbers and decide how much you want to bet, you're ready to mark your ticket. Because there is so little time between games, it saves everyone a lot of anxiety if you correctly mark all the numbers, or spots, you want to play on your ticket before placing your bet. Always use one of the crayons supplied instead of your own pen or pencil.

To mark a straight bet on a blank ticket, put an "X" through the number or numbers you want to play. Indicate how many numbers you're playing in the right margin (usually in an area marked #SPOTS/WAYS), and then write the amount of your bet in the PRICE PER GAME box and the number of games in the NUMBER OF GAMES box, like the ticket shown in the next figure. In some casinos, your keno ticket has a TOTAL PRICE box where you enter the total cost of the ticket by multiplying the number of games you're playing by the amount of your wager on each game. If your keno ticket doesn't have a TOTAL PRICE box, or you don't know how to fill it in, the keno runner or ticket writer can fill it in for you or write it in at the top of the ticket.

Best Bet

If you can't decide which numbers to play, many casinos offer a quick pick, which lets the computer select for you. All you have to do is decide how many numbers you want and then ask for "quick pick."

After you mark the ticket, give it to a keno runner or a ticket writer in the keno lounge before the start of the next game. (Ask the runner for help completing your ticket, if you need it. Just be sure to mark the numbers you want to bet.)

The ticket writer enters it in the computer and prints you an official ticket. Be sure to check your numbers and bet on the printed ticket before the game begins. Then sit back and relax! Don't lose the official ticket—it's like money in that if you lose it, someone else can use it. Soon after the numbers are drawn, the keno runner comes by to check your ticket, pay you your winnings, and see if you want to play again. If there's no keno runner around and you have a winning ticket, you *must* get to the counter in the keno lounge before the start of the next game to collect your winning money. Otherwise, you lose your payoff!

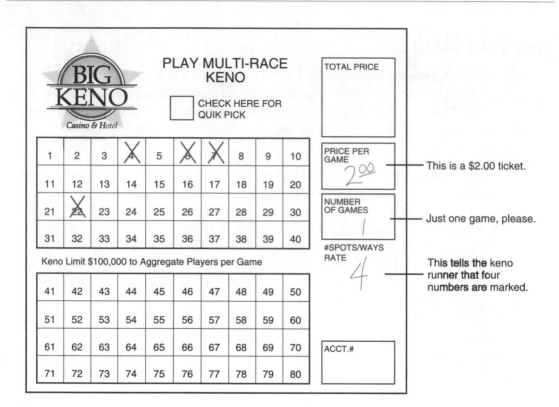

PLAY MULTI-RACE KENO

☐ CHECK HERE FOR QUIK PICK

TOTAL PRICE

PRICE PER GAME

2 00 ——— This is a $2.00 ticket.

NUMBER OF GAMES

1 ——— Just one game, please.

#SPOTS/WAYS RATE

4 ——— This **tells the** keno runner that four numbers **are** marked.

Keno Limit $100,000 to Aggregate Players per Game

ACCT.#

X Marks the spot!

Having It Your Way

Another way to increase your chances of winning at keno is to give yourself more betting options. *Way tickets* do that by allowing you to group numbers and pay for the number of "ways" each group can be used to win. Because many casinos lower the minimum bet on a way ticket, you can wager a smaller amount than the minimum for betting each number or combination of numbers on straight or split tickets. For example, on a 3-way ticket, you can mark two groups of three numbers and also include all the numbers marked on the ticket as another group of six numbers. If five of the six numbers come in on your 3-way ticket, you are paid for not only the 5 out of 6 win, but also the 3 out of 3 and 2 out of 3 groups.

The amount of your bet depends on how many ways you elect to *cover*, or purchase. In the 3-way example, you would have had to wager on all three possible ways to win the most money. (This bet is called a *combination way* ticket, and we'll tell you why later!) If you covered only one way, using two groups to cover 6 numbers, you would have been paid for only 5 out of 6 numbers, as in a straight bet. If you covered each group separately (that's two ways of getting 3 out of 3), you would have been paid only for hitting 3 out of 3 and 2 out of 3. You are not getting any bonus payouts on a combination way ticket compared to using straight tickets; if you cover more combinations, you pay more for the ticket, just as though you were covering those combinations with straight tickets.

You can create tickets with as many groups and possible ways of winning as you like, but the cost goes up considerably. To find out more about the cost of way tickets and how to determine the possible combinations you might want to cover, speak with a ticket writer in the keno lounge.

Make "Way" for a Winner!

To mark your way ticket, mark each spot with an "X" and then draw a circle around all the numbers in each group. You must bet the same amount on each group of numbers or ways selected.

Let's look at a real keno ticket to see how a simple way ticket is written. If you were betting three groups of three numbers each, your ticket would look like the one shown in the next figure. Notice how each set of numbers is circled to identify them as a group. You can bet each group of three numbers separately by simply writing this as a split ticket and entering "3/3" in the right margin, to indicate three separate bets on three groups of numbers. Or you can combine each group differently to come up with three ways of making a 6-spot ticket combination, like this:

> Group 1 + Group 2
>
> Group 1 + Group 3
>
> Group 2 + Group 3

Enter "3/6" in the right margin to indicate that you're placing three bets on six numbers each, and enter "50 cents" below that to indicate the amount of each wager. At 50 cents per way (which is lower than the minimum price of a straight bet), the total cost of your ticket would be $1.50 for three ways of hitting six numbers. If all the numbers in two groups are drawn, you are also paid for hitting three out of three in each of the winning groups. If all nine numbers happen to come in, you're paid for not only three six-out-of-six wins, but also three three-out-of-three tickets. That's more fun than just one 6-spot straight ticket, don't you think?

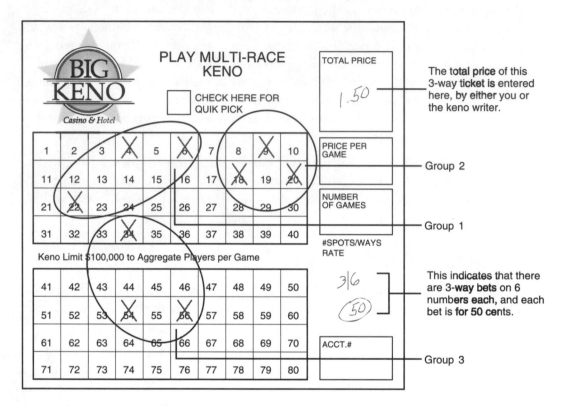

The **total price** of this 3-way **ticket is** entered here, **by either** you or the keno writer.

Group 2

Group 1

This **indicates that there** are 3-**way bets** on 6 numbers **each**, and each bet is **for 50 cents.**

Group 3

This is another "way" to go!

Let Me Count the Ways

In the 3/6 example just described, you could easily cover the possibility (and windfall profit potential) of nine out of nine numbers coming in by turning your ticket into a *combination way ticket*, which allows you to cover a different number of spots on the same ticket. In this case, you'd just add the additional nine out of nine way, or *grouping*, to the ticket, as shown in the next figure. To mark the additional bet, write "1/9" (for one way to win a 9-spot bet) in the right margin and the amount wagered under it. All way bets must be for the same amount. If you want to wager 50 cents on one way, you must wager 50 cents on all ways.

Gamb-lingo

A **combination way ticket** is a special type of keno ticket in which the groups contain different amounts of numbers.

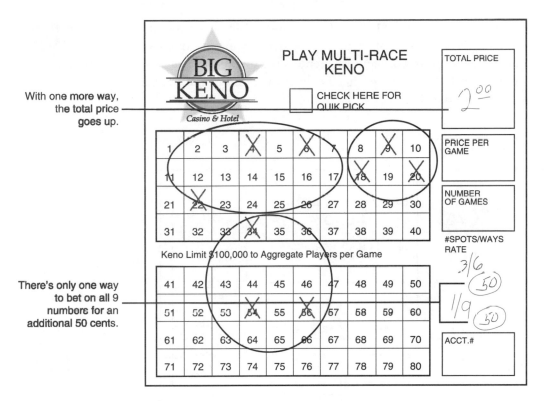

With one **more** way,
the **total** price
goes up.

There's only one way
to bet on all 9
numbers for an
additional 50 cents.

This may be the hard way—but it pays!

Splitting Your Ticket

When you want to place more than one straight keno bet at a time, you can save time and paper by writing a *split ticket*. A split ticket lets you write multiple straight bets on the same keno ticket instead of writing multiple tickets (and one ticket should be easier to keep track of). Just be sure to separate the different groups of numbers by a line, as we did on the ticket shown on the next page.

As you can see, you need to indicate how many bets you are placing per number of spots marked in the right margin. In this game, you marked four numbers in the top half and four numbers in the bottom half, but you want to bet one group of three numbers and one group of five numbers. So that the keno runner will know what you mean, you've separated the numbers for each separate bet

Best Bet

If you want to play the same numbers again for the next game, just present your original ticket to the keno runner or ticket writer. The writer will change the game number and issue a new ticket.

with a line and entered "1/3" and "1/5" in the right-hand margin. You also entered and circled the amount of each wager under the number of spots marked. The keno runner checks your work and then enters the total cost of the ticket ($2.10) in the TOTAL PRICE box. If you need help writing a split ticket, a keno runner or writer will be glad to assist!

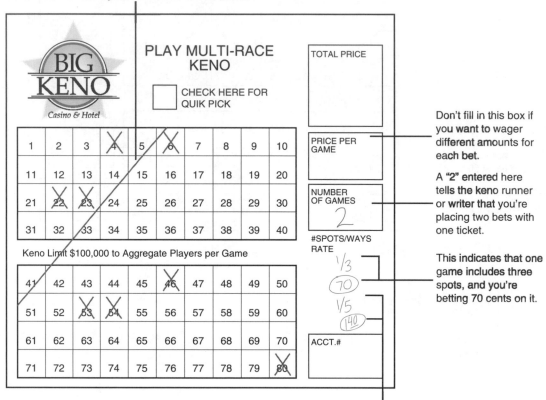

A line is drawn here to separate the three spots on one bet from the spots covered on the other bet.

Splitting a ticket for two straight bets.

Don't fill in this box if you want to wager different amounts for each bet.

A "2" entered here tells the keno runner or writer that you're placing two bets with one ticket.

This indicates that one game includes three spots, and you're betting 70 cents on it.

This indicates that the other game includes five spots, and you're betting $1.40 on it.

Keno to Go

You may be wondering why they make it so difficult to collect your keno winnings—requiring you to cash winning tickets before the start of the very next game. Good question! All we know is that's the state law in Nevada, so if you're playing there, be sure to follow the rule! Most casinos have found a way to ease your burden by letting you play anywhere from two to 20 games in a row on one ticket. This is called a *multi-game ticket*, and you don't need to collect your winnings for any game until your last game is played. At the end of the last game, if you bring your multi-game ticket to the keno counter, they'll run it through the computer to see what you've won. When you play a multi-game ticket, however, you must play that ticket for all games and remain on the premises in a restaurant or gaming area. You must also be sure to turn in the ticket to collect your winnings before the start of the next game after your last game. There, I said it!

If you really don't want to wait around, some casinos offer even better keno take-out by letting you bet 21 to 1,000 keno games in a row on the same ticket. All you need to do to collect your winnings for this multi-game ticket is come back within a year to collect. (And *no*, you can't mail it in! They want to see your smiling face, in person.)

While Waiting for Your Ship to Come In

By now you probably understand that there's more to keno than meets the eye. It might look relatively harmless and relaxing, but keep in mind that losing combinations pile up quickly. In keno, the house has a huge advantage (25 percent to 30 percent or more), and you face just about the worst odds out there. Most people play keno only every now and then to test their luck. When they do, they know it's a *very* long shot, but the possible payout makes it worth the risk. Here are some pointers that can help you stay afloat while waiting for your keno ship to come in:

> **There are other, more complex betting strategies (like "kings") and specialty games that we didn't cover in this chapter.** If you're really serious about keno and want to learn more, many in-depth books are available. One book we recommend is *The Facts of Keno*, by Casino Press, Inc. (But you still won't find a way to reduce the house edge!)

> *Don't* **sink all your money into keno.** The payoffs are incredible, but the odds against it are, too. Just play as a relaxing way to spend some time in a casino and enjoy the sights.

> **The 6-, 7-, and 8-spot tickets are more popular because they offer better odds of winning than the 9- or 10-spot tickets.**

> **The magic number for keno is $1,500.** When you win more than that, you'll have to show your identification and present your Social Security Number so that the casino can report your windfall to the IRS.

Stanford says the rest of these popular tips are nonsense (and I'm sure he's right—I've tried 'em all!). But if they help *you* play the game and you have a good time doing it, go for it and good luck!

Try to spot trends in previous games. Watch the keno board for numbers that come up frequently, and then try to go with them.

Because for some mysterious reason numbers seem to run in patterns on the keno board, many people select numbers that form groups or patterns. This is especially true in video keno, but it may help with live keno, too.

Find the numbers you like and stick with them. If you wait long enough (it may take forever!), any set of numbers will be drawn. If you keep switching around, you might miss the boat when your favorites come in.

The Least You Need to Know

- The house edge in keno is 25 percent or more.

- It's not easy to select 10 numbers out of 20 that will be drawn from a pool of 80, but it sure pays if you do!

- The fewer numbers you select, the easier it is to win.

- You can make three types of keno bets: straight, way, and combination way.

- Use only the crayons that are provided to mark your keno tickets. Use an × to mark the numbers you want to select on your keno ticket.

- Circle groups of numbers to indicate that you are playing them as a group on a way ticket.

- If you need help in marking your ticket, don't be embarrassed to ask the keno writer or runner. It's your money and you want to be sure you've done it right. Besides, helping you is their job!

Chapter 23

Lottery—The Mother of All Numbers Games

In This Chapter

- How to play most lotteries
- How millionaires are made
- How to get the most bang for your lottery buck
- Avoiding lotto burnout

Lotteries are one of the most popular forms of gambling in America today, and no gambling reference book would be complete without paying tribute to the mother of all numbers games.

The origins of gambling go as far back as the Bible, when lots were cast to divide up land. The *casting of lots* generally means "to take a chance," and that's probably where the term *lottery* comes from.

The lottery is as old as ancient Rome. History tells us that after Nero fiddled while Rome burned, a lottery was held to raise the money needed to rebuild the city. Since then, lotteries have been used in countries all over the world as a means of funding public projects. In the United States, lotteries are legal in most states and generate billions of dollars in annual revenue.

Winning by Numbers

The object of a lottery is to pick a winning combination of numbers that will be randomly selected from a larger pool of numbers. Your odds, or chances of winning, are based on how many numbers you have to pick and the size of the *number pool* (1 to 35, 1 to 45, and so on), *not* on the number of players. The bigger the number pool, the greater the odds against you. Most states run more than one type of lottery game, each with different odds and payouts. Take the time to learn about them all, so you can find the game that fits your style. As they say, "You have to *play* to win!"

Gamb-lingo

The lottery **jackpot** is a percentage of the revenues generated by the drawing and increases incrementally as more people play. If a prize level has more than one winner, the jackpot is divided equally. The **number pool** is the range of numbers (1 to 60, for example) from which you select. When no one matches the winning numbers, a jackpot **rolls over** and is added to the next drawing.

The biggest lottery game in each state is often called lotto. This is the game with a progressive *jackpot* (meaning it grows each week until someone wins) that has produced thousands of "instant" millionaires. To play, just select what you think will be this game's winning numbers and go down to your local convenience store, supermarket, or lottery center and ask the person in charge to print you a ticket with those numbers on it, or find a self-service terminal and print it yourself. Each lottery ticket costs from 50 cents to $1.00, depending on the state in which you play. There's usually one lotto game played per week, and if no one holds the winning ticket that matches all the numbers selected, the grand prize jackpot *rolls over* to the next game.

The Big Payoffs

The big jackpot lotto games are pari-mutuel systems. That means that, like your winning payoff at a horse race, you never really know how much you will win until everyone has purchased their tickets and the game is closed. During the days leading up to a lottery drawing, the jackpot figure increases as more players buy tickets. After the game is closed and the money collected from ticket sales has been counted, the state deducts the cost of conducting the game and any portion of lottery sales that has been earmarked for funding state projects. The money that remains in the lottery pool is used to pay off all winning ticket holders for that lottery drawing.

Best Bet

You have the best odds of winning lottery games that require you to pick fewer numbers and have a smaller number pool.

In the California lottery, for example, players must match six out of six numbers to win the big multi-million-dollar jackpot. If you matched five out of six numbers, you'd win a lesser prize, which is usually in the hundreds of thousands of dollars and still quite substantial. Winners who match four out of six numbers generally receive a few hundred or a thousand dollars. The only prize amount determined *before* every drawing is the $5 you win if you match three out of six numbers.

In each of the top prize categories—matching six out of six, five out of six, or four out of six numbers—more than one player can win. When that happens, the total prize money for that category is split among all the winning ticket holders. For example, if three people matched six out of six numbers on their winning tickets for a $6 million jackpot, the prize would be split three ways and each winner would receive $2 million.

Bet You Didn't Know ...

You're not the only one whose time is precious. Money also has a time value. Because of it, the gigantic prizes awarded to lotto winners aren't quite what they appear to be. Most lottery prizes of a million dollars or more are paid over a period of 20 years, just like an annuity. That means a million-dollar winner gets $50,000 a year for 20 years. I wouldn't turn it down, but, because a dollar received tomorrow can't be spent today, it's not worth as much as a dollar received today. A million dollars spread over the next 20 years is not nearly as rewarding as getting a million dollars *now*!

All's Fair in Love and Lottery

As we just mentioned, because lottery jackpots are pari-mutuel, if there is more than one winning lottery ticket in any drawing, the jackpot is split equally among the winning ticket holders. As a result, many lucky winners have had the misfortune of sharing their good fortune with total strangers!

The reason this happens has to do more with the popularity of the numbers people tend to select than with destiny or anything else. For example, most people like to choose their birthday, or their loved one's birthday, or the day they got their first car, and so on. (You get the idea.) What all of these days have in common as numbers is that they range from 1 to 31 (the days in a month). Other popular numbers are always 7 and 11 (not because that's where the ticket was bought, but because those

Best Bet

If you can't decide which numbers to play, ask for "Quick Pick" and have the computer choose for you. Many instant millionaires owe their fortunes to Quick Pick, and very few have ever had to share the prize with other winners.

are considered lucky numbers) and any numbers in a sequence, such as 1-2-3-4-5-6 or 5-10-15-20-25-30.

The best way to ensure your own private winner is to make sure at least some of your numbers fall outside the range of 1 to 31, pick them randomly, and don't use a logical numerical sequence that someone else might easily think of. If you don't want to share *your* jackpot with anyone, pick your numbers carefully!

Give Yourself a Bonus

If a lotto game offers bonus numbers or inexpensive ways to increase your payout, take them! They often give you additional ways or dollars to win at little or no extra cost. In California, for instance, a bonus ticket is given to you free when you buy five SuperLotto tickets (each ticket is a separate play) for one drawing. Your bonus play has seven numbers instead of the usual six, and if any six of the seven match the SuperLotto drawing, you get $200,000. Not bad for a free ticket!

Best Bet

Some state lotteries give you the choice of collecting your total winnings in 20 annual installments or as one lump-sum payment. Although the lump sum is less than the total of the 20 payments, it's almost always a better deal.

Oregon's Power Play option increases your winnings by quadrupling the value of a winning ticket when you hit three, four, or five out six numbers in each drawing. Although Power Play doubles the cost of your lottery ticket, the larger payout makes this option worth playing.

States are always coming up with different bonus gimmicks and special promotions to entice lottery players. Play smart and pay attention to these small variations so you don't overlook a free ride.

Comparison Shopping

Most people don't realize that each state's lotto game is different, so you might be able to find a real bargain in a neighboring state. In California's SuperLotto, for example, entrants have to pick 6 out of 51 numbers, and the odds against them are 18 million to 1. In neighboring Oregon, players pick 6 out of 54 numbers, which gives them odds of 26 million to 1.

On the surface, it looks like Oregonians would be better off crossing the state line to purchase the California SuperLotto tickets. But if you dig deeper, you'll find out that a lottery ticket in Oregon costs only 50 cents, which reduces their odds to 13 million to 1 for the same dollar. (Of course, you might also want to consider how big each state's jackpot is before you decide which one to play!)

State-ing the Odds

The odds for each state's lotto games are usually posted on their marketing material. If you know how much a ticket costs, you can compare your odds in different states and pinpoint the state closest to you that offers the best chances of winning.

States also have a way of changing the rules and the size of their number pools every so often, so your best bet is to keep track of the games played in neighboring states and compare the odds and relative size of the jackpots once or twice a year.

Most states now have a subscription service that lets you buy a year's worth of tickets in advance. You don't have to live in the state or be there to win. You just need to be *in* the state to buy the tickets or subscribe to the service.

A California lottery ticket is shown in this figure. Most state lottery tickets are similar.

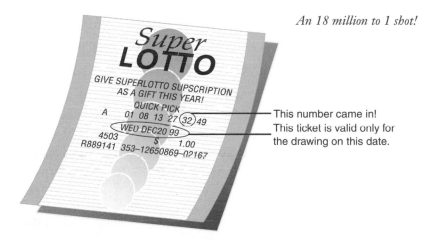

An 18 million to 1 shot!

This number came in!
This ticket is valid only for the drawing on this date.

Multi-state Mega-Jackpots

Some states pool their lottery fortunes in order to offer huge mega-jackpots. Players can purchase lottery tickets in any of the states that are part of the lottery pool.

The Powerball game is America's largest lottery, run jointly by 20 states and the District of Columbia. Players pick five numbers from a pool of 49 and a Powerball number from a field of 42. The chances of winning the Powerball lottery are 1 in 80,089,128.

On August 25, 2001, four lucky winners from four different states (New Hampshire, Delaware, Kentucky, and Minnesota) each held winning tickets to a $298 million

Powerball jackpot. In splitting the $298 million jackpot, which is the largest Power-ball jackpot to date, each winner receives $73.7 million, or $2.9 million per year for 25 years as an annuity. Or, they can elect one lump sum payment of $41.4 million, before taxes.

By the way, the richest lottery prize in U.S. history to date was $368 million won in the "Big Game Mega Millions" jackpot in 2000. Big Game Mega Millions is a multi-state lottery played by participants in nine states: Georgia, Illinois, Maryland, Massa-chusetts, Michigan, New Jersey, New York, Ohio, and Virginia.

A Ticket a Day

Many states operate "daily cash" games in addition to their weekly lotto drawings. The daily cash games don't offer the mega-jackpots that weekly lotto games do, but they give you a better shot at winning. Daily cash games include smaller versions of the regular lottery, so players pick fewer numbers from a smaller pool.

Take Your Pick!

Most states also offer "pick" games, which are daily cash games in which you pick only three or four numbers. No matter what state you play in, pick games always give you the same odds because you're selecting from the same size number pool. In Pick 3, the number pool ranges from 000 to 999. Because you are actually picking one number rather than three separate numbers (that is, 529 rather than 5-2-9), your odds are 1 in 1,000. In Pick 4, the number pool is from 0,000 to 9,999, and your odds of picking the winning number are 1 in 10,000.

Best Bet

Boxing lottery numbers on one pick ticket is the same thing as buying multiple smaller tickets. There is no advantage to boxing.

Risky Business

Don't ask a friend or relative to buy and send you lot-tery tickets from out of state. It is a federal offense to mail lottery tickets across state lines.

Most pick games cost either 50 cents or $1 to play. You can often increase your chances of winning a pick game, without spending more money, by *boxing* your bet. Boxing a bet means you are going to treat each digit in your number selection as a separate number (that is, 5-2-9, rather than 529). When you box a bet, as long as you have picked the winning digits, it doesn't matter what order they're in. If, for example, you boxed 5-2-9 and 295 came in, you'd win. Because boxing a three-digit number gives you six chances on the same ticket, however, the prize you win is one-sixth of what you would win by picking just one winning number. Boxing a four-digit number gives you 24 chances on the same ticket, and you are shooting for a prize that is $\frac{1}{24}$ of what you would win by picking just one number.

For That Sudden Itch

As the name implies, a scratch-off is a lottery ticket coated with latex that you scratch off to reveal a prize—or the lack of one. (I once received 30 scratch-offs for my birthday, and got nothing more than a dirty fingernail, one very BIG year older, and a little wiser). But all in all, scratch-offs do give you the best odds of winning a lottery prize. In fact, some states set their scratch-off odds as low as 1 in 3 or 4. One of the best prizes you can win with a scratch-off ticket is a shot at your state's bigger lottery or an appearance in a TV lottery game. Even though I lost 30 scratch-off games in a row, I still play occasionally and anxiously await the opportunity to win California's Big Spin—but now I use a coin to scratch!

Risky Business

Be careful *where* you scratch! Unlike a brand new pillow, which is still good if you remove the tag, if you scratch off the part of an instant ticket that says "Void If Removed," your winning ticket could be worthless.

What Have You Got to Lose?

Many people don't play the lottery because they think the odds against them are just too great. In reality, the odds of winning a lottery prize aren't that bad if you look at all the different lottery game choices and ways of winning. The only lottery game whose odds are substantially worse than, say, slot machines or hitting 10 out of 10 in keno are the big lotto games—and their jackpots more than make up for the adversity. If you shop carefully, you may find some states where you have to pick only six out of 35 or 39 numbers, which reduces the odds against you significantly. So other than a dollar or two, what *do* you have to lose? Your odds of being a lottery winner are the same as everyone else's, and *you* could wind up rich!

Waiting for the Phone to Ring?

When the big day comes and the lottery drawing is held (it may be that very same day if you play the daily cash games), *don't* sit by the phone waiting for that all-important call. Millions of dollars are just lying around lottery offices all over the country because winners never came forward to claim their prizes.

The only time a lottery office contacts *you* is if you entered a drawing through the lottery subscription. Most people buy their tickets before each game, and if you're one of them, it's up to you to check your ticket as soon as the lucky numbers are drawn. In some states the winning numbers are published in the next day's newspapers or flashed on your television screen. If you can't find the winners that way, you can always go back to where you bought the ticket (or any place tickets are sold) and get a daily update of winners. You can even pick up a sheet that tells you what numbers have won in the past few weeks or even months. In some states, there are toll free numbers you can call to find out. If you have access to the Internet, you can find the latest lottery numbers for each state at www.infospace.com. When you get to that web address, look under the "Fun" section and click on **Lottery**.

Risky Business

Most states give you between 30 and 360 days to turn in a winning lottery ticket, but the deadlines vary depending on the state and which game you're playing. *Always read the rules of the game before you buy your ticket, and be sure to check your ticket numbers before the time limit expires!*

When you *do* win, if your prize is $600 or less (the amount varies by state), you can go back to where you bought the ticket to collect. If it's more than $600 or so, you will probably have to mail your ticket in to the state lottery agency. Your lottery retailer can tell you specifically what to do. If you're mailing in a winning ticket, don't forget to keep a copy of it, and it's probably a good idea to send it registered mail with a return receipt.

Save Your Losing Tickets

There are two reasons it pays to save your losing lottery tickets:

First, you can use them to verify your gambling losses when you have a gambling win that you must report on your income taxes. For more information about IRS requirements for reporting gambling income, read Chapter 28.

Second, some states hold "last chance" lottery drawings for the holders of losing lotto or scratch-off tickets. Although these drawings usually aren't as well publicized as the regular lotto drawings (because they don't generate additional revenue), they do exist. If your state holds a "last" or "second chance" drawing, you can send in your losing tickets to enter. The prizes won't be as big as a multimillion-dollar jackpot, but you might win a car or thousands of dollars. Since fewer people enter these drawings, your chances of winning are greater than in the regular lotteries. Besides, what have you got to lose?

Play Smart and Win

There's certainly a variety of lottery games to choose from, and diversity should be part of your overall strategy. After you decide how much money you'd like to devote to the lottery, spread it around to the different games, so you don't get burned out not winning the Big One. A few Pick 3s and scratch-offs every now and then can restore your faith and help you feel like a winner. Eventually your lotto picks may come in! In the meantime:

> **Don't go overboard.** Buying 20,000 lotto tickets because the jackpot's never been this high before might seem like a winning strategy, but it's not. It's a real gamble, and it only reduces your odds to 20,000 in so many million! Buy 10 tickets and keep your fingers crossed. Remember, lotto starts with an *L* for "luck." (Of course, Stanford says the *L* in lottery is for "losers.")

> **If you buy multiple tickets, don't repeat the same numbers.** Mix them up.

> **Lotto jackpots are divided equally among all winners.** If you don't want to split your lotto prize with other entrants who also have winning tickets, select your numbers carefully and randomly or use Quick Pick. (There is less chance of duplication when you use Quick Pick.)

> **Read the rules of whatever lottery you decide to play** *carefully.* Each lottery game has different time limits and requirements for collecting on winning tickets. On smaller winnings, you might just need to return the ticket to the place where you bought it. On the bigger wins, you might have to mail it to a state lottery office.

Best Bet

If you are required to mail a winning ticket to a state lottery commission to receive your payoff, always make a duplicate copy of the ticket before mailing. If the sum is substantial, consider sending it registered mail, return receipt.

In addition to these strategies, many lotto games have been won by groups of people who pooled their money and bought more tickets. Thirteen co-workers from Ohio thought "pooling" was a fun and sensible thing to do when they put their money together and won $295.7 million.

Another way to win is to enter the game drawing when it's offered to you as a scratch-off game winner. Why pass up the opportunity to make a lot more money, at no cost to you?

The Least You Need to Know

- ◆ There are many different lottery games with different odds and payouts. Play them all so you can experience those "little" wins while you wait for your big number to come up!

- ◆ Your odds of winning a lotto game are *not* affected by the number of people who play. They are determined by the amount of numbers you have to pick and the size of the number pool from which you pick.

- ◆ Choose your lotto numbers carefully and randomly, or let Quick Pick do it for you.

- ◆ Some states have better odds. Shop around and play those states.

- ◆ The daily cash lottery games are a lot easier to win. With odds as low as 3 to 1, they're worth playing.

- ◆ If you think it's just a consolation prize to be entered in your state's Big Spin (TV) lottery drawing, guess again! You have a better chance of winning a lot of money in these smaller promotional games.

- ◆ Always check your lottery tickets for winners. If you find an old one lying around that you haven't checked, find out if it's a winner *before* you throw it away.

Chapter 24

Bingo—As American As Apple Pie

In This Chapter

- Where to play bingo and how much it costs
- What the object of the game is
- How matters can get complicated very quickly
- Playing bingo in the computer age

A lot has changed since those rainy camp days when we played bingo for candy and ice cream—and Annette played the beach-blanket variety with Frankie. Today, more than two million people play bingo on any given day at a cost of more than three billion dollars a year. It may be just a matter of time before bingo surpasses baseball as our national pastime.

In this chapter, we'll show you what to expect when you go to your first bingo session, how much it might cost you depending on where you play and the size of the jackpot, and how to play bingo, too. You'll also learn how to figure out your odds of winning and where and when you can get an advantage to help you win more often!

Big Bingo Business

Bingo was first legalized in New Jersey and New York in the 1950s and was originally used by churches to raise money for the needy during the Depression. Since then, many states have climbed aboard the bingo train after realizing how profitable it can be to get even a small percentage of each game's revenue back in licensing fees and taxes.

Today you can find a bingo game just about anywhere, from your local church or synagogue to almost any Indian reservation, casino—or even bingo halls. A typical night of bingo costs anywhere from $5 to $35, or slightly more if you buy more cards or bonus games for extra "chances."

Some states limit the top bingo prizes, but in other states the prize money for a night can top $10,000. (When the top prizes are in the thousands of dollars, it usually costs more to play.) Larger bingo halls and casinos even run progressive bingo games in which the jackpot on the final game of the session increases by a few hundred dollars each time it's played and not won. Not bad for a small investment!

Not Just Another Board Game

Bingo is a numbers game derived from lotteries, played with a field of 75 numbers and a game card. Twenty-four different numbers (and one free space) that decide your fate are preprinted on each game card. Although each game can have more than one winner, no two game cards are exactly alike at any bingo session. And, unlike the lottery, numbers are usually called until someone wins!

Gamb-lingo

The **caller** is responsible not only for keeping everyone awake, but also for choosing the game pattern, drawing each bingo ball, and reading the number clearly. A **session** is a series of 10 individual games (plus some extras) that takes about 2 or 3 hours, depending on breaks and how long each game takes (some games are won quickly, and others take longer).

A bingo *session* usually includes 10 to 15 individual bingo games and can last a few hours. During a single game, a *caller* selects a number from 1 through 75, and every player who has that number on his or her game card marks it off. Each game has a different winning game card pattern (more on these later in the chapter), which the caller identifies before the start of the game.

You can play more than one card per game by purchasing an additional game pack. Like the cost of the bingo session, the cost of an additional game pack varies depending on where you play, but it is usually about $1 for each additional game in the pack. So a pack that includes one additional card for 10 games would cost you $10 more. As you'll see later, there's no real advantage to playing additional cards, but many people enjoy the added thrill and excitement.

Once a player has filled in a pattern on his or her card from the numbers that have been called, he or she wins. *Bingo!* A *floor person*, or *checker*, verifies that the pattern is correct and that the numbers on the card match the numbers that have been called. If they do, the game is closed and a winner declared. If more than one player has won, the prize money is split among the victors.

> **Risk Business**
>
> Playing multiple game cards is harder than it looks! You have to pay careful attention to the numbers that are called, and then quickly check and mark each game card before the next number is called. It's easy to fall behind. We recommend that beginners start out with the basic bingo session package that includes one card per game before buying additional cards.

Tools of the Trade

Depending on where you play, bingo game cards are either paper throw-aways or hard plastic permanent cards. When throw-away cards are used, you get a separate card for each game, and the preprinted numbers on each game card are different. In bingo halls where the plastic permanent cards are used, you use one card for all games in the session, and consequently keep the same numbers for all bingo games.

The hard plastic cards are often called *shutter cards* because they have little shutters over each preprinted number. When a player has a number that's been called, he or she slides the shutter window over the number to mark it. These cards can be reused, but paper throw-aways can't. Players need a new paper game card for each game played because they use a crayon or a "professional" ink bingo *marker* (called a *dauber*) to mark off each number called.

No matter what the composition—throw-away or permanent—game cards are always set up in the following manner.

> **Gamb-lingo**
>
> A bingo **marker** can be a simple crayon or a serious, specially designed ink **dauber**, whose tip covers the number on a throw-away game card.
>
> The **shutter** is a window you pull down to mark each number called on a reusable bingo card.

Each column on a bingo card starts with one of the letters in the word *bingo*. The column letters are used to group and identify the numbers contained in each column below. When the pressure starts, knowing which numbers line up under each letter makes it easier to find the numbers as they are called:

The **B** column always contains five numbers, from 1 to 15.

The **I** column also contains five numbers, from 16 to 30.

The **N** column has only four numbers, ranging from 31 to 45, because the center spot is always free (everybody gets to mark off the free spot at the start of the game).

The **G** column has five numbers, from 46 to 60.

The **O** column has five numbers, from 61 to 75.

Bet You Didn't Know ...

With 75 possible numbers in a bingo field, you could actually print more bingo cards than the national budget deficit (what comes after trillion?) without repeating the same set of numbers. Because manufacturers generally print bingo cards in sets of 3,000, however, it's highly unlikely that you'll ever find any two identical cards in play at the same bingo session.

A bingo column runs up and down and always starts with a letter. In this case, it's O.

B	I	N	G	O
10	26	38	49	71
10	26	38	49	71
11	23	FREE	60	74
2	21	31	50	69
5	20	36	54	70

Bingo rows run left to right.

Don't wait 'til they call "Free"—it's yours for the taking!

This preprinted number is read "I-21."

Could this card be a winner?

Playing by Numbers

There are 75 bingo balls on which each possible letter-number combination (that is, B-1 through O-75) is written. The bingo balls are protected in either a ball cage or a glass blower, where they can be spun around to make sure that each pick is random and fair. After a bingo ball is selected, its number is announced by the caller and flashed on electronic boards so that everyone in the house can see the numbers called. As they're called, the balls are placed on a separate ball rack so they won't be called again.

Best Bet _____

Electronic boards are often posted high on the walls in large bingo halls. If you have a hearing problem or difficulty seeing at distances, sit close to the caller or one of the boards so you don't miss any of the action!

Every Game Has a Theme

Before a new bingo game begins, the caller selects a pattern, or theme, for the game. It's amazing how many shapes and patterns a creative caller can make out of one bingo card. Guess what this is:

This one takes the (3-layer) cake!

— Each row is a layer.

The simplest games may involve filling in only one row across the top or bottom or just the four corners of a card. Other patterns form letters, like *T*, *I*, *X*, *Y*, or *Z*, or words like *hi* (that's "little hi!") or *HI* (that's "BIG HI!"). The hardest game is usually left for last. That's the *coverall*, in which all 24 numbers have to be marked with only 48 or 50 numbers called. It's a lot harder to win than it seems, and frequently no one does win, so they just keep calling numbers until someone wins a consolation prize. The patterns themselves are fun and keep the game interesting. If you play more than one or two cards in a game with a complex pattern, it can be difficult to keep up!

> **Bet You Didn't Know ...**
>
> In a jurisdiction that allowed bingo but not blackjack, blackjack was dealt with 52 bingo balls. Each bingo ball represented a card in the deck. When a player got a natural 21, he or she shouted "Bingo!"

> **Best Bet**
>
> If you mark off the pattern on your paper bingo card before the game starts (which is a good idea if the pattern is difficult to remember), be sure to use a different color pen than the one you use for marking spots. Otherwise, you might forget which numbers were called and which were just part of the pattern.
>
> Some serious players use a pencil or crayon to run a thin line through the numbers that make up the pattern, so that the pattern is easier to remember.

And You Thought This Would Be Easy!

It's a good thing bingo is so popular because it's not as easy as it looks! Here are your odds of filling up a card in the coverall game when only 50 or fewer numbers are drawn:

> With 48 numbers, 1 in 799,399
>
> With 49 numbers, 1 in 407,857
>
> With 50 numbers, 1 in 212,086

The more numbers drawn, of course, the better your chances. With 55 or fewer numbers drawn, you have about a 1 in 10,359 shot. If you're one of the fortunate ones who's already won a coverall game in your lifetime, consider yourself lucky!

Fortunately, being the first to fill in a 5- or 10-spot pattern is a lot easier. To figure these odds, you just have to know how many game cards are in play. In a casino bingo hall or an Indian reservation, where the payouts are higher, it's not unusual to find people playing 10 or more cards. A good average to use is probably five cards per person. If there are 200 people playing approximately five cards each (with some people playing 10 cards, and others playing one), you have a 1 in 1,000 chance of winning (that is, $1/200 \times 1/5 = 1/1,000$). If you play four cards, your odds increase to only 4 in 1,000. It's up to you whether that small margin is worth the added confusion (and excitement!) that additional cards can bring.

Best Bet

You can increase your chances of winning by playing at unpopular times. With fewer players, you have better odds.

Bet You Didn't Know ...

In Nevada casinos, bingo is the only game that pays back more than 100 percent. Casinos run bingo at a loss to bring in slots players. (Many bingo players play the slots in the hour or two between bingo sessions.)

Bingo in the Information Age

For those of you who have a hard time playing two game cards, you might want to rent a computer at your next bingo session. Many casinos and Indian reservations supply computers (for a small fee, of course) that let you play up to 12 game cards at a time—without even breaking a sweat!

The bingo computer (sometimes misleadingly called "video bingo"—you still play against people, not against the computer) automatically keeps track of all your game cards. All you have to do is touch the video bingo screen to indicate which number has been called, and the computer does the rest. It automatically looks for the number on all your computer cards and marks the ones in which the number appears in the correct spot for the game pattern. Now *that's* progress!

The Least You Need to Know

- ◆ What was once just a charitable form of recreation has become *big* business.

- ◆ Bingo is derived from the lottery, but in this game, someone always wins!

- ◆ To find the numbers on your card quickly, remember which range of numbers fall within each lettered column at the top.

♦ You want to be the first one to fill in the correct pattern with numbers that have been called. When you are, yell "*Bingo!*"

♦ In the high-paying coverall game, you want to cover all spaces on your card within the first 48 or 50 numbers called. Don't worry if you can't; it's a 212,085-to-1 shot against it.

♦ Some coverall games are progressive. That means the jackpot keeps growing and growing each time it's not won.

♦ Playing multiple cards increases your odds of winning only slightly, but it certainly keeps you on your toes!

Chapter 25

Video Keno—A Numbers Machine

In This Chapter

- ◆ How is video keno related to slot machines?
- ◆ A word about the video revolution
- ◆ What's the difference between live keno and video keno?
- ◆ How do video keno machines differ, and which ones should *you* play?

I tend to gauge the popularity of video machine games by the number of casino employees I see playing them during their breaks. Video poker was the most popular among blackjack dealers for a long time, but video keno is catching up. In fact, many casino patrons seem to have acquired a taste for video keno (myself included), and I suspect this has something to do with the huge payoffs when you're lucky enough to win! Unfortunately, like keno, it's not really a beatable game, and in this chapter, we'll explain why. We'll also show you how easy it is to play.

What's So Special About Video Keno?

Video keno is derived from the live, "big-board" keno you learned about in Chapter 22. Here are the main differences between the live and video versions:

- Like slot machines, video keno is played independently on a computer-operated machine.

- Each video keno game takes only a few seconds to finish, so it's much quicker than live keno.

- Because you can squeeze a lot more video games into an hour than live keno games, you have more chances to win—but it also costs you more per hour.

- The minimum bet is usually a quarter, which is lower than most minimums for live keno.

Best Bet

When you play a multi-game machine, it doesn't matter whether you select your game first and then put your money in, or vice versa. If you don't like the game you're playing, use your remaining credits on another game by pressing **EXIT** and selecting a different game from the main menu.

- Payouts for winning video keno combinations vary according to the type of machine and the kind of video keno game you're playing. The newest multi-game video machines sometimes offer you the choice of different keno games that have different minimum bets, payout schedules, and bonuses. We'll talk more about the multi-game machines next.

We're not going to repeat all the basics of keno, so you might want to review Chapter 22.

Bring On the Machine!

It seems that our insatiable appetite for gaming entertainment, especially the desire to go one-on-one with a machine, has sparked a mini-revolution in game design. As a result, there are many varieties of both standalone video keno machines and video machines that include many different games, including keno. Video machines that offer players the opportunity to play more than one game, or switch from game to game, are known as *multi-game* machines.

Bet You Didn't Know ...

One reason video keno is so popular is that the payouts can be very large for a small investment. If you read a typical video keno payout schedule, you'll notice that the payouts are listed in dollars, *not* credits. That means hitting eight out of eight on a minimum 25-cent bet can win you as much as $2,000—worth 8,000 *credits*! Read payout schedules on machines carefully to make sure your video keno payouts are paid in dollars, or at least in equivalent coin credits. The odds against you in keno are just too high to give up any amount of return.

Many of the multi-game machines contain basic video keno (often with a *progressive* jackpot) as well as variations that require higher minimum bets and provide larger payouts, or offer the chance to increase your winnings when your winning combination happens to include a superball. The superball quadruples your payout if it bounces on one of your winning numbers. When you play a multi-game machine, be sure to read the game instructions to find out what your minimum bet, winning payouts, and keno variations are *before* you decide which game to play.

Gamb-lingo

A **progressive** slot or video machine's jackpot keeps increasing each time a coin is played. When the jackpot finally hits, the amount goes back to the starting number. A **touch wand** is a pointing device used on some video keno machines to select numbers.

Which Machine Is Which?

It's easy to distinguish between the standalone video keno machines and the multi-game types: Generally, the standalone machines take up a lot more space and require the use of a penlike device (called a *touch wand*) to select the numbers to be played. The touch wand isn't shown in the following figure, but otherwise most standalone video keno machines look like the one shown here. Multi-game machines, on the other hand, look more modern and are about the same size as a regular slot machine. Instead of touch wands, they usually have touch screens, which allow you to merely touch the number or button you want right on the screen. Screens can get really dirty by the end of a long day, but when you're playing you'll hardly notice!

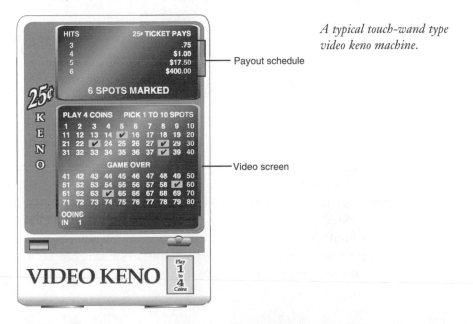

A typical touch-wand type video keno machine.

How to Play Either Way

The older standalone machines accepted only coins; today, most have been changed so that you can insert a $1, $5, $10, $20, or $100 bill and receive game credits, or use coins instead. On some of the newer multi-game machines found in California's Indian casinos, you may not even find a coin slot, so you have to insert cash for game credits. On these machines, when you're ready to cash out, the machine prints you a credit ticket showing how many credits you had left, and you go to the cashier window to get your money. When you do use cash, always check the machine's credit meter to be sure you got the correct amount of game credits—a good habit to get into whenever you use cash on any type of video or slot machine. After you insert your money, press the **ERASE** or **WIPE** button to clear the numbers selected by the previous player. The video keno field has the same numbers (from 1 to 80) as the live keno game. You can use the touch wand on a standalone machine or your finger on a touch screen to select the numbers you want to play. You can choose as many numbers as the game allows (usually ten is the maximum), or as few as one. The payout schedule is posted above the keno number board and changes with each number you select. It also changes as you increase or decrease your bet by pressing the **BET** selection button or by inserting more money.

Bet You Didn't Know ...

Statistically, the odds of scoring a big win in keno are the same whether you play the live game or a computerized video version, but you'll find that what each one *pays* for winning combinations differs quite a bit, and varies from one video keno machine to another.

Most older touch wand machines give a higher payout for hitting, say, eight out of eight numbers, but they don't give you anything for hitting three out of eight. Although the eight-out-of-eight payout on the newer multi-game video keno machines is smaller (but still large!), at least you get your money back when you hit three out of eight. You don't need to be a rocket scientist to figure out that you're gonna hit three out of eight more often, so why not look for the machines that pay you when you do?

When you're ready to roll, press the **PLAY** or **START** button and 20 numbers will be randomly drawn from the pool of 80. As the numbers are drawn, they are highlighted on the keno board in front of you. Every number you selected that matches one drawn is indicated by either a checkmark or a change in the video color surrounding the winning number. If enough of your numbers match any of those that were drawn, you win according to the game's payout schedule. Winning credits are automatically added to your credit meter or coins are dropped into a coin machine's coin basket.

If you want to continue, either insert more coins or press the **BET** selection button to use credits. You can continue to bet the same numbers, or change them by erasing the board and selecting new ones. When you're ready to *cash out* (collect your winnings), just press the **CASH OUT** button if you have been playing with credits.

Making It Through the Dry Spells

Like any other video or slot-machine game, video keno has its ups and downs. But because the odds against you are so great, it sometimes seems as though the downs in video keno last longer than in other games. This is a game of patience as well as chance.

The keno strategies you learned in Chapter 22 apply equally to video keno, and some of them are worth repeating here. You'll also recognize some of these tips from Chapters 5 and 6 on slot machines. That, of course, is simply because, even though you're playing a video game that has different screens, colors, and pictures than a slot machine, it still operates on the same underlying technology and principles. This means: (1) Don't marry a machine, (2) It's *not* your personal piggy bank, and (3) When you finally get the chance, take your money and *run!*

Here are some more strategic hints:

- Play only the denomination (nickel, quarter, dollar, and so on) and number of coins you can afford to play.

- Set your limits for the session. When the money you set aside for a session expires, or your allotted time is up, leave! There will be other chances.

- Unlike a slot machine, it's totally irrelevant whether you load up a video keno machine (play maximum coins), unless you're shooting for a progressive jackpot.

- The odds for keno and video keno are pretty much the same (although the payouts vary).

 Best Bet

If you can't decide which numbers to play, most machines have a quick pick button that will select numbers for you.

- Pick the numbers you want to play and stick with them. Some people make a science out of choosing the right numbers—you'll see them change numbers when they don't work, and even change them again if they *do* win. The numbers you choose don't affect your probability of winning because mathematics dictates that past events have no influence over future events.

Here are some tips that might not make sense to a mathematician, but some gamblers use them successfully:

♦ If you watch the numbers that are drawn when you lose, you'll see that they seem to land on the board in groups or patterns. However, those patterns cannot be predicted. I've won many times by playing the numbers in my family's birthdays scattered all across the board. I've also won on numbers that were in a straight line or wrapped around a corner.

♦ If you can't seem to hit the broad side of a barn with six numbers, try making a bigger target by adding more numbers. The opposite is also true. If you can't win on eight numbers, move down to six or seven, or even four or five. Try to find the "spot" where your numbers start coming in.

♦ Once you hit a jackpot on a certain amount of numbers, say six out of six, you may have expended all the luck you're going to catch on a 6-spot. That might be a good time to switch to seven or eight numbers, change machines, or take your winnings home!

♦ Don't feed all your money into just one machine. It just may be that your machine is having a bad day! Hunt for one that isn't.

Progressive Advice

Many casinos offer progressive video keno machines, and the jackpots can grow into the tens of thousands. When they climb that high, it's not uncommon to see players lined up waiting for seats. Here's some advice for progressive players (although most will tell you they don't need it):

♦ Play as many coins and as few numbers as it takes to get a shot at the jackpot. For example, some machines won't pay the progressive unless you play four or more coins per game and either eight, nine, or ten numbers. If you don't have to play ten numbers to win the progressive, don't, unless hitting nine out of ten will also win it. If eight pays the progressive jackpot with just one more coin than is required on the 9- or 10-spot, it's probably worth the extra money to improve your odds substantially. Study the payout sheet carefully to find the most logical and economical way to shoot for a progressive jackpot.

♦ If there are several progressive machines in the casino, play the machines with the largest jackpot.

◆ If you really don't want to play as many coins as are needed for the progressive jackpot, don't. But if you are not playing for the progressive jackpot and someone offers you money for the chance to play at your machine, take the money and consider yourself lucky!

The Least You Need to Know

◆ Video keno has the same odds as "live," big-board keno. Review Chapter 22 to check some of them out.

◆ Video keno payouts are usually posted and paid in real dollars—not machine credits.

◆ If you're playing to win a progressive, play as many coins as you need to win the progressive in as few numbers as possible: eight out of eight rather than ten out of ten.

◆ It really doesn't matter *what* numbers you play.

◆ Video keno games are really just souped-up slot machines, so don't forget to take the money and *run* when you get the chance!

Part 6

Virtual Gambling (The Last Frontier?)

Gambling may not be legal everywhere, but it IS in cyberspace. Or is it? We'll discuss some of the controversy that still surrounds online, or Internet, gambling in Chapter 26. You'll also learn about websites and which ones will let you gamble for fun and/or money. If you want to learn more about gambling and get the latest up-to-date information on your favorite gambling getaway, we'll show you where to look online in Chapter 27.

Gambling Gets Wired

In This Chapter

- ◆ What is Internet gambling?
- ◆ How do you do it?
- ◆ Is it safe?
- ◆ How do you find gambling websites?

Imagine turning on the television in your living room and tuning in to your favorite casino, playing some blackjack before dinner or taking a few spins on the mega-millions slot machine while waiting for your next appointment.

If you have a home computer with Internet access, you can experience online gambling right now. In fact, we'll show you how in this chapter. But be careful—it's still a bit like the Wild West!

What's Online Gambling?

Gambling online means gambling over the Internet. For those of you who have never been online and visited a *virtual casino*, it may be difficult to imagine why it's fun. But today's Internet entrepreneurs are working very hard to make the online gaming experience as exciting as a visit to your favorite casino. They're doing it with elaborate three-dimensional graphics, a lot of flashy colors, sights, sounds, and even free contests and giveaways for signing on to their website.

Virtual casinos are among the most interactive and entertaining sites in *cyberspace* and, once inside, you can bet on sports or play slot machines, roulette, craps, blackjack, keno, lottery, video poker, and other video-gambling games. Many of the online games look and act like the video machines you play in Las Vegas casinos or the gaming software you can use to practice your blackjack and poker skills on your home computer.

If They Build It, Will *You* Come?

While there's no doubt that the Internet is here to stay, the success of online gambling is still anybody's guess. Many obstacles must be overcome before online gambling can become the multibillion-dollar industry that promoters foresee. First, there is the question of legality. Gambling is legal in only some countries of the world, yet the Internet reaches every country. In many countries where gambling is illegal, online gambling isn't an issue because access to the Internet is also restricted. In free and democratic countries like the United States, debate rages over the moral and social implications of legalized Internet gambling. Should it be legalized so we can regulate it and protect our citizens from unscrupulous operators and from their own gambling addictions? Or should we ban it outright? If we ban it, how can we enforce the ban—can we restrict any activities in cyberspace, which has no boundaries or law?

As the debate continues, there are already laws in the United States that can be used to prohibit online gambling. Individual states, for example, are free to make their own gambling laws, and some have already enacted laws making it illegal for people to make bets with online casinos. At the federal level, the Wire Act of 1960 limits the transmission of wagers over the telephone or other wire communications lines, but it doesn't specifically spell out Internet gambling. As of this writing, no one has ever been convicted under the Wire Act of placing a bet in an online casino (although there have been a few arrests of people operating virtual casinos from within the United States).

Another federal regulation, the Internet Gambling Prohibition Act, has been stalled in Congress for the past few years. When and if it ever passes, online gambling would clearly be illegal in the United States, but what will that really mean?

Gamb-lingo

A casino that operates on the Internet is a **virtual casino**, an **online casino**, or an **Internet casino**. Internet casinos offer software versions of most casino games, including blackjack, poker, slots, craps, and baccarat. Some Internet casinos accept sports bets on live sporting events. **Cyberspace** is where the Internet is located.

> **Bet You Didn't Know ...**
>
> The Federal Wire Act is primarily aimed at the people "engaged in the business of betting or wagering"—the bookies and casino operators. The government does not intend to go after the people who make the bets, so those who use a telephone or modem to make football bets with an Internet casino are not *likely* to be arrested by the feds. However, the people who are on the casino side of that call could be arrested and accused of violating the Wire Act.

A Walk on the Wild Side

If online gambling is illegal in the United States, will it be illegal for me to sit at my desk in California and access a virtual casino that operates out of a foreign country where gambling *is* legal? And if it is illegal, who will enforce it and how? What will the penalties be? The United States is not the only country grappling with these Internet-related issues. For now, the answers are unclear and the Internet remains a virtual new frontier.

Most of today's online casinos get around this in one of two ways. They either operate out of a country such as the Bahamas where gambling and Internet gambling are legal, or let you play for free, with the opportunity to win prizes instead of cash.

If, during your web adventures, you encounter a virtual casino where you are required to provide your credit card or bank account number or send cash before playing, you have probably entered an online casino that expects you to play for money. Before deciding to dive in, at least finish reading the next few sections.

Update: Online Gambling Legislation as of 2002

On July 17, 2000 the House of Representatives voted against HR 3125, the Internet Gambling Prohibition Act. HR 3125 would have banned some, but not all, forms of gambling on the Internet. A similar bill, S 692, sponsored by Sen. Jon Kyl of Arizona, passed the Senate in November 1999.

Although a majority of representatives in Congress and the Senate favor a ban on Internet gambling, they have been unable to agree upon legislation as of this writing. There seems to be increased pressure from existing online casinos, Indian tribes, and even organizations that oppose limiting the Internet in any way, to regulate online gambling rather than prohibit it. As the debate continues, it appears that the focus will always be on the operators of online casinos rather than the gambling participants—which is good news for you if you like to gamble in the comfort of your own home!

What's in a Name?

When you gamble in Nevada and Atlantic City (two of the most heavily regulated and, therefore, player-friendly places to gamble), you are likely to be seated in a casino owned and operated by one of the largest shareholder-owned corporations in the entertainment and lodging industries: Starwood, Hilton, MGM, Mirage Resorts, and so forth. When you sit at your desk and gamble on the Internet, you are likely to be playing in a virtual casino that is not run by any major corporation. In fact, your virtual casino is probably run by a company you have never heard of before, one that has been created specifically for Internet gambling. Many Internet casino companies have already disappeared, and many more will fold in the years ahead. Having a fancy website is no guarantee that an Internet casino will be in existence when you try to collect your winnings. If an Internet casino that owes you money goes bankrupt or is a criminal operation, you will never collect.

Some virtual casinos try to fool you into thinking they are affiliated with a large company or well-established legitimate casino by selecting a name that is similar. For example, there is an Internet casino called Starluck, which closely resembles Stardust, the name of the well-known Las Vegas casino. But if you win money from "Starluck," you won't be able to collect your winnings from the Stardust. The tremendous financial resources of the Stardust casino in Las Vegas do not guarantee your bets at the Starluck casino on the Internet.

Is There Truth in Virtual Advertising?

Log on to any virtual casino and you're likely to find a very big, bold claim extolling the honesty of the casino you're about to enter. But the truth is, there is no international law to protect you online. Virtual casino ads can claim honest games whether the games are honest or not.

Remember, the video games played in virtual casinos use computer programs like those that operate slot machines and video games found in live casinos. It is just as easy to program a computer to cheat as it is to program an honest game. How are you protected in a casino? The programming code of every machine placed in service in Nevada and Atlantic City must be inspected and approved by Gaming Commission inspectors before the machine can be set up on the casino floor! It costs little to set up an attractive website, so you can't judge honesty or financial stability by the quality of the graphics. And there are no regulations or programming inspections required of online casinos in cyberspace!

There are crooks in this world, and historically, crooks have gravitated toward the fast, easy buck. Unfortunately, Internet casinos may be today's best source of easy money.

An Internet casino that has been honest for a while can suddenly turn dishonest. Here's how it might work when placing a sports bet, when you're not betting against a computer program, but a real, live sporting event: You log on to a virtual casino where you've placed other sports bets before, and you place your bet on the Super Bowl game. The casino accepts your bet and thousands of other people's bets as well. In fact, they've collected $2 million in Super Bowl bets, $1 million on each team. The bettors who have picked the winning team stand to collect $1,904,762 after the Super Bowl. The Internet casino, if it is honest and pays the holders of the winning tickets, will see its $2 million bank account dwindle to $95,238. If the casino has accepted more bets on the winning team than on the loser, its $2 million bank account will shrink to less than $95,238. Two million dollars shrinking to less than $100,000 the day after the Super Bowl is huge incentive for the proprietors of an online casino to disappear with all the money during the Super Bowl.

The day after the Super Bowl, you log on to the Internet to credit your winnings to your account, and the casino website is gone. What can you do? Nothing.

The Cards Just Don't Add Up!

You might have figured out by now that we're not online gambling enthusiasts. The legality of it isn't the issue. There's just *too* much risk to consider.

How safe is it? If I give you my credit card number, how do I know you won't fraudulently charge huge sums of money to my credit card and then disappear? If I win, how do I know for sure that you'll pay me? If I lose, how do I know for sure the game wasn't rigged?

There's no FDIC for Internet casinos and no agency that insures your deposits as there is for banks. If you deposit funds with an Internet casino and it goes broke, your money is gone just as surely as though you had lost it gambling.

Likewise, there is no Internet Casino Control Commission. There is no agency that handles

Bet You Didn't Know ...
One of the reasons governments seem to be dragging their feet about Internet gambling is that they lack the technology needed to regulate and control it. Governments can't even impose age restrictions on online gambling because a simple and effective way to verify identification over the Internet has not yet been developed.

disputes gamblers have with Internet casinos. If you have a dispute with one, it's just you against the casino with nobody to help you.

When you sign up to play for real money in a virtual casino, you're playing at your own risk. All we can say is be sure to read the rules and fine print and be willing to lose it all.

Logging On to the Wild West

For the fearless ones among us who'd like to experience a bit of the Wild West before it's tamed, there are virtual casinos popping up all the time. Your experience should go something like this:

Best Bet

Whenever you download files or software from the Internet, you risk having your computer infected by viruses that may inhabit the files you are downloading. A virus is a bug in a software program that can destroy some or all of the files on your computer. It's always a good idea to purchase a virus protection program and install it on your computer if you plan on using the Internet to transfer files.

Risky Business

If you ever forget your password or lose contact with a virtual casino where you've left a deposit, you might not get your money back. It's a good idea to withdraw your money after each online session or at least keep track of your accounts and passwords.

◆ Search the web (we'll show you how soon) for interesting casino sites, and look at the rules of play and payment before deciding to play.

◆ Check the deposit and minimum bet requirements, too. Make sure these amounts are within the range you're willing to put at risk.

◆ When you've selected a casino, sign on to their site. Most casinos ask you to enter your name, address, and email address. If you have any hesitations about supplying this information, consider finding a casino where you can remain anonymous. There are fewer of them, but they do exist.

◆ Select a *user name* and *password*. You need to remember them so you can access your account and money each time you play.

◆ Deposit some money! Virtual casinos require money up front and usually accept any of the following forms of payment: a valid credit card, debit card, bank account number, or wire transfer. If you don't mind waiting until they receive it, you can also send a cashier's check or money order.

◆ After the casino has received your money, you're ready to play. As you win, money is credited to your account. As you lose, it's taken out of your account. You can let all your money sit in the account until your next session, or you can withdraw it at the end of each session. The casino either credits your credit card or sends you a check. Of course, they may charge a small fee for this service!

Where To Start Playing for Free

If you're determined to go online to gamble, buy yourself a copy of Mark Balestra's *The Complete Idiot's Guide to Online Gambling* first. Mark has a very entertaining way of explaining the virtues and pitfalls of online gambling, and his research and commentary can save you lots of time, money, and aggravation.

As Mark points out "Online gambling businesses are extremely aggressive when it comes to advertising. They'd reach through the monitor and pull you into their websites if it were possible. If you started your gambling search without a clue of where to go, it wouldn't be long before you were bombarded with banners, buttons, and icons leading to all kinds of real-money wagering sites."

The safest place to start your online gambling quest is to go to some of the free, moneyless gambling sites—although they are getting harder and harder to find. Some of the online casinos we listed later in this chapter will let you test drive their games before you have to sign on or leave a deposit. So don't worry that just because you've landed in a pay-to-play casino, you can't get out without paying. You can. (Besides, you can always click the Back button to exit!)

Many of the free-play casinos offer prizes for the highest scores, but you might need to sign on and choose a password first. Always remember to read the fine print and check out the instructions before you jump in. And do be careful about giving out your credit card numbers.

These websites offer free gambling software or preview access to virtual casinos:

Video Poker	www.videopoker.com
Fantasy Sports	www.2play.com
Free Software Downloads and play	www.gamblehouse.com
Slot Players Insider	www.slotplayer.com
Mining Co.	www.miningco.com (Click on Hobbies/ Games and then Pastimes/Casino Gambling
Virtual Vegas	www.casinophrophet.com
Free gambling online	www.dorcino.com

Gamb-lingo

When you sign on to a computer system that many people use, you might need a **user name** and **password** to identify yourself. Many people choose their first or last names or a combination of parts of both for their user name. A password should be a word or number that only you would know, or a series of nonsense characters that you record carefully. It's not a good idea to share your password with other people.

Finding a Safe Casino in Cyberspace

If you're determined to play online with real money, do your homework first! There are several Internet websites and publications that cover online gambling extensively. Not only can you find out what's new and exciting, you can keep an eye on what's happening on the 'dark side.' … When players are ripped off or treated poorly, sometimes they turn to gambling information or news websites with hopes of applying some pressure on the assailants. It's not the most sophisticated crime prevention system, but it's gotten results.

Mark Balestras recommends the following sites because they contain the latest online gambling information, such as online casino reviews, player testimonials, and online gambling news that can steer you in the right direction:

Casino News and Information	Website Address
Covers.com (Lou's casino news)	www.covers.com
Casino Wire	www.casinowire.com
Gamblers Den	www.gamblersden.com
Gamblink.com	www.gamblink.com
Rolling Good Times Online	www.rgtonline.com
WINNERonline	www.winneronline.com

Avoiding Trouble

In *The Complete Idiot's Guide to Online Gambling*, Mark Balestra provides a very valuable checklist that you should use to evaluate potential casinos. It's worth summarizing here:

- Find out if the casino website is licensed by any international jurisdiction. Licensing is good.

- Are the policies reasonable? Read them! And if they're not reasonable, move on. Pay particular attention to their payout policies—how payouts are made and how long it takes to get a payout.

- Do the operators of the site post e-mail addresses and phone numbers that work?

- What do other players have to say about the site? Go to the discussion groups and newsgroups listed in the previous section to see if there's any mention of the casino you're checking out.

- Does the site offer deals that are too good to be true? Be suspicious if the free prizes and signup bonuses are ridiculously high or if the betting spreads and posted odds are way out of line with the general consensus.

- Does the site spend money on advertising? Sites that do are likely to be legitimate because they've made their presence well known and have invested in it.

- Are the games audited? Some of the most reputable online casinos use third parties (not Price Waterhouse, I hope) to audit their payout percentages and gambling transactions. Look for a link to the auditing firm, too, so that you can check their credentials.

- Make sure the deposit and payment transactions are secure.

- Is 24/7 tech support available over the phone? If so, do the support operators speak your language?

- Are they members of the Interactive Gaming Council (IGC)? All members of the IGC have agreed to adhere to a code of ethical conduct to instill a level of consumer confidence.

- When you find a safe place to wager, stick with it!

Bet You Didn't Know ...

When you use a credit card to gamble on the Internet, the casino charges the amount you wager from the credit card. If you win, however, they can only credit the amount of your original wager back to the credit card. Any additional winnings must be paid to you by check or wire transfer. This is where the whole process can seem shady even when it's legitimate. It takes time to set up a wire transfer, and you know how long it can take to receive a check in the mail. So, while you're waiting to get paid it's easy to think you're getting cheated. But be patient before jumping to any conclusion because as of yet, getting paid isn't as easy as it should be!

You're On Your Own!

The following sites can lead you to casinos that will gladly take your money. Remember, this is not an endorsement or a recommendation for any of the establishments listed. Do your homework (and due diligence) first. Then, sign up. Good luck!

Casino	Website Address
AnteUp Gambling Links	www.gamblinglinks.com
Gambling.com	www.gambling.com
Gambling Registry	www.gamblingregistry.com
Rolling Good Times	www.RGTonline.com
Casino City	www.casinocity.com
Casino on the Net	http://casionoonnet.com or http://entercasino.com
Gambling Information	http://www.casino.com
Gold Club Casino	http://us.goldclubcasino.com
Offshore Gambling	http://www.wheretobet.com
Top Ten Casinos	http://www.10topcasinos.com
Online Casino Search	http://www.online-gambling.com

The Least You Need to Know

- There are many new and exciting virtual casinos on the Internet.

- When you gamble for money in a virtual casino, you usually have to deposit upfront money first. Don't forget to withdraw any money you have left when you're done playing.

- When you gamble for money in a virtual casino, you are completely on your own. There is no guarantee that you will get the money you deposited or your winnings back.

- There *are* websites on the Internet where you can get valuable online gambling information or free gambling software.

- Whether you're playing for free or for money, always read the policies, rules, and fine print before signing on to a virtual casino.

- When looking for a safe online casino, use Mark Balestra's 11-point checklist.

Chapter 27

Gambling and the Information Age

In This Chapter

♦ Surfing the web

♦ Using the Internet to plan your next gambling excursion

♦ Getting information from the World Wide Web

♦ Finding the best gambling advice

In the previous chapter, we jumped right into cyberspace and showed you how to find virtual casinos where you can gamble online in the comfort of your own home. But if you're like us, you'd probably rather spend your gambling dollars more judiciously in a well-regulated casino where you can enjoy all the sights and sounds of the real thing!

You can still get plenty of information online about your favorite casino games, gaming centers, hotel accommodations, show tickets, and more. We'll show you how in this chapter.

Lost In CyberSpace?

Have you ever spent hours roaming through stacks of books in the library, jumping from one topic to the next as each book started you down a different path of discovery? Well, that's what the Internet is like. It's a World Wide Web of information and you can get caught up in it for hours. That's why it's a good idea to start out with a plan, or at least an idea of where you want to go.

The best way to start is to use one of the *search engines* we mentioned in the previous chapter, including Yahoo!, Lycos, Infoseek, AltaVista, Savvy Search, and Excite. To access a search engine, just enter one of the following addresses in the Internet address field:

Best Bet

All you need to access the Internet is a home computer, browser software such as Netscape or Microsoft Explorer, a modem, and an Internet Service Provider (ISP), such as AOL, the Microsoft Network, or a local provider you can find by checking the Yellow Pages.

www.yahoo.com

www.infoseek.com

www.altavista.com

www.savvysearch.com

www.excite.com

Next, type in what you're looking for in the search field. For example, if you want to find the latest information about gambling in general, enter *gambling* and then click the **Search** button. A list of thousands of websites with information about gambling will be displayed. Some websites will be useful, and others won't, but many will have links to other websites that might have just the information you're looking for.

Gamb-lingo

An Internet **search engine** lets you sort through the millions of websites in cyberspace to find the ones with the information you're looking for.

You can save time by being more specific with your search criteria. If you'd really like to find only websites that offer advice and how-to information about gambling, try entering *gambling advice*.

Something to *Chat* About

It's not fair to launch you any further into cyberspace without a brief description of what you'll encounter there. Basically, there are two distinct sources of information on the Internet: Usenet newsgroups and websites. The word *newsgroup* is a misnomer.

Newsgroups are really discussion groups in which people like you and me chat about a common subject. They converse from all over the world by "posting" messages back and forth. Posts can be read by anyone in the world, and anyone can join in the conversation by posting his or her own message. One popular newsgroup is rec.gambling. poker, which is a collection of posts related to poker. The "rec" refers to recreational subjects, "gambling" is a subset of recreation, and "poker" is a subset of gambling.

Anyone with access to a computer can post a message to a newsgroup, which leaves newsgroups open to all kinds of interesting conversation and information, as well as abusive language and inappropriate content on occasion. There are currently ten gambling newsgroups. To access one, just enter one of the following addresses in the Internet address field:

news:rec.gambling.blackjack

news:rec.gambling.blackjack.moderated

news:rec.gambling.poker

news:rec.gambling.craps

news:rec.gambling.racing

news:rec.gambling.sports

news:rec.gambling.lottery

news:rec.gambling.other-games

news:rec.gambling.misc

news:alt.gambling

Gamb-lingo

In a **moderated** newsgroup, you send your post to a moderator who decides whether to add your message to the newsgroup. The moderator makes sure there's no repetition, in addition to making sure nothing inappropriate is posted. A moderated newsgroup may make better reading.

Bet You Didn't Know ...

There are tens of thousands of newsgroups in cyberspace. A newsgroup is like a written conversation that is broadcast over the Internet to anyone who subscribes to it. Each major Internet Service Provider, such as AOL, carries a selection of newsgroups. When someone posts a new message to a newsgroup, the ISP that receives the message sends it to other ISPs that also carry that newsgroup, and they in turn pass the new message on to still other ISPs. Newsgroups, like the Internet itself, are not controlled by a central computer. Instead, newsgroups are sent like e-mail from computer to computer across the world. No one person or company is responsible for a given newsgroup. Usenet was set up this way with war and other disasters in mind; if any group of computers were blown out of existence, the information on them would not be lost because it would still exist on many other surviving computers.

What *Is* a Website?

Unlike newsgroups, websites exist on only one computer, and everybody who visits that website is in contact with that one computer. If that computer has problems, you won't be able to contact the website. Each website is owned and operated by an individual or company, or some other identifiable entity. ISPs own many computers that are used only to host the websites of their customers.

Bet You Didn't Know ...

What's so great about the Internet? Speed. Information is transferred instantaneously. It's the same advantage that television and radio have over newspapers and magazines. Television and radio bring you mass-market programming, but on the Internet, you choose what you want to receive and when you want to receive it. The Internet is especially useful for people who are interested in a specific subject that television does not cover, such as detailed weather reports from Rome. (I used it to find out if I had to dress up to gamble at the casino in Monte Carlo. The answer is no.) On the Internet, you can do more than merely get information; you can also send information to other people. In that respect, it is similar to the telephone, but a telephone call reaches only one or a few people, while one post on the Internet can easily reach thousands of people.

Some websites have a message board that works like a newsgroup. You can post messages to a message board in the same way you can post messages to a newsgroup, and that message is then available to people all over the world who are viewing that website. Unlike a newsgroup, messages posted to a message board are available immediately. Also, any message posted on a message board on a website can be amended or deleted at any time by the people who control the website. An inappropriate message could be posted to a website, but if the people in charge are on their toes, that inappropriate message will be deleted quickly.

Gamb-lingo

When you move from website to website by way of **links**, you're **surfing** the Net. *Links* are the buttons or highlighted words on a website that automatically connect you to another website when you click them with your mouse. Once you find a website or newsgroup you like and want to remember, **bookmark** it so you can return there by selecting the site from a list of your favorite places, instead of typing in the address.

Joy Riding

Part of the fun of using the Internet is "surfing", which is going from site to site using links you find in each site you visit. You're wandering around a neighborhood, but this is a neighborhood in cyberspace dedicated to everything that you're interested in! It's more fun than using a search engine to find what you need, and it's often just as efficient. To surf, first go to a site related to a subject of interest to you, such as gambling. (There are a few gambling sites listed in the following sections.) Then look around in that site for links to other sites, and click on one that looks interesting. If you happen to advance to a dead-end site, one that contains no links to other sites, just back up to the last site you visited by clicking the Back button. Keep backing up with the Back button until you find one of the sites you visited that had a good collection of links, and then set off on a different path. When you come across a site you really like, bookmark it so you can visit it again without having to remember its web address.

Another Saturday Night and No Reservations?

One of the things I like to do on the Internet is plan vacations and getaways. The Internet is a great place to find out what's happening in your favorite gambling town, for instance. You can check out who's appearing on stage and who's got hotel rooms available at the last minute, book flights in and out of major resort areas, and even find special vacation package deals. These websites can help you plan your next gambling trip, and some of them have great links to other sites:

Website	Address
All Las Vegas Travel—Official Tourist Bureau	www.golasvegas.cc/golasvegas/
Las Vegas Online	www.lvol.com
Las Vegas Vacations Longhorn Cattle Company (Take a cattle drive while you're there!)	www.longhorncattleco.com/gambler.html
Discount Las Vegas Reservations—Hotels and Casinos	www.vacationweb.com/userx/ goodpages3.html
Nevada Camping and Travel Adventures	www.rvn4fun.com/travelby/nevada.html
Southwestern Gaming (Tucson-area casinos and links to Nevada casinos)	www.azstarnet.com/azgaming

continues

continued

Website	Address
Junkets and overnights to Mississippi gambling casinos	www.casinoairlink.com
Cripple Creek, Colorado, Bed and Breakfasts	www.indra.com/fallline/bandb/ auto/cc.html
I Love Atlantic City Online— Lodging and Campgrounds	Iloveac.com/sleep.shtml
Accommodations Express	www.accommodationsexpress.com/
Florida Gambling Cruises	www.funandsun.com

Gambling Information

In the information age, those with valuable information can sell it. In the gambling world, people who take the game seriously or play professionally are more than willing to pay for the latest information about current gambling conditions and for good, sound advice.

Stanford offers such a service to serious blackjack players through his own website at www.BJ21.com. BJ21 offers four levels of participation: free, CBJN (the *Current Blackjack News* newsletter), green chip membership, and black chip membership. All visitors to Stanford's website can participate in the free pages, which include links to other gambling-related websites and, most important, bulletin boards for participants to post gambling questions or information they'd like to share with other players.

CBJN is an online version of Stanford's *Current Blackjack News* newsletter, which you can subscribe to. Green chip members are paying for the right to exchange messages with other *green chippers*, which means people who are serious about blackjack. (Many of the free messages are posted by people who are less serious or less knowledgeable about the game.) *Black chippers* are paying for the right to find out quickly about emerging beatable games and the strategies for beating them and for the right to exchange information with other black chippers.

Here are some more sites with quality gambling information. Some of these websites have message boards and some do not. Some charge a fee.

Website	Address
Stanford Wong's blackjack site	www.BJ21.com
Michael Dalton's blackjack site	www.BJRnet.com
Arnold Snyder's blackjack site	www.RGE21.com

Website	Address
Richard Reid on mathematics of blackjack	www.bjmath.com
GameMaster on casino games in general	www.GameMasteronline.com
Lodestone's site covering video poker, comps, and more	www.flash.net/~mchino/
David Slanksky and Mason Malmuth's poker site	www.twoplustwo.com/forum.html
Sportspot for sportslines and news	sports.dbc.com
Video poker by Skip Hughes	www.vid-poker.com
Video poker by Jazbo	www.Jazbo.com
A site dedicated to casino law	www.Casinolaw.com

There are many more gambling advice and information websites than we could possibly cover, and new ones are added all the time. Now that you know what to look for and how to search, you're on your own. Surf's up—get out there and ride the waves!

Bet You Didn't Know ...

Most newsgroups and websites with message boards develop into "virtual communities" with a core group of people who are interested in the topic and visit and post frequently. There are thousands of virtual communities online.

Stanford's BJ21 has become a major blackjack community with thousands of active participants. Counting cards at blackjack is a lonesome activity. Many card counters don't know anyone with whom they can discuss card counting; their spouses, neighbors, colleagues at work, relatives, and friends have no interest in the subject. In the BJ21 community, they find kindred spirits. Members of the BJ21 community not only socialize online, they also get together in person for parties in Las Vegas and elsewhere.

Something to Think About

With so much stuff on the web, how do you know what's good information and what's not? Sure, a website sponsored by a public company is likely to contain good news about the company, but is it always accurate? And what about a website sponsored by an individual who doesn't happen to like that company? What about postings that you read in message boards and newsgroups? Sometimes it's hard to separate opinion from fact.

Best Bet

Many states have lottery websites where you can check the winning numbers for the past few weeks or months. To see if your state has its own lottery website, just add your state's abbreviation to the phrase "lottery.com." For example, to check the California (CA) state lottery, enter this address: www.calottery.com. Or, go to www.infospace.com and click on **Lotteries.**

That's why it's good to surf the web as though you were listening to a politician; keep in mind that some of what you hear and see may not be completely accurate. A liberal sense of humor sprinkled with a healthy dose of skepticism is very useful, *especially* when the information is from someone neither you nor I have ever heard of! Here's a list of some of my favorite examples. Some of them are strictly "infotainment"—part information and part entertainment. (It's up to *you* to decide which part is which!)

Website	Address
Las Vegas Hack Attack: Las Vegas cab drivers pick the "best" of Las Vegas and offer advice on gambling and what to do in Vegas. (This one is my personal infotainment favorite!)	www.lasvegastaxi.com
Slot Players Insider: A wealth of slot playing information.	www.slotplayers.com
Let's Go Gambling: "A high tech gambling information site."	www.letsgogambling.com
Where to Bet Online: Lists casinos and offers free games and gambling advice from Dan. Also advertises "Share Your Systems and Win Cash!" (Bring a large grain of salt when checking out "shared" systems!)	www.wheretobet.com
Mike's Gambling Page: The Wizard of Odds	www.charm.net/~shack/ game/index.html

The Least You Need to Know

- You can use any one of many search engines to locate gambling-related websites and newsgroups.

- Newsgroups provide a forum for participants on a variety of subjects and are not owned by anybody. Individuals, companies, and organizations own and operate websites. Websites often have message boards, which are similar to newsgroups.

- Use the Internet to plan gambling vacations (or any kind of vacation, for that matter).

- Some gambling websites are more entertainment than information.

- Don't always trust the advice and strategies that you find on gambling websites or newsgroups. Few web operators or message posters invest the time or money in statistically analyzing gambling games. They may just be average players, not experts.

- There are many gambling sites operated by proven experts that serious players and professional gamblers pay to access.

Part 7

Money Management

Though it comes at the end of the book, this section shows you how money management is no small part of the gambling equation, and something a smart player doesn't overlook. In Chapter 28, you'll learn how to manage your gambling dollars by setting a realistic budget and loss limits. Chapter 29 teaches you how to protect yourself so you won't wind up the unsuspecting victim of dishonesty or crime. In Chapter 30, you'll see how easy it is to take advantage of the freebies and promotions available to you, to offset the cost of your good time. Finally, you get a lesson on casino etiquette.

Managing Your Gambling Money

In This Chapter

- ◆ How to budget your gambling dollars
- ◆ Mapping out a vacation plan
- ◆ How to avoid sinking to new lows
- ◆ Why keeping records is important

Money is a very personal subject. We all need it; there's no doubt about that. But how you use it and what it means to different people varies considerably. Some people would never dream of entertaining themselves by gambling with *real* money, yet they would gladly spend hundreds on a night out on the town or on a single bottle of wine (imagine the cost per sip of a $100 bottle of wine).

It's hard to tell people how to manage their gambling money because everyone's situation is different. Most gambling books avoid the subject entirely. Until someone opens a casino that guarantees your money back at the end of the night, however, it's a subject that only the wealthy can afford to ignore. In this chapter, we'll try to give you some general advice about budgeting your gambling dollars, preserving your capital, refueling if you have to, and more.

Planning the Escape

You know what your financial situation is. You know how much money comes in on a weekly basis and how much goes out to pay monthly bills. You know how much you're socking away for the kids' college fund and your own retirement account. And if anything's left after paying off credit cards, regular bills, incidentals, and building a nest egg, that's yours to spend as you please.

Many people budget a portion of what's left over (their *discretionary income)* for entertainment, which includes vacations, dining out, movies, shows, and—you guessed it—gambling. If you like to vacation in a gambling mecca, the good news is that even if you're not a "Comp Wizard" (more about *comps* in Chapter 30), the hotels and meals can be pretty inexpensive, considering all the attractions you get. You still have to figure in the cost of your fun, and that—the money you can afford to spend at the tables or machines—should be figured separately.

Try this: Say you plan on taking three vacations this year—two with the kids and one to Las Vegas. You can afford to spend approximately $1,000 on each vacation, so that's your limit on the Vegas trip. Based on the way you like to play, you know you're not going to get the room comped, but you *are* savvy enough to get yourself the casino rate in a great hotel. (If you don't know what comps and rates are all about, read Chapter 30 next and learn how to *save money*!)

Gamb-lingo

Casinos issue free gifts and incentives called **comps** to entice players to gamble. "Comp" is short for "complimentary," meaning "free."

Best Bet

A good way to start any Las Vegas vacation is to get a bird's-eye view of the city from the Stratosphere Tower. You can also enjoy one of the finest meals in town in the revolving restaurant at the top.

You prefer a long weekend in Vegas. Any longer and you go nuts and broke, so figure three nights and four days. Depending on the availability of discount air fares, skipping the champagne until you win, and porking out at those sumptuous buffets, you should be able to swing the trip for $400 or less, which leaves you $600 to gamble with. That's approximately $300 for each of you to enjoy.

The day you arrive, it's late; you worked all day, the casino's packed, and you may not even feel like playing. Great—go eat. Check out the latest sights and take it easy. The next morning, you're up bright and early, refreshed and ready to play.

You have $300, and two and a half days to spend it. You could take out your calculator and figure that you have $120 each for Saturday and Sunday, and $60 more before the plane leaves on Monday. Or, you can decide to forget Monday and spend $150 on Saturday and Sunday. Either way, you've set your limits. What matters most is that you *plan* to stop gambling when your $300 is gone, and *stick with it!*

Playing Within Your Means

Okay, you've got your daily gambling budget. You've skimmed Chapters 3 and 4 you know which games you want to play, and you have a general idea of the odds against you in each game. Start out by cruising the casino to determine the minimum bets at each game. If you want to play in this casino and the minimum bet on each game is between $3 and $5 per table, that's what you've got to work with. If you want to play slots and video poker primarily, on a $150 bankroll, you should look for quarter machines. Unless, of course, you don't care how long the $150 lasts and you're willing to find something else to do if the money runs out fast. In that case, go ahead and play for higher stakes—*but stop when today's bankroll is gone.*

Bet You Didn't Know ...

You can calculate approximately how long your gambling money will last, depending on which games you play and which bets you make. In Chapter 3 and the individual game chapters, we discuss the house edge and how it varies from game to game. If you multiply each bet you make by the house edge and then multiply that result by the number of bets you can make in each playing session, you can get a pretty good idea of how much playing the game will cost you. For example, if you're playing $5 blackjack against a house edge of 2 percent, at the rate of 60 hands per hour, you can expect to lose about $6 per hour: ($5 × .02) × 60 = $6.

Of course, your actual results can vary substantially in either direction, based on your level of skill, the playing conditions, and any number of random factors. However, doing the math can help you figure out how long your bankroll should last and where to set your minimum or maximum bet levels based on your bankroll.

If you want to stretch your bankroll as far as it will go, break your $150 into different playing sessions. For instance, it's early morning and the casino's nice and quiet—great time to play blackjack. You know your husband wants to watch a game sometime after lunch and then probably go for a swim before dinner. That'll take up at least 3 to 4 hours. So, you've got this wonderful 2- to 3-hour morning session, maybe an hour or so before dinner, and then one final session after dinner.

You can divide your bankroll into $50 for each session, or divvy it up according to the amount of time you'll spend playing, something like this: $65, $30, $55. Be creative! The point is, try to get the maximum entertainment value out of your gambling dollar, and plan to play when you'll enjoy it the most.

Now, we haven't said a word about winning, and you're going to have to do some of that to play as much as you've planned. Because you budgeted the trip so nicely, there's really no reason you shouldn't play your winnings. Heck, the whole point of budgeting and planning is to have a good time.

If you don't use the winnings for anything else—you don't really want that bottle of champagne, you don't have to buy gifts for anyone, and you want to keep playing—go ahead and add them to your bankroll. If you'd rather hold your winnings from each session in reserve in case you need them tomorrow or the next day, that's not a bad idea either. Or, stash them away and use them to cover the expenses. Winnings aren't a problem. You'll always think of something to do with them.

When Your Escape Moves Next Door

As more and more states legalize gambling and bring casinos closer to home, recreational players face tougher gambling decisions, such as how often to play, how much to spend when playing more frequently, and whether to spend their gambling dollars nearby or still make the usual trek to Nevada or Atlantic City.

If you decide you'd like to play more often now that there's gambling just down the road, it's even more important to set your limits and stick with them. You should probably play shorter sessions and spend fewer dollars each time than you would if you still played only a couple of times a year on vacation.

Bet You Didn't Know ...

There are now three Native American casinos within 20 miles of my home in San Diego's east county. I've pledged allegiance to one of them, Barona, because they know how to treat regular players, they've put a lot of effort into running their operations like a Las Vegas casino—smooth and customer-focused! And, they let me win once in a while! The downside is that I haven't been to Las Vegas in a long time, simply because there's only so much money to go around.

In addition, consider which dollars you're playing with. If you're not really getting away, does your weekly "good time" count as vacation? Does that mean if you lose your local gaming money, you won't take a vacation? Or is it separate from your vacation budget? You'll be way ahead of the game at the end of the year if you budget your gambling dollars as entertainment expenses and then stick to whatever plan you come up with. That way, although you may have had plenty of fun gambling at home, you won't be wondering where all your money went and why you can't join your friends in Barbados.

> **Best Bet**
>
> Before deciding whether to spend your gambling dollars at your local casino, consider that casinos in Nevada and Atlantic City are more heavily regulated than those in other states. That doesn't guarantee you'll hang on to your money any longer, but it just might help!

Casino Credit: *Not* Your Private Reserve!

There are times in any player's gaming experience when you lose your bankroll. Unfortunately, your money sometimes runs out before your time does. That's usually no problem when you're only 20 miles from home—you just drive home and stay there. But what do you do when you're on vacation? Smart players find something else to do, and there's usually plenty of that. But let's face it: If you can afford it, and you're determined, you'll try to find a way to replenish the funds and start all over again. Casinos make it easy for you. You should make it difficult! For starters, don't bring more than the one credit card you're charging the room on. Nothing feels worse than paying for a temporary lapse in judgment for months to come. You might as well leave the ATM card at home, too, because both the bank and the casino charge as much as they can get away with to give you your own money.

The next bit of advice, believe it or not, is *don't bring any cash!* Years ago, I learned how the credit game worked, and when I ran out of cash, I'd foolishly go over to the cage and use my credit to get more. Now I know that's much too easy to abuse, so I bring only enough money to travel with safely. When I'm at the hotel and ready to play, I tap into my limited casino credit. Once that's gone, I'm done.

> **Best Bet**
>
> To establish casino credit while you're still in the planning stages of your vacation, call the hotel/casino operator and ask to speak with the casino cashier, or cage. Tell them you'd like a credit application so that you can cash checks (day or night and on weekends) on your next visit. Then fill out the application and return it before your next trip.

It's easy to establish casino credit, which can also help you earn *comps*. (There's that word again. Read Chapter 30!) *Casino credit* is just a fancy term for check-cashing privileges. After you fill out the necessary application at the *casino cage* or the VIP desk—or phone for an application from home—the casino checks your bank references and balance and your credit history. Then, in a few hours or a day or two (depending on whether it's a weekday or weekend and your bank is open or closed), they'll tell you what your credit line is. Usually you can get at least a limited amount of credit even if your bank is closed for the weekend. If you are offered more credit than you want, ask them to restrict the line to your own limits. They should oblige, even though they'll note that you're worth more. In the interim before the final bank approval arrives, the hotel usually lets you cash a "courtesy" check for a few hundred dollars.

After your credit line is set up, you can cash personal checks up to your limit at the casino cage or take a *marker* right at the gaming table. A marker is a casino check that you sign to borrow money against your credit line. You can pay it off before you leave or withdraw it from your bank like a regular check. You might also be given a VIP card to use at each game to earn comps. If (after reading Chapter 30) you're interested in earning comps and they haven't already offered, you might want to request the VIP card when you establish credit.

Gamb-lingo

The cashier's desk, where you can often cash checks, establish credit, and turn your gaming chips back into the real thing, is referred to as the **casino cage**. A player who has established credit with the casino can write a **marker**, which is essentially a check, at the gaming tables.

Anyway, if the only money you have to play with is the amount of credit you establish for yourself, you'll be forced to stop playing when you reach your self-imposed limit. Don't make the mistake of taking all your credit out at once. You'll want to reserve a cushion in case you want it later because once it's gone, it's gone!

Alternative Lifestyles (in America's Playlands)

What if you're on vacation in Las Vegas for example and the money runs out, but you don't want no stinkin' credit? Good for you! There's plenty to do, and you can start by going down to the pool and renting a raft. For just $5 a day (that's just one single bet!), you can float your cares away, keep one foot in the water to cool off, and learn to appreciate the dry desert heat the way I do.

I used to float with my significant other for hours at a time, betting on how high and how quickly the temperature would rise. He'd check his watch and then we'd make our bets and at the appointed hour, glance over at the huge thermometer conveniently posted on an adjacent rooftop to see who won! (Of course, he never paid up!)

If you're not into basking, basting, and broiling in the heat (or even betting on it), go to the spa and spend the day pampering yourself for much less than it would cost to keep gambling. Then charge all that much-needed rest and relaxation to your room.

Or, if you're tired of all the decadence and want a bit of fresh air, take a stroll down the Strip in Vegas. Too hot? Go downtown and sit under the canopy for the Fremont Street experience. Got a car? Go see Red Rock Canyon, Hoover Dam, Mt. Charleston, or the desert flowers out on I-15. Drive to Laughlin, and in only 90 minutes, you'll be rollin' on the Colorado River.

Feel like hanging around the casinos but don't want to play anymore? How about sitting in on some of those free gaming classes? Park yourself in a comfortable chair at the bar and watch all the people! Las Vegas has better people-watching than almost anywhere else. Or go see the sights in some other hotel. Cruise the "indoor city" at the MGM Grand, and then walk across the street and check out the pool (and great waterfall) at the Tropicana.

Risky Business

Don't even consider using more money than you planned to gamble with on any one trip. Most people *don't* win their money back, and some wind up going into debt. The worst time to double up your bets is when you're losing (that's called "chasing" your money). Playing catch-up is more of a dream than a reality.

Best Bet

Enjoy the beauty and charm of an Italian villa on your next trip to Las Vegas by taking a stroll around the 8-acre lake at Bellagio.

There's always something going on in a gambling town. If yours happens to be Atlantic City instead of Las Vegas, then you've got the whole Atlantic Ocean and miles of beach to explore. If you're lucky enough to be in Lake Tahoe, you've got one of the world's most breathtaking views, the highest alpine lake in the country, and all the fresh mountain air your lungs can take in, right at your doorstep.

The best thing you can do for yourself—wherever you are, even *before* the money runs out—is spend some of your time relaxing. Although most people visit gambling meccas to get away from it all and have a good time, they seldom rest. Don't make the mistake of returning from your vacation exhausted!

It's easy to forget that gambling isn't always all fun and games. Sometimes it's a lot of work, and the stimulation (read that as "occasional pressure") can take its toll. With all the excitement and your adrenaline pumping, it's sometimes next to impossible to get to sleep in the "city that never sleeps"; by the time you do, somebody always slams a door. Maybe that's why I have this affinity for oceans, lakes, and pools—I can always catch a few ZZZs around water!

Anyway, you get the picture. A big part of money management is holding on to it longer, finding other ways to have fun (and there are plenty), and getting your money's worth from a great vacation. Eventually you'll get the hang of how to mix the gambling fun with the relaxation, and your money will last a little longer. You'll wind up feeling and playing better and have more pleasant memories to bring home, too.

When the Taxman Cometh

Before you go spending all your windfall profits, remember there's someone out there waiting for a piece of your action. The IRS considers all gambling gains to be income, so you—and possibly the casino where you win—are obligated to report them. For all the sordid details, we advise you to talk to your tax accountant or advisor. We'll just give you some of the highlights.

Basically, you have to report *any* money you win through gambling to the IRS. To make your reporting job easier when you win a substantial amount, casino personnel will pay you your winnings by check or cash (not coins, even if you've won a slot machine jackpot). They will also record and report your name, Social Security Number (SSN), and the amount of your winnings to the IRS if they equal or exceed the following limits:

- $1,200 or more won in a single bingo game or a slot-machine jackpot, which includes the one-armed bandits as well as video poker, keno, blackjack, and so on.

- $1,500 or more won in a live-action keno game.

After the casino representative completes the paperwork, he or she gives you a copy, which you should keep with your tax records until an official IRS form W-2G is mailed to you by the casino at the end of the year.

In all other games, which include sports betting, horse racing, lotteries, craps, blackjack, and other table games, taxes are automatically withheld if you cash in winnings in excess of $5,000. You can also elect to have taxes withheld from slot machine and keno winnings. When taxes are withheld, the casino deducts the proper amount of taxes based on the size of your winnings and sends the deduction and appropriate paperwork to the IRS.

When you have a win that the casino has reported to the IRS, you have two choices: (1) Pay income taxes on that win either when you win it or at the end of the tax year, or (2) Offset part or all of that win with your gambling losses, which you must be able to document.

After your gambling winnings have been reported to the IRS by a gambling establishment or lottery commission, you get a copy of the W-2G tax form at the end of the year. You must include this tax form, like any other tax form used to report income, in your annual income-tax filing to the IRS.

A number of good tax books are available that deal specifically with gambling, and many of them provide examples of forms you can use to record and substantiate your losses. Keeping good records of each gambling session is a good habit to get into anyway, not only because it helps reduce your tax obligations on big wins, but also because it helps you keep tabs on how much you spend and lose in the course of a year. If you plan to gamble a few times a year, good advice would be to talk to a tax expert *and* start keeping records.

The sample record shown in the next illustration demonstrates how easy it is to keep track of your wins and losses for each gambling session. Record the date and each machine or table game you play. Keep track of the amount of time you spend playing each game, too. Then record the total amount of money wagered on that game and how much you walked away with. To figure out how much you won or lost, subtract your total stake from the amount you walked away with. If the figure is a positive number, you won. If the figure is negative, you lost and should enter the amount lost in parentheses.

Tally up how you did for each gambling session by adding all the wins and losses for all the games you played that day, and enter the result in the Session Bal. column. You can keep track of how you're doing cumulatively throughout the year by totaling all the wins and losses recorded in that last column. If you keep good records, it will be easy for you to see when you've reached your budgeted limit and ought to stop gambling—until next year!

For those of you who would like to use this form, we've provided a blank one. Feel free to copy or modify it. However, if you intend to use it for tax purposes, run it by your tax advisor first.

| Date | Casino | Time | Machine or Table # | Total Stake | | | Result | | | |
				Buy-In	Extra	Total	Left With	Won	(Lost)	Session Bal.
4/22/96	Nugget	5p - 7p	VP #1234	80	60	140	80		(60)	
		7p - 9p	BJ#3	60		60	85	25		
		9p-10p	VP #4567	60		60	30		(30)	(65)
6/4/96	Luxor	12p-1p	VP #7666	40	40	80	228	148		
		3p-3:15	Slot # 5213	60		60	30		(30)	118

To keep track of your progress, keep good records of each gambling session, as shown here.

Date	Casino	Time	Machine or Table #	Total Stake			Result			
				Buy-In	Extra	Total	Left With	Won	(Lost)	Session Bal.

Use a worksheet like this blank one to track your gambling winnings and losses.

The Least You Need to Know

- After you budget the money you have to spend on a gambling vacation or weekly trips to a local casino, you've set your limit. Don't let yourself go over it.

- There are many other things to do on a gambling vacation besides gamble. Don't forget to take time to relax and enjoy yourself doing some of them.

- When you establish casino credit, you are allowed to cash personal checks up to your credit limit. You will probably also start earning comps on the money you play, which is a sensible reason for establishing credit.

- When you win, you have to pay the piper. To avoid overpaying your IRS tax on winnings (and to keep track of the money you spend), keep careful records of each gambling session.

Chapter 29

Looking Out for #1

In This Chapter

- Why you're less likely to be cheated in today's casino than in days gone by
- Who regulates gambling and how the public is protected
- When to suspect cheating
- How to protect yourself and your money in a casino

When Stanford first started out as a gambling whiz in 1964, he spent the summer in Reno and entertained visiting friends by taking them to a local casino that cheated. There they would amuse themselves by watching the blatant peeking and dealing of seconds by the blackjack dealers—cheating methods we'll discuss later. As Stanford recalls, Las Vegas was worse—it was difficult to find an honest blackjack game in Las Vegas back then. That was the bad old days; nowadays, Nevada gambling is strictly honest. Although cheating is no longer a problem in states such as Nevada and New Jersey that have adequate control over their casinos, new gambling facilities are springing up in other states all the time, and their regulatory controls have yet to be tested and proven.

Consequently, no book on casino gambling would be complete without a chapter on cheating and protecting yourself. In this chapter, we'll not only explain why gambling is generally much safer and honest today, but we'll also show you how to spot a gambling cheat or scam in the unlikely event that one stares you in the face. And, because we're talking about *your* money, we'll show you how to guard against theft when you visit a gambling mecca. To borrow from an old expression: You can never be too rich—*or* too careful!

How Far Have We Come?

As you learned way back in Chapter 1, before gambling was legalized in Nevada, then Atlantic City, and now many of the towns, cities, and states in between, it was going on anyway everywhere in the United States. In addition to the craps games and card games played among friends in the privacy of their own homes, there were plenty of illegal gaming establishments in the back rooms of bars and storefronts. Many of these operations were run by mobsters, hustlers, cons, and cheats.

Now that gambling *is* legal, it's one of America's most prosperous and heavily regulated industries. In fact, many casinos are owned and operated by some of the largest shareholder-owned corporations in the entertainment and hospitality industries—companies such as Starwood Lodging, MGM, Hilton, Mirage, Circus Circus, and so on. Even those that aren't owned by huge conglomerates are dedicated to increasing shareholder value by maintaining the same high levels of standards, ethics, professional service, and customer satisfaction as their competition does.

If the gaming industry has learned one thing over the years, it's that if they provide an honest game, people will play. That alone should allay any fears you may have that a prominent gaming establishment might be running a crooked ship. If that's not enough, know that any gaming establishment *within the jurisdiction of state gaming authorities and their regulations* can be shut down at a moment's notice if cheating is uncovered in any form on their premises. None are foolish enough to risk their most valuable possession—a state gaming license—to make a few measly bucks on the side.

How Gambling Regulations Protect *You*

Gambling is regulated by the states rather than the federal government. In each state that has legalized gambling of any kind, state gambling commissions decide which games are allowed, monitor gambling activities, and enforce gaming regulations and laws to ensure that casinos operate honest games. In Atlantic City, for example, an agent of the New Jersey Casino Control Commission is required by law to remain on site in each casino at all times. In Nevada, on-site agents are not required, but casinos are frequently monitored and audited by the Nevada Gaming Control Board.

Federal regulations govern the operation of gambling facilities on overseas military installations, the transport of gaming equipment such as slot machines between states, and the transmission of gambling information over public communication lines. Federal regulations also govern gambling on Indian reservations, which are sovereign nations and, therefore, not under the control of state regulation. Some, but not all, Indian reservations have agreed to abide by the rules and regulations of state gaming commissions.

Cruise ships, which are often owned and operated by foreign interests, are restricted to gambling outside the boundaries of United States territorial waters. As such, gambling interests are regulated and monitored by the cruise ship lines themselves. They do, however, have a vested interest in keeping on-board gaming fair and square; otherwise, fewer patrons would participate.

Caution: What Sovereignty Means to You

As sovereign nations, Indian tribes are self-governing. What that means to you is that although they have established general gaming agreements with the federal government and the states in which they reside, they are *not* subject to the same regulations and scrutiny as casinos in Nevada and Atlantic City. In Nevada, for example, all slot machines must be programmed to pay back a minimum of 75 percent and are regularly inspected by Gaming Commission agents. Indian casinos, on the other hand, are free to set their own minimum payback percentages and monitor the programming and performance of their slot machines (and video machines) themselves.

It also means that if you have any kind of dispute with an Indian casino, your case must be settled within the tribal government system. Here's how the system might work: Suppose you get lucky on a slot machine in an Indian casino and line up a collection of symbols that is supposed to pay you $300,000. Next, suppose that the Indians refuse to pay you the $300,000, claiming that the machine malfunctioned. You cannot go to the police or the FBI because they do not have jurisdiction. You can sue, but not in the same court you would use if you had a dispute with a non-Indian business; you must sue in a tribal court, and that tribe may not have any laws covering slot jackpots or whatever your problem is. Tribal courts are set to handle domestic disputes, not casino-related problems. You may have difficulty finding a lawyer who can and will represent you in a tribal court. You are going up against the Indians in their own court, which is not the same thing as having a case decided by a court that has no ties to either party. If you are going up against an Indian casino, you are going against the major income producer for the tribe. Do you really think a tribal court is going to tell its own casino to pay you the $300,000? It's something to think about!

Finding Safety in Numbers

Obviously, if you stick to the casinos that are regulated by the state to protect gambling customers, you should be able to find an honest game in a safe environment. In fact, the major problem casinos have with cheating is with players and employees who try to steal from the house. That's why you'll find security cameras hidden in plastic domes (commonly referred to as "the eye in the sky") on the ceiling of most gambling establishments.

With that huge disclaimer out of the way, it doesn't hurt for you to be aware of, and alert to, the treatment you get in any casino. Most questionable practices are usually the result of an individual employee and *not* the policy of the house. Casinos spend small fortunes protecting their interests and their customers from unscrupulous employees. Consider the enormous sums of money that cross the palms of slot-change people, table-game dealers, and casino cashiers every day—a lot more than your average McDonald's employee handles in a year! What about the hundreds of technicians who not only know how to fix, but can open and reprogram, slot machines with multimillion-dollar jackpots?

To ensure the integrity and character of their staffs, casinos in most states are required to follow state-approved security regulations that involve strict hiring and screening practices, as well as routine inspections to make sure security processes are well-documented, maintained, and followed. In Nevada, every employee—from the highest-ranking casino official to the housekeeper who cleans your room—is required to get a work card from the local sheriff's department. The work card is issued only after doing a complete background check and careful screening for prior violations. A Nevada employee caught stealing or cheating is usually fired immediately and arrested and prosecuted as well.

Gamb-lingo

A player leaving a game often **colors up**, exchanging smaller denomination chips for larger denomination chips; they're easier to carry since there are fewer of them. You can transport and count large-denomination coins, slot-machine tokens, and casino chips in wood or plastic containers called **racks**.

Making Change

The most obvious mistake you may encounter is when an employee changes your cash into playing chips or slot-machine coins, and then again when changing them back after you're done. When you're playing a table game or craps, *always* count the change passed to you when you buy in, or when you *color up* (exchange lower denomination chips for higher denomination chips when you leave or decide to bet bigger). Mistakes do happen, and sometimes, especially in a fast game or with a novice dealer, you might not get as many chips as you deserve. If you count up as soon as the chips are passed to you, or while the dealer is stacking them, and call an error to the dealer's attention, it will be corrected immediately. The same goes for any incorrect payoffs you might receive on a bet or errors a dealer might make deciding who won a hand.

One reason to point out a mistake immediately is the possibility of instant replay. The casino videotapes almost everything that happens (no, not in the restrooms), but most of those tapes are never viewed. So if you think you gave the dealer $100 and received chips for only $20, the appropriate tape can be found immediately and played. Either the tape will show you proffering a $20 bill, or you will get the extra $80 in chips you should have gotten in the first place.

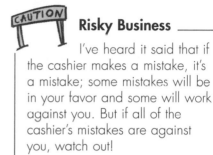

Risky Business

I've heard it said that if the cashier makes a mistake, it's a mistake; some mistakes will be in your favor and some will work against you. But if all of the cashier's mistakes are against you, watch out!

It's much harder for slot-machine change people to make mistakes or incorrect change because most people buy rolls or racks of coins. Here's what you should get when you buy a roll of coins:

One Roll of	Costs This Much	For This Many Coins
Nickels	$2	40
Dimes	$5	50
Quarters	$10	40
Half dollars	$10	20
Dollars	$20	20
$5 tokens	$100	20

You can also purchase dollars and $5 tokens by the *rack* at the change booth. A rack generally has five rows, with each holding the equivalent of a roll of the same coin or token. A rack of dollars costs $100, and a rack of $5 tokens costs $500. An easy way to make sure you got a full rack is to jiggle each row of coins or tokens. There shouldn't be room for another coin in any row, so they shouldn't jiggle. If they do, a coin may be missing. Before you walk away from the change booth, check your rack. If there's a discrepancy, tell the attendant immediately.

Usually, when you finish playing a slot machine, you collect your winnings in a bucket and the change-booth attendant dumps them into an automated coin-counting machine, which is faster and more reliable than counting by hand. If you're playing dollars or higher-denomination tokens, you may have to stack your winnings back into the racks, which can be tedious and time-consuming but is a dependable way to count your money. Many casinos still require you to re-rack large coins because their coin-counting machines haven't been adapted to accommodate larger coins and tokens. No doubt they will be modified eventually, as the higher-denomination machines become more popular.

Card Tricks

We've all seen magicians do mind-boggling card tricks with sleight-of-hand—and whatever else it takes to pull an ace out of nowhere. Many of the tricks we're about to describe are deceptions that gambling halls used to be famous for, especially when dealing from one deck of cards. It's much more difficult to manipulate eight decks of cards than one deck of cards!

Watch Out for Second-Hand Rose

Dealing seconds used to be the most common form of card cheating when blackjack was played with one handheld deck. Now that most blackjack games are dealt from a shoe, dealing seconds is uncommon—but it is something to be aware of. Seconds can be dealt in any card game (including the ones you play at home) in which the cards are dealt from the dealer's hand and not a shoe.

As the name implies, *dealing seconds* means the dealer deals the second card rather than the top card. There are many ways to deal seconds. One easy way to do it is to hold the deck in one hand and use the thumb of that hand to pull the top card back slightly, and then deal the next card. Voilà! You've dealt a second. With practice, you can learn to do it so quickly that the human eye can't detect it.

Dealing seconds hurts the player only if the dealer has done so to take a peek at the top card. For example, if the top card is an ace, and the game is blackjack, the dealer could deal seconds to the players, and then deal the ace to the dealer's hand. (Peeking at the top card is much easier to catch than dealing seconds.) If you ever see a space appear between the top card and the rest of the pack, you're probably being cheated.

There are many ways to cheat besides peeking and dealing seconds. Several skillful cheats have made videotapes demonstrating their talents. Stanford particularly recommends the *Gambling Protection Series* by Steve Forte.

A casino where one type of cheating takes place probably condones other types. If you see any form of cheating, your best bet is to do your gambling in a different casino.

Not Playing with a Full Deck

In multiple-deck blackjack games, an effective form of deception that even an unskilled dealer can get away with is altering the mix of cards used. Aces and tens favor the player, and twos through sixes favor the casino. Adding extra twos through sixes or removing aces or tens cheats the players. Removing a dozen 10-count cards from a six-deck blackjack shoe gives the casino an extra and unfair 1 percent advantage. If you learn to count cards (as mentioned in Chapter 11 and covered in Stanford's book *Professional Blackjack*), you can detect whether cards are missing from a shoe.

The Shuffle Off to Buffalo

Stacking the deck is another trick *card sharpers* have used to influence card games. You've probably seen it done in poker games on the movie screen; the *mark* (carnival talk for "victim") gets four aces dealt and bets the ranch, only to lose to a straight flush.

When a deck is *stacked*, the cards are arranged in an order that benefits the sharper or an accomplice, and then the order is preserved through the shuffle and cut. Some sharpers practice long hours to maintain their skills. Again, the best advice is to limit your gambling to legal casinos, where you are highly unlikely to encounter dealers with such skills. (Casinos don't like to hire skillful cheats because the casinos themselves are equally likely to be the victims of cheating.)

Gamb-lingo _____

A **card sharp** is a person skilled at cards. A **card sharper** is a person or dealer who can manipulate cards to cheat. Some card sharps are card sharpers.

A Final Word to the Wise

Although an abundance of security personnel and surveillance cameras ensure the safety of casino patrons, *you* can still do a lot to protect yourself. For starters, realize that any criminal element in a gambling establishment is usually after money—either yours or the casino's. And when gambling, most players carry more money than they do at any other time. To enjoy your gambling experience without becoming the unsuspecting victim of crime or theft, follow these simple suggestions and stay alert and informed:

◆ If you brought a large amount of cash, deposit it in a free hotel safe instead of carrying it with you or keeping it in your room. Deposit unneeded credit cards in the safe as well, or better yet, leave them at home.

◆ Don't flash your wallet, cash, or credit cards around. Bring to the tables only as much money as you intend to use for each playing session.

◆ Don't carry a purse. A "belly bag" (a.k.a. "fanny pack" worn backward, resting in front of you where you can see it) is a perfect substitute for both men and women. It has a zipper, wraps around your waist (leaving your arms free), and can be worn in front where you can see it. It's hard to imagine anyone running off with a belly bag while it's wrapped around you, or even getting close to the zipper without you knowing it. Similarly, if you carry anything around, make sure you're always touching it. If someone takes something from you but you notice the theft immediately, and you're in a casino, the thief will probably be caught and the theft captured on video.

◆ If you're too tired to pay attention to your game *and* your surroundings, stop playing.

◆ If you're playing slot machines, don't play more machines than you can easily keep track of or reach. It's too easy for passers-by to reach into a coin tray and grab a handful. Be even more careful when playing near an entrance.

◆ When playing slot machines, don't let buckets of coins pile up. Cash them in frequently and then *stash the cash*!

◆ Keep track of your chips at the gaming tables. Although dealers will look out for your interests while you take a short break from the table, it's generally wise to take a quick count of what you leave on the table before you go. If there's too much on the table, bring most of it with you and leave a small portion on the table to reserve your seat.

Best Bet _____

Money isn't the only thing casino crooks are after. Occasionally you'll hear about expensive jewelry, camera equipment, laptop computers, and anything of value being stolen from a hotel room. Play it smart and always store your valuables in a hotel safe deposit box.

◆ The top rail of a craps table is a convenient place to store your chips as you play. However, as the action heats up and you get caught up in the game, your chips can become an easy target for an unscrupulous player. To protect your chips, stand close to them and even keep a hand over them if you're suspicious of a nearby player. Or, better yet, as your chips pile up, put some in your pocket and hold some in your hand. Always keep track of how many and what color chips you have resting on the rail at all times.

◆ If you get lucky and win a bundle, ask for a security person to accompany you to your car instead of walking out to the parking lot alone. Or accept your winnings in the form of a check. Another alternative is to deposit your big win at the cage and come back to get it later—after the people who saw you win it are gone.

◆ If you do decide to drive home with a lot of cash, be cautious when leaving the casino. There have been cases of people leaving casinos safely but not making it home with the money because they were run off the road and robbed. This has occurred more frequently to customers of casinos located in rural areas.

◆ Be discreet about your home address. If you need to give it to a casino employee after a big win, write it down for them or whisper! You don't need a stranger showing up at your door to steal your winnings when you arrive home.

◆ Stick to your budget. That way, all that can happen if you become a victim of cheating is you'll lose your money sooner—you won't lose *more* money than you would at an honest game.

◆ Don't gamble in jurisdictions with inadequate regulations.

◆ Stick to legal casinos. Avoid illegal games.

◆ If you're curious and committed to protecting yourself against cheating, many videotapes are available to show you what to look out for. Steve Forte's are among the best.

◆ If you've been cheated or robbed, or witness a casino crime, report it to casino security immediately.

The Least You Need to Know

◆ Cheating is generally not a problem in well-regulated states, such as Nevada and New Jersey. In states where gambling has recently been legalized and on Indian reservations, which are not under state jurisdiction, only time will tell.

◆ It's important to protect yourself from mistakes that can happen whenever a casino employee makes change for you, cashes in your chips, pays winning hands, or sells you coins and tokens for the slot machines.

◆ Criminals know that when gambling, most players carry more money than they do at any other time. Be very careful!

◆ Bring only as much money to the gaming area as you need for one playing session. If a criminal element is in a casino, they're after money, so don't flaunt it.

Chapter 30

On the House (Comps)

In This Chapter

- ◆ What happens when you get "comped"?
- ◆ Getting full RFB
- ◆ How to get a great room, cheap
- ◆ Why you would (or wouldn't) want to join a slot club

Why is it that the guy who drops hundreds, maybe even *thousands*, of dollars at the craps tables and slot machines gets everything (well, almost everything) his heart could possibly desire—*free*—while you sit in your airplane seat meticulously adding up the cost of three nights' lodging, meals, snacks, tips, the spa, Siegfried and Roy, taxis to and from the airport, and plane tickets (don't forget the raft rental), and trying to figure out how much you really won (or lost) at the tables? The answer lies in what you know and who you know, not how you played the game.

In this chapter, we'll show you how to cash in on some of those freebies and let you figure out for yourself whether it's worth it. Stick around; the price is right.

Who Says There's No Free Lunch?

Comped, a small word that means so much to so many recreational gamblers, is short for *complimentary*, as in, "This one's on us!" Casinos are famous for doling out free gifts and services that are worth a lot of money to their most loyal and high-rolling clientele. But it isn't the pure joy of giving that inspires such benevolence—it's the desire to have you stay and play at their house exclusively.

Comps come in all sizes and packages, designed to accommodate all gambling budgets and styles: the honeymooners, vacationing couples, swinging singles, entrepreneurs, the lonely and forlorn, the young and restless, weekend "regulars," tourists, retirees—you name it, there's a comp waiting somewhere with your name on it. All you need to do is know where to look—and then ask!

It's What's Up Front That Counts

The idea of comping players for their playing time and devotion originated back in the '60s with gambling junkets. Junkets were initially designed to lure groups of high-rolling VIPs from far-away places (mostly the east coast) by providing limousine and chartered jet service, followed by a free run-of-the-house (room, meal, booze, and so on) upon arrival. The catch was that players had to put up *front* money to qualify and guarantee the casino a certain amount of playing time at high stakes. The front-money requirement assured the casino that the customer was either establishing credit or bringing enough cash to be able to gamble if he (there weren't too many VIP women back in those days) chose to. If the player chose not to gamble, he simply wouldn't be invited back.

Gamb-lingo

Casinos issue complimentary gifts called **comps** to entice players to gamble. Typical comps include free room (R), food (F), beverage (B), and sometimes even air fare, depending on a player's level of play. A customer who is worthy of full complimentary treatment is considered a **Very Important Player** (**VIP**) in the casino's book.

Casinos decided to expand their junket propositions to low rollers (like most of us) when they started offering cheap turnarounds and overnight getaways (at usually less than half the regular cost of airfare) in the late '70s. Granted, we didn't get chartered flights, but we did wind up with a free room and a meal or two if we played our cards right. All a low roller had to do to qualify was give the hosting casino four hours of play at a $5 minimum table, and then the rest of the town was ours until the plane left. (Heck, a real "player" could qualify in his or her sleep. In fact, *I* usually did!)

Another way to get freebies was to cash in on all the coupons and funbooks you could collect on your drive into town. Just about every restaurant and gas station from Victorville to Vegas had racks full of casino giveaways, from free shrimp cocktails and cheap rooms to slot machine pulls and lucky-buck coupons you could use as cash at the tables. There are still plenty of coupons out there; in fact, many of them get mailed right to your door if your name finds its way onto the appropriate mailing list. But most of the airline junkets have gone by the wayside, replaced by bus turnarounds, overnights, and plain old casino comps!

Best Bet

Besides getting to stuff your face for free, a meal comp entitles the user to stand in shorter VIP lines at crowded casino restaurants. Sometimes that can be worth more than the meal itself!

How *Comp*assionate Are They?

Comps fall into different categories. If you're a slot player, you earn your comps by joining a slot club, which usually has its own requirements and reward structure that we'll cover later. If you're a table-game player (blackjack, craps, roulette, baccarat, and so on), the level of *complimentaries* showered on you is limited only by how often you frequent the tables and your average bet size. The extent of your bankroll also figures heavily into the comping equation: a 20-pound bag of gold dropped at the casino cage should be worth something somewhere; a one-inch stack of $100s will earn you free room and board most everywhere; and a suitcase filled with $100s should cover a decadent week in paradise for your whole entourage including a private plane, limos, suites, feasts—the works!

For the rest of us (those whose bankrolls end in fewer zeros), here's how the equation works: You decide you'd like to cash in on whatever free *RFBs* (room, food, beverages) you're entitled to. When arriving at your favorite mecca, you tell the pit boss at the game you want to play (or the casino host at the VIP desk) that you'd like to get rated and start earning comps. They'll take your name and essentials and give you a little plastic card to hand to the pit boss at each table game you play. The pit boss then watches your action from time to time, checking how much you buy-in

Best Bet

The level of play required to earn comps varies greatly from casino to casino. You may get full comps at one casino and not even earn a free meal at another. Not only is it important to shop around, but you should also contact a slot or casino host or hostess right away, so they can explain the requirements and look after your best interests.

for, the amount of your average bet, and how long you play. (Some people increase their bet temporarily when the pit boss comes over to their table to chat in order to get a higher rating and better comp.) When you're ready to leave—which shouldn't be too soon if you really want comps!—ask for your card back and the pit boss will enter the information gathered about you into a computer.

> **Risky Business**
>
> Don't even *think* about playing higher limit games or risking more money than you'd planned just to earn a comp. The money you save in room and board isn't worth the money you may wind up losing in the process of earning it! Remember, casinos give out comps to try to lure you into spending more. You should use comps to help you spend less.

In *Comp City*, Max Rubin, the "Comp Wizard," has turned getting comped into an art form. He advises readers to bet bigger only when the pit boss is watching, tip the dealers now and then, and never stiff the cocktail waitress. These little things add up, and when the pit boss records what he or she has noticed about you into the computer, his or her favorable attitude can make the difference between whether you earn a free buffet dinner for two (which most players can get after just a few hours of play) or a full RFB for the weekend.

You won't earn your comps after just an hour or two of play. In fact, to get the whole enchilada, you'll either have to bet more than $75 per hand for eight hours or more or settle for just a free room at around $25 to $50 per bet. Some places may let you bet half (or less) of the required amount and spend twice as much time earning the comp, but others won't. Do yourself a favor and check first. Most casinos are upfront with you about their comp requirements, but you have to *ask*—and be willing to shop around! (By the way, long hard hours at a much lower minimum bet should still earn you a free mercy meal for the asking. If it doesn't, you're definitely at the wrong place!)

> **Best Bet**
>
> The end of the twentieth century marks yet another metamorphosis for Las Vegas as it's transformed from the fun family destination of the 1990's into an opulent desert oasis and playground for the rich. With more than 9,000 high-priced luxury suites coming on line by the turn of the century, what does it mean for you, the average player? More comps and lower room rates as today's top-tier hotels, such as Caesars, Mirage, Bally's, the MGM, and others, compete with the likes of the Bellagio, the Venetian, and the Paris Las Vegas. If we play our cards right, we can all upgrade. See you there!

Casinos calculate your comp worthiness by determining how much they can expect to profit from you. First, they calculate your total action by multiplying your average bet size by the average number of hands played in an hour. Then they multiply your total action by what they can expect to win (that is, the normal house edge for the bets you make). Most casinos give you back 30 percent to 50 percent of what they expect to win in R, F, or B comps. For example, say you're a blackjack player playing $25 per hand, 60 hands per hour, for 8 hours. If the casino figures its expected win (or house edge) at about 2 percent, your play is worth the following:

$$\$25 \times 60/\text{hr.} \times 8 \text{ hr.} \times 2\% = \mathbf{\$240}$$

When a casino expects to earn $240 from you, it's usually willing to give you back $75 to $120 worth of complimentary room or meal credits. This level of play probably won't get you R *and* F in a luxury hotel like Caesars Palace, the MGM Grand, or the Mirage, but it should certainly earn you dinner for two and the *casino rate* on a room. At a less opulent palace, the same level of play could be worth a whole lot more in comps. When you're done playing for a session, ask the pit boss what he or she can do for you. You'll either find out on the spot, or you'll be hooked up with a casino host who can map out the whole comp program.

If you're unsure of your comp worthiness or unwilling to bet at these levels, your best bet is to speak with the folks in casino marketing when you make your travel plans. They can tell you what it takes to qualify for different comps and how your style of play would rate. Most casino marketing departments have their own toll-free 800 number. Call the 800 operator at 1-800-555-1212 and ask for the number of the casino's marketing department, specifically. These days, you can also get some casino phone numbers online. Get to know the Internet, and the Internet will help you!

Gamb-lingo

The highest rollers usually get the full **RFB** comp treatment, which includes room, food, beverage (meaning booze with meals), and sometimes airfare and more. Moderate rollers usually qualify for food comps and sometimes room comps, too, depending on their level of play. The **casino rate** is a reduced room rate that casinos usually offer rated players who do not qualify for full room comps.

Sleep Cheap Anyway

Even if you don't qualify to get your room comped, you can usually get about 50 percent off the regular price of a room by getting the *casino rate*. In most casinos, playing $5 to $25 bets at the tables for four hours will qualify you for cheap sleep.

In fact, most slot clubs give the casino rate to their slot players. The downtown Las Vegas hotel/casinos are usually more liberal with both their slots and their casino room rates than the Strip hotels. Again, your best bet is to call casino marketing

Best Bet

It pays to shop around when playing the comp game. It's easy for me to earn a free room and a meal or two at the Rio, the Golden Nugget, or even the Mirage. But when I play at the Stratosphere, I get a two-room suite and the royal treatment (not to mention machines that seem to let me play and play all day!).

wherever you're going (Atlantic City, Nevada, or any other gambling destination) and ask how to get the casino rate. Or, when you check in, ask who you need to speak with about getting the casino rate. The front desk will usually change your original reservation to the casino rate upon check out, if you qualified during your stay. When you're approved for cheap sleep, you can generally stay on the casino-rate list for a year or so, regardless of how much you play.

You don't have to be a player to cash in on Las Vegas. Plenty of visitors and townies make their own good time going from place to place using coupons and collecting the latest giveaways and bargains. Here are just a few examples of how to work the comp game in Vegas:

- Walk through Glitter Gulch downtown and take a free pull on the world's biggest slot machine at the Four Queens.

- Check out the computerized light-show experience above Fremont Street.

- Experience the luxury and ambience of an Italian villa at the Bellagio. Pay an extra $10 to view the Bellagio's $300 million art collection, which includes paintings by Gauguin, Matisse, Van Gogh, Cezanne, Warhol, and even Frank Sinatra.

- Meet me at the Horseshoe for the midnight special: T-bone, baked potato, and salad for three bucks.

- Watch the traffic-stopping pirate show at Treasure Island, the live circus act at Circus Circus, or the fiery volcano and Siegfried and Roy's white Bengal tigers at the Mirage.

- Get a bird's-eye view of the city that never sleeps from atop the Stratosphere Tower.

All in the Family (Slot Clubs)

More than 60 percent of today's casino revenue is generated by slot players alone, and casinos have gotten smart about that. No longer are slot players relegated to the farthest reaches of the house. Now they are the *most* sought-after guests of just about every casino on the mainland. To prove their adoration, casinos compete ruthlessly for your slot-playing business.

According to Jeffrey Compton, whose *Las Vegas Guide to Slot Clubs* is a must if you're into the one-armed bandits, the overwhelming majority of casinos in Sin City and Atlantic City have slot clubs, and you'll be doing yourself a favor by joining as many of them as you can. Shortly thereafter, you'll receive invitations to participate in slot tournaments and get reduced room rates, special birthday cards, party invitations, and more.

Once you join the family, you'll immediately earn casino credits for cash and comps each time you play a slot or video-poker machine. To start, just visit the casino slot club booth and ask to sign up. The host or hostess will tell you how the program works, ask you to fill out an application, and give you your own plastic club card. When you sit down at a slot machine from that moment on, insert the club card into the special card reader. The reader automatically registers the total amount of coins you've played into the slot club's central computer. When you leave one machine, don't forget to take your card with you. Then insert it into the next machine you play, or you'll miss earning more valuable credits.

Many slot players like to play two and even three machines at a time. (Any more than that and it's very hard to stand guard over your money.) Most slot clubs are glad to accommodate multi-machine players by giving you additional plastic cards for the asking. When you have more than one card, there's no reason why you can't loan a card to a friend and start earning credits on his or her play, too.

Best Bet

If you visit a gambling town during a busy weekend (Presidents' Day weekend is one of the worst!) and can't find a room, sit down at a table and start playing. Then ask the pit boss for help and look like you really want to keep playing. It's surprising how fast a room opens up even for $5 bettors. Of course, it's safer to call ahead for reservations.

Best Bet

When you win $1,200 or more playing slots, the casino reports your winnings to the IRS. You can, however, offset the taxes by reporting your losses—if you keep good records. Many slot clubs are automated and may be able to supply documentation about machines you played and how much you won and lost. Discuss the possibility with your tax advisor and a slot club host/hostess.

Life in the Information Fast Lane

When your casino has a fully automated player-tracking system, the casino can keep track of how much action you're giving them at all times. In fact, the casino can use its computer and your card to collect valuable marketing information, such as which machines you like to play, how much you've "invested," and how you're doing at any hour of the day. The tracking system also helps the casino identify the most popular machines and how often they pay out.

All the data collected helps management find players who deserve the royal treatment. It also helps the casino make informed decisions about how to best use limited floor space by providing machines that customers *really* want to play. Shades of Big Brother? Maybe—but this is a system that has advantages for you, too. Besides, rumor has it that these state-of-the-art, profit-driven fortresses of fun will soon be installing player-tracking systems at gaming tables, too. So you can run, but you can't always hide. You might as well cash in!

Proceed with Caution

Before we leave you with a burning desire to join every slot club in your path, here's something you should seriously consider: Some clubs allow you to earn credits and comps by playing quarter machines and higher. Others require you play on dollar machines or higher. If you are a quarter-machine player, do *not* step up to the dollar machines simply to earn slot club comps and bonuses. You will be playing beyond your risk level and bankroll, and any credits and comps you earn will *not* be worth the added risk and potential losses. If you play quarters, join slot clubs that reward quarter players. There are fewer of them, but they *do* exist.

If you already play dollar slots, you have much greater choice and freedom of movement, but don't let the added comps entice you to go over your limit. Join slot clubs to reap what is rightfully yours—the bonuses you get for playing machines you'd be playing anyway—but *don't* join just to get freebies that could wind up costing you more than they're worth.

The Least You Need to Know

◆ You qualify for comps (complimentaries) by getting your play and your credit rated. If you pass the test, the house picks up the tab for a lot of stuff.

◆ If you don't qualify for the big comps, you should still be able to earn meal comps and the casino rate on your room.

◆ Slot players can earn comps *and* cash when they join a slot club. But if you have to play higher denomination machines or play longer than you would without earning comps, then the freebies aren't worth the eventual cost.

◆ After you're in the comping pipeline, the casinos can gather information about the games you enjoy and the way you play. It also helps them reward you appropriately for your loyalty *and* perseverance.

Can't We All Get Along?
(Casino Etiquette)

In This Chapter

- Why casino rules, protocol, and etiquette are so important

- How to behave at the tables

- How the emotional swings of machine play should guide your behavior when playing slots and video poker

- What responsibilities you have when you walk the casino floor

Now that casinos are everywhere, especially in my Southern California backyard, I've become more and more aware of casino etiquette, or the lack thereof. It seems to me that as we find ourselves spending more time in our local casinos—simply because they are a new and inviting source of local entertainment—visitors could use an introductory or refresher course in casino protocol and manners. That's what you'll get in this chapter.

Who's Not in It for the *Money?*

Casinos offer a little bit of everything for everyone and as a result, there are often thousands of people from all walks of life doing their own thing at any given time. Most are playing slot or video machines, some are playing table games, and others are wandering around drinking in the atmosphere—so to speak.

If you're a serious player, it could be easier to read a book in Penn Station at rush hour than to find your zone in a crowded casino. Even casual players find that too much time around a rude and obnoxious player eventually spoils their fun.

For everyone in a casino, the common denominator is *money!* Whether you've an ample sum for the evening that you're just trying to hold on to, or a suitcase full that you're hoping to parlay into a small fortune, there are certain rules of decorum that need to be followed. That doesn't mean you have to act like you're in a bank or the library. Just act responsibly, respect other people's time and space, and know that the house is looking to protect everyone and their money!

At the Tables

In addition to civilized rules of courtesy, there are standard house rules that must be followed at gaming tables. We've covered many of these rules in their respective chapters, but here's a reminder:

- Wait 'til the game or hand in progress has finished before you join a table game.

- When you join a game, buy-in your chips for the game if you don't already have some. Just place the amount of money you want to buy-in for on the table and the dealer will exchange it for chips.

- Use only one hand to touch your cards. Never put both hands on your cards or the playing table. This makes the dealer and pit bosses very nervous about cheating.

- Don't bend, scratch, nick, or mark the cards in any way. Doing so is a sign of cheating to the house.

- If the game you're playing deals the cards face up, don't touch the cards at all.

- If shooting craps, never touch the dice unless you are the shooter.

- Don't touch your bet after the cards have been dealt. This also makes dealers and pit bosses very nervous.

- Use the proper hand signals to tell the dealer what you want to do next.

- Learn the rules and protocols for each game before you sit down to play. A good place to start is by reading this book.

◆ Don't sit down at a crowded table if you don't know how to play. Questions and frequent interruptions can really slow a game down and annoy other players who were probably enjoying the pace before you arrived. Play to learn when the casino is less busy.

◆ Don't expect other players to teach you. They're there to have fun, too.

◆ Don't ask the dealer how you should play your hand. They will gladly explain the mechanics of the game but they don't want to be responsible or involved in your playing decisions.

◆ Don't give advice to other players. You don't want to feel responsible for their results, do you?

> **Bet You Didn't Know ...**
>
> In some foreign countries tables get so crowded that bystanders line up three deep behind seated players and actually wager on the players' hands. I've actually had this happen to me here in the good old U.S.A. But this is definitely a no no in most American casinos, unless local custom accepts it. If you don't see this being done, don't do it. If you're compelled to do it, ask first!

◆ Don't get annoyed when another player gets the card you need. That's part of the game, and no one likes a poor sport.

◆ When the game is over, place your cards down in front of you and let the dealer pick them up. Do not hand them to the dealer.

◆ Don't be a sore loser or blame the dealer for your play. There are ups and downs in gambling and you have merely experienced one. If you can not accept losing gracefully, perhaps you shouldn't be gambling.

◆ Don't get drunk, loud, or obnoxious. Unlike a bar, there's money to be won and lost in a casino and most people take that seriously. It's no fun to be around an idiot when you're playing for keeps.

◆ Seats at the tables are for players. Don't take a seat unless you are playing. If you are watching a friend and the table is not crowded, ask the dealer if it is alright to sit down. They will usually say yes.

◆ Nowadays, if you're a smoker, try to take a seat on either side of a table so that your smoke will bother fewer players.

At the Machines

I think you'd have to be almost dead not to get an adrenalin high playing slots or video machines. It's exciting, frustrating, and undoubtedly emotional. So, tread lightly with fellow players; they may not be in their right mind! The Golden Rule definitely applies at the machines. Here's a few house rules and Golden Rules to live by:

◆ Read the warnings posted on your machine, such as: Malfunction voids all play; One machine per player at certain times; Progressive jackpots paid out in 20 annual payments, etc.

◆ If you like to play two machines at a time, resist the urge when the casino is crowded. Other people are there to play, too. Save your two-machine playing to off-hours when the casino isn't crowded.

◆ When most of the machines are taken at peak times, don't occupy a machine and only play one coin at a time versus maximum bet. Plenty of other players who can't find a machine would jump at the chance to play max bet at that machine if it were available. Drop down to a lower denomination machine and load it up!

◆ Don't bang, punch, or whack the buttons on a slot or video machine so hard that it distracts other players. I sometimes wonder whether people who do this treat their kids the same way. Psychologically speaking, it indicates anger that you probably shouldn't be taking out on the machine or other people. And, there's absolutely no correlation between the release of hostility and jackpots. Lighten up and get some help!

◆ Don't tap, rub, or punch a machine's screen in a manner that other players find distracting. This is a superstitious, voodoo-ish behavior that doesn't work, unless you're trying to distract those around you.

◆ *Don't* under *any* circumstances sit down next to a player who is sitting quietly, peacefully minding his/her own business at a machine and start doing any of the previously two distracting behaviors.

◆ Unlike a table game where you merely leave some of your chips on the table and excuse yourself when you need to take a restroom break, there's not much you can do about saving your machine when playing slots. Many players push their seat in toward the machine and leave a plastic cup on it, or on the handle. Some leave their Player's card in the slot, too, indicating that the machine is still being used. Don't start playing a machine that has been left in a similar manner. Someone is probably playing it.

◆ If you happen to start playing a machine that was in use by someone who was merely taking a temporary break, offer to give them back the machine. First, try to establish evidence that they intended to return to the machine.

◆ If you need to take a short break while playing at a machine, ask a floor person to stand by your machine for a few moments or get you a "Reserved" sign. (Reserved signs are not available at all casinos. But it doesn't hurt to ask.) If all else fails, try the seat and cup routine explained previously.

◆ Don't assume that the people playing near you will gladly guard your machine when you need to take a break. Ask them to do so, nicely.

◆ Don't covet your neighbor's machine. Be happy for everyone who beats the casino. Eventually, you will be the winner of the moment!

◆ Do play quietly by yourself. That's the beauty of playing against a machine.

The Wanderers

Casino wanderers are a special breed of people watchers. They often soak up a casino's excitement by participating vicariously. Which is fine, provided the person whose excitement they're soaking up doesn't mind being watched.

I for one can't stand it! I find it to be an invasion of my privacy and one of the most unnerving distractions there is in a casino. I can literally feel a person's eyes on the back of my neck as they watch over my shoulder. If I'm their entertainment, shouldn't they be paying me? I'm paying the house.

Wanderers should keep wandering. Don't stand back and stare at someone playing a machine or table game. Most likely the one being stared at or watched knows you're there, and doesn't like it. They're probably nervous, like me.

And, while we're on the subject, please try to keep loud or boisterous conversation away from players. You never know when someone has a big bet riding and they're trying to concentrate, focus, or pray. Other than that, enjoy your walk!

What About a Tip?

Tipping in a casino is one of those gray areas. What applies in your local casino doesn't necessarily apply in Las Vegas or Atlantic City, and vice versa.

For example, I know most of the customer service people at my local casino and they always go out of their way to be nice to me. I often get my regular beverage handed to me before I have to ask, employees I don't even know ask how I'm doing today, and I can always get a Reserved sign when I want it. So, I tip! I give a small token tip to the change person and the floor person when I hit a jackpot that has to be "written up." I don't, however, do this in Las Vegas where I don't even know the floor people.

(Although I have tipped the change person when he or she has shown me to the winning machine.)

Gamb-lingo

Whenever you hit a jackpot over $1,999 on a slot or video machine, the win has to be "written up," which means reported to the IRS on a Form W2G. A casino floor person prepares the paperwork for your signature and gives you a copy. Then, they send the original to the IRS at the end of the tax year.

I generally tip blackjack dealers and other table game dealers when they've been nice and I've had a good run or hand. But the only really hard and fast rule I have is that I *always* tip beverage servers wherever I am. (Probably because I like a steady stream of half water, half Sprite with plenty of ice, please.)

The bottom line about tipping is that you just have to trust your own judgment and be who you are. If you would like to share in your good fortune, no one is going to stop you. Except, of course the casino hosts, hostesses, and pit bosses who aren't allowed to accept tips at all.

The Least You Need to Know

♦ Many rules of table game protocol are designed to protect against cheating and theft.

♦ After you've placed your bet in a table game, don't touch the bet until the dealer pays you.

♦ Be considerate of neighboring players when playing slot and video machines.

♦ If the casino is crowded and there are very few machines available, limit yourself to only playing one at a time.

♦ Don't interrupt or distract players when walking through the casino. They're playing with *money!*

♦ There are no clear-cut rules on tipping in a casino. If you feel like tipping, do it!

Gamb-lingo Glossary

action   The amount of money wagered is defined as the action a game is getting at any given time.

ante   Poker players ante when they place a small portion of the minimum bet into the pot before a new hand starts.

baccarat (American style)   An adaptation of a card game that originated in France. Sometimes referred to as Nevada-style baccarat, or *punto banco*.

baccarat pit   An area in a casino that is specially set aside for one or more large baccarat tables.

banker   A card-game banker is someone who books the action of the other bettors at the table. The banker can be the casino or it can be another player.

bar the 12   When the house "bars the 12" in a crap game, that means that a twelve is a tie bet for don't pass and don't come bettors on the come-out roll. Some casinos "bar the 2," in which case the two is a tie.

basic strategy   Basic strategy for blackjack is the set of plays you should make to maximize your advantage, using no information about cards remaining in the deck except that the cards in your hand and the dealer's upcard are not among them. You are presumed to know the number of decks used in the game, the house rules, and what procedures the dealer must follow.

bet down   When an extra-large amount of money has been wagered on one horse, that horse is said to be bet down. If the horse wins, the win payoff will be less than if the horse had not been bet down.

betting limits   In a table game, the betting limits establish the minimum and maximum amounts of money that you can wager on one bet. You cannot wager less than the minimum or more than the maximum amount posted. The betting limits will vary from game to game, and often from table to table in the same casino.

bias   If a horse is more likely to win if it runs on one part of the running surface rather than on another part, the surface is said to have a bias or be biased.

bingo marker   A bingo marker can be a simple crayon, or as fancy as the specially designed ink daubers whose tip covers the number on a game card precisely.

blind bet   A blind bet is a bet that certain poker players are required to make because of their betting positions.

bluffing   A poker player bluffs by raising with a weak hand in hopes of driving out players with stronger hands.

board   The community cards that are dealt face-up in the center of a poker table are referred to as on the "board."

bookmark   Marking the web address of a favorite website so that you can return to it by clicking the name of the site, rather than typing in the address.

box   The box is the center section of the crap table layout where center bets are placed.

boxcars   A roll of two 6s in a crap game is called boxcars, like on a train.

break-even point   The break-even point is the point at which if you played forever, the bets you made would approximately equal the payoffs you'd receive.

bring-in   In seven-card stud, the bring-in is a mandatory bet made by the player with the lowest upcard in the first round of betting.

burn card   After a shuffle and cut, one card is placed on the bottom of the deck or in the discard tray. This procedure is called burning a card, and the card temporarily removed from play is called the burn card.

bust   To bust is to go over twenty-one in blackjack. If you bust, you lose. If the dealer busts and you don't, you win. If both you and the dealer bust, you lose anyway.

button   A button is a small marker that is moved from player to player after each hand of hold 'em poker to designate the dealer position.

call   In poker, a call is when a player makes a bet equal to the previous bet. Sometimes this is referred to as *seeing a bet*. In keno and bingo, to call means to draw the numbers for each game.

caller   The caller is the person at a bingo game who is not only responsible for keeping everyone awake, but also choosing the game pattern, drawing each bingo ball, and reading the number clearly so that everyone can hear and understand. A caller at poker is someone who has called a bet.

card counting   Card counting means keeping track of a summary statistic that describes which cards have been played since the shuffle. Card counters in blackjack generally vary bet size and playing strategy as the composition of the remaining deck changes.

card sharp   A card sharp is a person who is an expert at cards. Sometimes card sharp is used to mean card sharper, a person who can manipulate cards in order to cheat.

carousel   A group of slot machines that are positioned in a circle or ring, so that a change person can stand in the center and supervise the action. (He or she can also change a hundred-dollar bill quicker than you can blink an eye!)

casino cage   The cashier's fortress, where you cash checks, establish credit, and turn your gaming chips back into the real thing, is referred to as the cage.

casino rate   The casino rate is a reduced hotel-room rate that casinos offer good customers.

catch   Catching a keno number means that a number you've marked on your keno ticket has been drawn.

center bets   Center bets, sometimes referred to as proposition bets, are wagers on any of the center propositions on the crap table.

check   In casino gambling, a check is another term for a *chip*. In poker, a player can "check" in order to stay in the game but not bet. This can only be done when no other bets have been made yet on this round.

chip tray   The chip tray in front of a dealer holds that table's inventory of chips.

chips   Chips are tokens of gaming pleasure that are used on casino gaming tables in lieu of cash. You buy chips, or *checks* as they're sometimes called, when you enter a game.

claimer   A claimer is a horse entered in a claiming race.

claiming race   In a claiming race, all the horses are for sale at a set price.

cold   When a slot machine won't let you win anything or quickly takes back what it gave you, it's cold. A player who can't win no matter what also is cold.

color up   A player leaving a game will often color up to exchange smaller-denomination chips for chips of a larger denomination (and a different color). Fewer chips mean less chance of dropping them on the way to the cashier.

colt   A colt is an uncastrated male horse aged four or less.

combination way ticket   A combination way ticket is a keno ticket in which groups of numbers are bet several different ways, allowing the customer to sprinkle money over more combinations.

come-out roll   A crapshooter's first roll(s) before establishing a point, or after making a point, is a come-out roll.

comps   Casinos issue complimentary gifts called comps in order to entice players to gamble. Typical comps include free room (R), food (F), beverage (B), and sometimes even airfare, depending on a player's level of play.

copy   A copy in pai gow poker is when a player and the banker have the same two-card hand, or the same five-card hand. Copies go to the banker, giving him or her a natural advantage over the player.

crapping out   A shooter craps-out by rolling "craps," which is a two, three, or twelve on a come out roll.

croupier   The French word for dealer, the croupier in baccarat controls the drawing and dealing, calls the cards, and collects and pays off player bets. In roulette, the croupier is the person who spins the wheel, sells you chips, and picks them up after you lose them.

cut   When you cut a deck, you divide it into two parts. The dealer then inverts the order of the two parts.

cut card   A card of a different color that is used to cut a deck of cards.

cyberspace   Another term for the Internet.

designated dealer   In poker games like Texas hold 'em, the player to the left of the dealer bets first. In a poker room where each game has a resident dealer, a different player serves as the designated dealer for each hand.

dice   Two identical numbered cubes, a "pair of dice," which are used by a shooter in a crap game.

die   A cube, singular for dice, with sides numbered from 1 to 6.

discard tray   The discard tray is a tray on the dealer's right side that holds all of the cards that have been played or discarded.

double down   When you double down in blackjack, you turn your cards face-up, double your bet, and receive one and only one more card.

down   At craps, to take a bet down is to remove it from the table. Not all bets can be taken down. Specifically, after a point is established, a line bet cannot be taken down, and a come bet that has been moved to a number cannot be taken down. Any other bet can be taken down.

draw   The draw is the second round of cards that are dealt in draw poker.

drop box   The drop box serves as repository for cash, markers, and chip receipts on a gaming table.

entry   An entry is two or more horses linked together for betting purposes. Typically this means both horses have the same owner.

even money   A bet that pays you back the same amount that you wagered, plus your original wager, or 1 to 1. In blackjack, taking even money when you have a natural and the dealer has an ace is the same thing as taking insurance with a natural; no matter what the dealer's hole card, you win even money.

exacta   An exacta is a bet in which you select the first two horses in the correct order of finish.

exacta box   An exacta box is a way to combine multiple bets on one ticket, betting all possible exactas involving two, three, or four horses.

exacta wheel   An exacta wheel is a way to make multiple exacta bets with your favorite horse as the first place winner and other horses as second place finishers.

expected win rate   The expected win rate is a percentage of the total amount of money wagered that you can expect to win or lose over time.

face cards   The jack, queen, and king of any suit of cards.

fast rail   A fast rail is a bias in which horses running close to the rail have an edge over horses running away from the rail.

fifth street   The third round of betting in seven-card stud is called fifth street because players have five cards. In hold 'em, fifth street is the fifth card on board and the final round of betting.

filly   A filly is a female horse, four years old or younger. (*Not yet the "steak sandwich."*)

first base   You're at first base on a blackjack table if you're playing the spot nearest the dealer's left hand; your hand will be played first, before the dealer moves on to the next player.

fishing   A player who stays in a poker game longer than advisable generally is fishing for the card or two that will make the hand a winner.

flat top   A flat top is a slot machine whose jackpot is always a fixed amount. Though the jackpot may vary based on the number of coins you play, it does not progress with each coin that is lost.

flop   The three cards dealt face-up in the center of the table in a game of hold 'em are called the flop.

fold   A player folds by tossing in his or her cards and giving up any claim on the pot in exchange for not having to throw more money into the pot.

foul   A pai gow poker hand is fouled when the two-card low hand is set higher than the five-card high hand, or when the hands are set with the wrong number of cards. A fouled hand is a losing hand.

fourth street   The second round of betting in seven-card stud is called fourth street because players have four cards. In hold 'em, fourth street is the fourth card on board and the third round of betting.

furlongs   A furlong is 220 yards. Eight furlongs equal one mile.

gait   Gait refers to the style in which a horse has been trained to move its legs while running. Standardbreds (harness horses) are required to move two legs in unison in either a trot or a pace, while thoroughbreds are allowed to gallop.

gelding   A gelding is a colt that has been castrated, generally to settle it down for racing.

giving odds   In craps, when you've made a don't pass or don't come bet, you can back it up by giving odds after the point has been established. This allows you to get more money in action without increasing your expected loss.

handicapper   A handicapper is a person who analyzes statistics and information to predict the outcome of a sporting event or horse race.

handicapping   Handicapping involves using available information to assign a probability to a sports team or horse's chance of winning.

hard hand   Any blackjack hand that does not contain an ace valued at eleven is a hard hand; for example, 6-7 is hard thirteen. A hand with an ace can be hard if the hand totals twelve or more and each ace in the hand counts as one—5-10-A is hard sixteen. The term hard is not used with hands of eleven or less.

harness racing   A harness race is a type of horse race in which standardbred horses pull a driver and sulky around a track.

high poker   High poker is standard poker, as compared to low poker or lowball. In high poker, high hands win.

high roller   A high roller is a big bettor.

hit   To hit a blackjack hand is to take another card. The card received is also called a hit.

hole card   When the blackjack dealer gets a card face-up and a card face-down, the hole card is the card that is face-down. You are not supposed to know the value of the hole card until after you play your hand.

horse   Though they all look like horses to me, in racing the term *horse* refers to uncastrated males five years old or older.

hot   When a slot machine is letting you win, it's considered hot. A player who keeps winning is also considered hot.

house edge   The house edge is a percentage of each bet you make that the house takes in. It's regarded as payment for letting you play, like an entertainment tax. For the house to get this edge, winning bets are paid off at less than the true odds.

inside bets   An inside bet is a roulette bet placed on any number or small combination of numbers.

insurance   Insurance at blackjack is a side bet that the dealer has a natural. Insurance is offered only when the dealer's up card is an ace. If the dealer has a natural, the insurance bet wins double. If the dealer doesn't have a natural, the insurance bet loses. If the player has a natural, insurance is also called even money.

jackpot   This is the moment you've been waiting for. A jackpot is a big win on a slot machine—the winning combination of symbols that will supposedly pay you back for all your time and effort.

jockey   A jockey is the rider of a thoroughbred horse in a race.

keno board   Large electronic keno boards are posted in many places throughout a casino to display the winning numbers.

keno lounge   The keno lounge is the main area within a casino where keno is played.

keno runner A keno runner is a casino employee who shuttles your keno bet from wherever you are to the keno lounge counter, and also delivers payment for winning tickets.

kicker In a draw poker game, a kicker is an odd high card held, usually an ace or king.

laying odds A person betting on the favorite in a sporting event must bet a lot to win a little; this is called laying odds or giving odds. At craps, making an odds bet on the don't pass or don't come is called laying odds.

line An athletic contest often pits two teams of unequal abilities. The line is the sports book's method of dealing with this inequality to attract wagers on both sides.

load up To play the maximum coins per spin that a slot machine or video game will allow is to load it up.

lottery jackpot The grand prize offered in a lottery is the lottery jackpot. It is a percentage of the sales revenues generated by that lottery drawing, and increases incrementally as more people play. If there is more than one winner, the jackpot is divided equally among all winners.

low poker Low poker, also called lowball, is poker in which the pot is awarded to the hand with the lowest poker value, as opposed to high poker.

maiden race A maiden race is restricted to horses that have never won a race.

mare A mare is a female horse, five years old or older.

markers A player who has established credit with the casino can write a marker, which is essentially a check, at the gaming tables.

mini-baccarat Mini-baccarat is a scaled-down, lower-limit version of baccarat, played with fewer players and dealers but following the same rules as American baccarat.

money line The money line is the betting line that's quoted in some sports. A bet on the favorite involves laying odds, or putting up more money than will be won. A bet on the underdog involves taking odds.

morning line An employee of the track handicaps each race, and the resulting estimates of the win odds for each horse are known as the morning line.

natural In blackjack, a natural is a two-card hand of twenty-one points. The only way to make a twenty-one in two cards is to be dealt an ace and a 10 or face card. Sometimes a natural is referred to as a blackjack. In baccarat a natural is a two-card total of eight (*le petit* natural) or nine (*le grande* natural).

number pool The number pool is the range of numbers from which you select the ones you want to play. A typical lottery number pool ranges from 1 to 60, and the keno pool is 1 to 80.

off In craps, a bet that is off is still on the table layout and looks like a working bet, but both the player and the dealer know that it will not be at risk (won or lost) until the player claims it to be *working* again. Only odds and place bets can be temporarily off.

open In poker, the player who bets first is said to open.

outside bets Outside bets are roulette bets located on the outside part of the layout. They involve betting 12 to 18 numbers at one time.

over An over is a sports bet that the combined total of points scored by both teams during a game will be over a specified total.

overlay An overlay is a good bet. To find an overlay is to find a bet where you have an edge over the casino.

pair A pair is any two cards that have the same rank, such as 3-3 or 10-10. At blackjack, whether two unlike 10s (such as Q-K) is a pair is up to the casino management. Generally, a pair may be split and played as two hands. In poker, the rank must be the same in order for two cards to be considered a pair (such as Q-Q).

pari-mutuel system In a pari-mutuel betting system, or pool, the odds are set by the bettors. In horse racing, the track takes a fixed percentage of wagers off the top and distributes the remainder to winning ticket holders.

parley A sports or racing bet in which two or more games or races are tied together is called a parley. All games/races must be won in order to win the parley.

pat In blackjack, a pat hand is an unbusted hand worth at least seventeen points. You should not hit a pat hand.

pay cycle A pay cycle is a theoretical expression that reflects the number of plays required for the machine to cycle through all possible winning and nonwinning combinations. But payouts are randomized; a machine doesn't actually hit each possible combination exactly once per number of plays corresponding to a play cycle. For example, if the frequency of a jackpot is once per pay cycle, and the pay cycle is 8,000 pulls, the probability of a jackpot is always 1/8,000 regardless of how many times the handle has been pulled since the last jackpot.

payline The payline is the line on a slot machine window on which the symbols from each reel must line up. Slot machines can have as many as eight (or more!) paylines, although most only have one. The more paylines, the more coins you need to play.

payoff   Your payoff, or payback, is the return you receive on a wager.

payout percentage   The payout percentage, which is also referred to as the "payback" percentage, is the percent of each dollar played in a video or slot machine that the machine is programmed to return to the player. Included in the payout percentage is the money returned as the result of hitting the jackpot. Payback percentage is 100 percent minus the house edge.

payout table   A payout table, or schedule, is a posting somewhere on the front of a video poker machine, or on the screen itself, that tells you what each winning hand will pay for the number of coins or credits played.

pit   A pit is an area of a casino in which a group of table games are arranged. Dealers and supervisors stand in the center, which is restricted to casino personnel, while players sit or stand along the outside edges of the gaming tables.

pit boss   The pit boss is the person who supervises all of the games and casino personnel associated with a pit area during a particular work shift. Pit bosses watch out for cheating, settle disputes, and give comps to big bettors. They also handle some of the paperwork required by tax collectors, casino accounting, and credit departments.

place   At craps, to place a number is to bet that the number will roll before a seven rolls. In a race book, a place bet is a bet that a particular horse will finish first or second.

point   In craps, the point is a number (four, five, six, eight, nine, or ten) that a shooter is trying to roll to make a winner of pass-line bets.

point-spread   The point-spread is the betting line that's quoted for football, basketball, and hockey, where the favorite gives up points or the underdog takes points in order to equalize the attractiveness of bets on either side. The outcome of a point-spread bet is determined by adjusting the final game score by the points.

post position   Horses start a race abreast, and where a horse starts is its post position. Post positions are numbered consecutively, with number 1 being closest to the rail.

post time   The time at which the race starts is the post time. Horses line up at the starting gate a minute or two before post time.

pot   The pot is the pile of chips that accumulates in a poker game as each player antes, bets, and raises. The pot goes to the winner of the hand.

pressing   A bettor who lets winnings ride by wagering them along with the original bet is pressing the bet and luck!

probability   Probability is a branch of mathematics that measures the likelihood that an event will occur. Probabilities are expressed as numbers between 0 and 1. The probability of an impossible event is 0, while an event that is certain to occur has a probability of 1.

progressive   A progressive is a slot machine (or video machine) whose jackpot keeps increasing each time a coin is played. When the progressive jackpot finally hits, the amount goes back to the starting number.

puck   A puck is a marker (white on one side and black on the other) that is used to indicate the point that has been established in a crap game.

purse   The purse is the total prize money distributed to the owners of first- through fifth-place horses in a race.

push   A push is a tie hand between a dealer and a player and no money changes hands. A push at blackjack occurs when both you and the dealer have unbusted hands with the same total points. If you bust, you cannot push.

quinella   A quinella is a bet in which you select two horses in a race, and your bet wins if the horses finish 1-2 or 2-1.

rack   You can transport and count large-denomination coins, slot-machine tokens, and casino chips in plastic containers called racks.

rail   The rail is the inside edge of the racetrack and the spectator gallery in a poker room.

raise   A player raises in poker by matching the previous bet and then betting more, to increase the stake for remaining players.

rake   The rake is the money that the casino/card room charges for each hand of poker. It is usually a percentage or flat fee that is taken from the pot after each round of betting.

reel   A wheel inside a slot machine window on which the slot machine symbols are printed. The number of reels per slot machine varies. The more reels and symbols, the harder it is for you to win. In slots, the more the merrier doesn't apply!

RFB   High rollers who get an RFB comp get free room, food, and beverage.

right bettor   A right bettor is a crap player who makes pass and come bets.

river   Staying in until the fifth and final round of betting in seven-card stud is called going to the river.

roll   To roll is to toss the dice at craps. A proper roll requires that the dice bounce off the far (or side) wall of the crap table before coming to rest. Bouncing off a wall helps ensure the casino that the resulting numbers are random.

roll-over   A roll-over is the part of a lottery jackpot that is carried over to the next lottery drawing if no one matches the numbers needed to win. The jackpot increases each time it rolls over.

saddlecloth   A saddlecloth is a piece of fabric between the horse and saddle in which weights can be placed.

scratched   When a horse has been scratched, it probably didn't just have an itch. But whatever it had has caused it to be withdrawn from the race.

search engine   Internet browser software that lets you sort through all of the thousands, and maybe even millions, of websites and newsgroups in cyberspace to find the ones that contain the information you're looking for.

sequence bets   In craps, sequence bets are bets that may require multiple rolls of the dice to reach a decision, as opposed to one-roll bets that are always decided on the very next roll of the dice.

session   A session is a series of 10 individual bingo games (plus some extras) that take about two to three hours to complete, depending on the number of breaks taken and how long it takes to find each game's winner. A session is also a series of plays at any other gambling game.

set   A pai gow poker player skillfully sets seven cards into two separate hands of two and five cards each.

seven out   At craps, when a point has been established and then a seven rolls, the shooter has sevened-out and the dice pass to the next shooter.

seventh street   The fifth and final round of betting in seven-card stud is called seventh street because players have seven cards.

shoe   A shoe is a plastic or wooden box that holds multiple decks of cards for dealing. Since dealing with more than two decks held in the hand is awkward, three or more decks are dealt out of a shoe.

shooter   The lucky crap shooter holds the dice and the fate of the entire table in the palm of his or her hands, and rolls the dice.

show   A show bet is a bet that wins if a horse finishes first, second, or third.

showdown   After the last betting round, the players who remain in a poker pot show their hands in the showdown to determine the winner.

shutter   A shutter is a window covering a number on a reusable bingo card. The shutter can be pulled down to mark each number as called.

singleton   In poker, a card that is the only one of its rank is called a singleton.

sixth street   The fourth round of betting in seven-card stud is called sixth street because players have six cards.

slow rail   A slow rail is a bias in which horses running away from the rail have an edge over horses running close to it.

snake eyes   When you roll a two in craps it's called snake eyes, for the obvious reason.

soft hand   In blackjack, any hand that contains an ace counted as eleven is called a soft hand. An ace and a 6, for example, is called a soft seventeen.

speed rating   Comparisons among horses are complicated due to past races having been run at a variety of distances and track conditions, and sometimes on a variety of tracks. The *speed rating* is a method of dealing with this problem. The speed rating relates how fast a horse ran to some standard that allows comparison between different past races. Historically, a speed rating of 100 means the horse tied the track record.

sports book   A facility that accepts wagers on sporting events is called a sports book.

spot   A spot can be any number (from 1 to 80) that a player selects on a keno ticket, as in "X marks the *spot*." It also refers to the number of numbers that are marked on a ticket, as in a "6-spot" or "10-spot" ticket.

stakes race   A stakes race is the highest echelon of thoroughbred horse races, offering the highest purses, which in turn attract the best horses.

stand   In blackjack, to stand is to refrain from taking another card.

stiff   In blackjack, a stiff is a hand that is not *pat* and that may bust if hit once. Stiffs include hard twelve through sixteen.

straight keno   Straight keno is the basic keno game, played by marking individual numbers or "spots" on a keno ticket.

surfing   Moving from one linked website on the Internet to another by clicking on links.

surrender   In blackjack, to surrender is to give up half of your bet for the privilege of not playing out a hand. In roulette, surrender means you effectively lose only half on an even-money bet when the ball lands on 0 (or 00, if there is one).

take   The take is the amount of money deducted from the pari-mutuel pool for track revenue, purses, and taxes.

taking odds   A sports bettor takes odds when betting the underdog, betting a little to win a lot. In craps, when you have a pass with a point established or a come bet that has been moved to a number, you can make an additional no-vig bet called taking odds.

teaser   A teaser is a sports parlay that uses different spreads than those that are used for regular parlays. A typical teaser card gives each team an extra six points.

third base   You are in third base if you are playing the spot nearest the dealer's right hand. If you are playing third base your hand will be played last before the dealer's hand is played.

third street   The first round of betting in seven-card stud is called third street because players have three cards.

thoroughbred racing   A thoroughbred race is a type of horse race in which jockeys are mounted atop thoroughbred horses.

toke   To toke is to give money or chips as a tip.

total   In some sports you can wager on the total, which is the combined total of points scored by both teams during a game. You can bet that the actual score will be *under* the total or that it will be *over* the total.

tote board   The tote board is a display of the totals bet on the various horses to win, place, and show, and the odds a bettor is likely to receive on win bets. It is updated generally at one-minute intervals before the start of the race.

touch wand   A touch wand is a pointing device used on some video keno machines to select numbers.

trifecta   A trifecta is a bet in which you pick the first three finishers of a race in the correct order of finish (1-2-3).

trips   When a poker player has trips of anything, it's three of a kind.

true odds   The true odds, commonly referred to as odds, is the ratio of the number of times one event will occur to the number of times another event will occur.

under   An under bet is a sports bet that the combined total of points scored by both teams during a game will be under a specified total.

underlay   An underlay is a bad bet, an event that has more money bet on its happening than can be justified by the probability of it happening.

up card   The up card is the card in the blackjack dealer's hand that is face-up for all the players to see before they play their hands.

vigorish (a.k.a. **vig**)   Vigorish is the fee, or commission, taken by the house.

VIP   A big bettor is worthy of full complimentary treatment and is considered a Very Important Player (VIP) in any casino's book.

virtual casino   A casino that operates on the Internet is often referred to as a virtual casino, an online casino, or an Internet casino. Virtual casinos offer software-based video versions of most casino games, including blackjack, poker, slots, craps, and baccarat. Some virtual casinos accept sports bets on live sporting events.

way ticket   A way ticket is a keno ticket that groups different numbers to create more than one way to win. Each group contains the same number of numbers.

win   A win bet is a bet that the horse will finish first.

working   In craps, when a bet is working, it is at risk on the next roll of the dice. If you have taken an odds or place bet *off* you can turn it back on by telling the dealer that it is working.

wrong bettor   At craps, a wrong bettor bets on don't pass and don't come.

Appendix B

Selected Reading

Alice Fleming, *Something for Nothing: A History of Gambling*, 1978, Delecorte Press, New York, NY.

Anthony Curtis, *Bargain City*, 1993, Huntington Press, Las Vegas, NV.

Avery Cardoza, *Winning Caribbean Stud Poker & Let It Ride*, 1998, Cardoza Publishing, New York, NY.

Doyle Brunson, *Super/System*, 1978, B & G Publishing, Las Vegas, NV.

Dwight and Louise Crevelt, *Slot Mania*, 1989, Gollehon Books, Grand Rapids, MI.

Edward O. Thorp, *Beat the Dealer*, 1966, Random House, New York, NY.

Jeffrey Compton, *The Las Vegas Advisor Guide to Slot Clubs*, 1995, Huntington Press, Las Vegas, NV.

Mark Balestra, *The Complete Idiot's Guide to Online Gambling*, 2000, Que Publishing, Indianapolis, IN.

Mason Malmuth and Lynne Loomis, *Fundamentals of Craps*, 1995, Two Plus Two Publishing, Henderson, NV.

Max Rubin, *Comp City*, 1994, Huntington Press, Las Vegas, NV.

Olaf Vancura, *Smart Casino Gambling*, 1996, Index Publishing Group, San Diego, CA.

Peter A. Griffin, *The Theory of Blackjack*, 1996, Huntington Press, Las Vegas, NV.

Stanford Wong, *Basic Blackjack*, 1995, Pi Yee Press, La Jolla, CA.

————*Betting Cheap Claimers*, 1992, Pi Yee Press, La Jolla, CA.

————*Blackjack Secrets*, 1993, Pi Yee Press, La Jolla, CA.

————*Casino Tournament Strategy*, 1993, Pi Yee Press, La Jolla, CA.

————*Optimal Strategy for Pai Gow Poker*, 1992, Pi Yee Press, La Jolla, CA.

————*Professional Blackjack*, 1994, Pi Yee Press, La Jolla, CA.

————*Professional Video Poker*, 1993, Pi Yee Press, La Jolla, CA.

Stanley Ko, *Mastering the Game of Let It Ride*, 1995, Gambology, Las Vegas, NV.

Steve Bourie, *American Casino Guide*, 1996, Casino Vacations, Dania, FL.

Walter I. Nolan, *The Facts of Keno*, 1984, Casino Press, Inc., New York, NY.

The Ten Commandments of Gambling

1. Thou shalt not pray before spotted cubes of ivory.

2. Thou shalt not speak the name of the Lord until all else has failed.

3. Thou shalt not worship thy winnings.

4. Thou shalt not play seven days in a row. Thou shalt rest at least once.

5. Thou shalt honor thy mother and father and forgive them for gambling away thy inheritance.

6. Thou shalt not kill third-base players who know not what they have done.

7. Thou shalt not adulterate thy cards, cubes, or coins.

8. Thou shalt not steal thy gambling money from thy children's college fund.

9. Thou shalt not falsely accuse thy dealer of cheating.

10. Thou shalt not covet thy neighbor's machine.

Index

W–X–Y–Z